What Is *Your* Heritage and the State of Its Preservation?

Volume 3
Putting Theory into Practice

Edited by

Barry L. Stiefel

HERITAGE BOOKS
2018

HERITAGE BOOKS

AN IMPRINT OF HERITAGE BOOKS, INC.

Books, CDs, and more—Worldwide

For our listing of thousands of titles see our website
at
www.HeritageBooks.com

Published 2018 by
HERITAGE BOOKS, INC.
Publishing Division
5810 Ruatan Street
Berwyn Heights, Md. 20740

Heritage Books by the author:

What Is Your Heritage and the State of Its Preservation?
Essays on Family History Exploration from the Field

What Is Your Heritage and the State of Its Preservation?
Volume 2: Collaborations with Storyboard America

What Is Your Heritage and the State of Its Preservation?
Volume 3: Putting Theory into Practice

Front Cover Credit:
"Family Record", Terre-Haute, Indiana: J. M. Vickroy & Co., 1889.
Library of Congress, Prints and Photographs Division.

International Standard Book Numbers
Paperbound: 978-0-7884-5848-4

Dedication

To our ancestors and the cultural patrimony that they bequeathed to us. Their stories continue with us.

Acknowledgements

Thank you to Susan Kammeraad-Campbell for the help, encouragement, and inspiration you give our students.

Table of Contents

List of Figures

Introduction by Barry L. Stiefel

During the Spring 2018 semester several students at the College of Charleston's Historic Preservation and Community Planning program participated in their Senior Seminar titled "What Is *Your* Heritage and the State of Its Preservation?". This was the third time this seminar topic had been taught at the College of Charleston, with the first taking place in 2014 and the second in 2016. For this class, each student had to conduct a lengthy in-depth research paper on the state of preservation of heritage sites, material objects, or traditions associated with their family's history. The assignment used genealogical research in an unconventional way by elevating the assessment of ancestors beyond typical names, dates, and generational succession; so commonly found on most family trees. The students had to ask profound questions to guide their inquiry, such as "Where (as in a specific spot) did my ancestors come from?"; "What was life like for them?"; and "What cultural traditions were important for them?". In this way the researcher becomes connected with their cultural forbearers, who are contextualized within time, place, and society. Moreover, the students had to utilize and synthesize the knowledge, skills, and experiences they acquired in previous classes. The class of 2018 was also able to read and discuss the essays of their predecessors from 2016, which were published in the second edited volume of this series.

Following some understanding of their family history background the students then had to investigate "What is the current state of preservation?" of these places, customs, and artifacts related to their ancestor(s). They learned how to evaluate significance of place or artifact in respect to their family history, both within a personal framework as well as larger meaning within society as a whole. In some instances, the answer was easy because a student's ancestor of study was well known to contemporary historians, and the place(s), things, or customs associated with them were being well cared for. In other instances, students focused on a more vernacular past, where detailed records were often not always readily available or never existed in the first place. While some of the students were descended from famous people of the past, it became important for the students to recognize the achievements of those whose names have almost or have become forgotten; especially considering that this is where the bulk of humanity comes from. Thus, the ethical question we came to postulate (the students and myself) is if one does not investigate and advocate for the preservation of one's own history and heritage, who will? And, if not now, when? Documenting our stories was the first step, and we all have a story to share.

During the semester Susan Kammeraad-Campbell of Storyboard America worked with the class a second time (the first in 2016) to hold a series of writing workshops on the topic, which was of great help for many of the students. The stance of Storyboard America is that "Everybody has a story. What's yours? We all have moments that matter. Write them down. Share. We'll show you how."[1] This outlook on documenting heritage meshed well for the students within the 2018 class. Several students incorporated their first-person accounts into their essays, which you will read about.

Within this book are six essays volunteered by the students after the semester had ended, with each committing some additional time for revision and research after graduation. Many of the essays have a geographical interest in the southern United States. The first chapter, *Cultivating Heritage in North Carolina Soil,* Rebecca Lawing, examines the relationship between a sense of place and one's heritage through the analysis of physical landscapes and the intangible cultural heritage found in cultural landscapes. In order to accomplish this

2

objective, Lawing delved into her own heritage by studying the town of Lincolnton, North Carolina's economic and physical development in the late nineteenth and early twentieth centuries. She investigates how development affected the values and interests of town residents, who are extended members of her family. Lawing concludes her research with a call to action for more rural landscape and intangible heritage preservation.

In *What's in a Name: Establishing My Heritage through the Perpetuation of a Neglected Surname*, we learn from Flannery Wood the unusual phenomenon of a misplaced surname. By delving into the very reasons surnames are important to us, and the origins behind them, she explores her own neglected surname, Minich, along with two other extended family names to better understand how her family's heritage connections to the textile industry of the South Carolina upstate region. Through analyzing each name, the genealogy behind it via the documents and pieces of the past they contain, Wood develops ideas related to the intangible preservation meaning of places and items associated with this history. The result is a construction of identity formation relating to places and material culture, and the realization that stewardship begins with herself and her family in order to continue their presence into the future.

For the third chapter by Ellen Feringa, *New Orleans Mardi Gras: More Than Just a Wild Party* we are introduced to the milieu of intangible traditions and material culture of the carnival festival of Mardi Gras. This annual event attracts hundreds of thousands of people to New Orleans, bringing attention to the city and boosting the economy. The entire city shuts down for the legal holiday, so all can participate. As public as Mardi Gras is today, it used to be a very exclusive event. The exclusivity and traditional component still exist today, but Mardi Gras has evolved into a more diverse and more inclusive celebration. The centuries-old traditions are reflective of both the old and new organizations. For example, the School of Design, better known as the Krewe of Rex, is the oldest parading organization and second oldest organization. Feringa's family history in Rex traces as far back as the late nineteenth century, but for other New Orleans natives, the lineage is far more extensive. Documentation, preservation, and continuation of Mardi Gras cultural heritage is essential because it allows us to connect to the past and understand how the unique cultural heritage of New Orleans functions. Through the history of Mardi Gras, the Rex Organization, Feringa's family stories, and pictures as a case study, this thesis explains how Mardi Gras is more than a wild parade, but a traditional cultural celebration of artistic expression.

In chapter four, *Landscapes of Memory: Exploring Family Heritage Through Place*, Madison Alspector looks at the relationship between landscape and memory. She dives into interviews with family members, old family photo albums, recipe books, travel itineraries, and rummages through her own memories, as a means of developing a case study on which we define one's family within a heritage framework. Alspector concludes that we create the cultural heritage we identify with through memories and connections to certain landscapes, activities, and values. Memories of traditions serve as physical reminders that also define one's own conceptualization of family, regardless of biological connection, at an individual as well as societal level.

For the fifth chapter Madison Moga looks at the tradition of her relatives who worked in a watch factory, in *A Pilcher Tradition: The Legacy of the Elgin National Watch Company*. Moga's great-great-great-grandfather George Pilcher, immigrated to the United States with his family from England in 1888. Once here, he and other members of the family worked much of their careers at the Elgin National Watch Company, which was a leading manufacturer of pocket watches in the United States, with a global market. She investigates the history of this remarkable company, the factory's architecture, and the socioeconomic impact the company had on the city of Elgin, Illinois. Moga then evaluates the preservation concerns of what remains of this company's legacy and built environment. While her ancestor, George Pilcher, lived in Elgin and worked at the watch factory, he began taking his family for picnics in the year 1897. This tradition of annual picnics has been embraced and preserved in her family for over a century. Therefore, Moga also discusses the importance of the annual Pilcher family picnics and how it connects her to George Pilcher and the Elgin National Watch Company, even though she resides in South Carolina.

The last chapter, *The Trinkets We Carry*, by Alec Meier, investigates oral histories passed down through generations that have a connection to specific heirloom material artifacts. Therefore, Meier researches his Irish cultural heritage in a way that provides a greater understanding of heritage appreciation that incorporates both the material and the intangible. This process allows for a connection for those in the present with the ancestors of the past. Meier's study thus allows for these objects and their associated stories to remain intact for future generations to appreciate by providing context to one another, even if one resides in South Carolina, far from Ireland. Stories gain meaning through artifacts. Heirlooms get meaning from stories that are retold across generations, which endows a modern appreciation.

Since this is the third volume of this series of published student papers, the subtitle of *Putting Theory into Practice* for the book has been used. The reason for this is that after the past two experiments in 2014 and 2016, the approach of investigating one's own heritage to both serve as a capstone experience within the Historic Preservation and Community Planning program and as a pedagogical tool for preparing preservation students to be better preservation advocates is no longer a theoretical discussion, but something that educators such as myself are doing. For example, in *Genealogy and the Librarian*: *Perspectives on Research, Instruction, Outreach and Management,* co-edited by Carol Smallwood and Vera Gubnitskaia, appears the chapter "Beyond Names and Dates on a Tree: How Librarians Can Help Explore Family Heritage and Preservation."[2] More can be read about this in the recently published chapter "The Places My Granddad Built': Using Popular Interest in Genealogy as a Pedagogical Segway for Historic Preservation," which I wrote and appears in *Human Centered Built Environment Heritage Preservation: Theory and Evidence-Based Practice,* co-edited by Jeremy C. Wells and myself (see Appendix).[3] So, hopefully what we have emerging is a more dynamic, critical way to approach the fields of heritage preservation and genealogy. Because ultimately, if the preservation of cultural heritage is not in some way personal to someone, then why are we doing it? Making a twist on the National Trust for Historic Preservation's campaign for "This Place Matters," the act of preserving *must* matter as well.

In closing, this sample of published papers reflects the students who volunteered their research from the Spring 2018 semester. A list of the other research papers is included to demonstrate the breadth and diversity of the students who took the class and decided not to publish. It is our hope – both my own as well as the students' – that our work can serve as an inspiration to others to think more comprehensively about one's own family history and heritage. To think beyond names, dates, and generational succession so that the lives of our ancestors can be better understood; as well as to foster and promote the preservation of the places, heirlooms, and traditions that formed what we have today and for future generations. As Susan Kammeraad-Campbell has demonstrated, stories endure. Write yours as part of the preservation process.

List of Student Papers Not Published Here from 2018:

Automobiles Generation to Generation, by Samantha Kloss

Entrepreneurs with a Serving Heart, by Megan Masters

Bringing the Lost Past to Light, by Anna Arkins

Raconteur, by Drew Whittle

Figure 0.1: The Caroline and Albert Simons Jr. Center for Historic Preservation at the College of Charleston, where the students spent a significant amount of time on their Bachelor of Arts degrees in Historic Preservation and Community Planning. Photograph by the editor.

Chapter 1: Cultivating Heritage in North Carolina Soil

By Rebecca Lawing

Every year at Thanksgiving my family would make the drive to my parent's hometown of Lincolnton, North Carolina, about four hours away from we lived in Charleston, South Carolina. Every year we would peel out of the driveways at least an hour later than we meant to with my dad, Robert, driving and my mom, Jeri, clutching her third cup of coffee for the morning. My older sister, Margaret, always used her free time during the car ride advantageously by reading the newest book in her ever-growing collection. As the younger sibling, naturally I tugged at the still crisp pages of her newly found source of entertainment and kicked at her heels until she agreed to read to me while I steadily grew impatient for Thanksgiving lunch. As we neared our grandparent's house, the desperate growling of my stomach almost deafened the sound of my sister's reading and my parents reminiscing about their youths.

As I reflected on the steam coming off my grandma's homemade bread, my mom would motion to a house near the top of a hill, which once belonged to her grandmother. While my sister and I argued about who would get the biggest piece of pumpkin pie my dad would point out the pharmacy his granddad had once owned. On one side of the road was the home of my mother's childhood best friend, now painted a different color than what she remembered. On the other side was a fire hydrant which marked the farthest distance my father's sled reached during his childhood's winters. As a young child some of these landmarks were lost on me. Yet, as I grew older, hearing of my parent's experiences with these personal landmarks gave me a sense of anemoia for the late nineteenth and early twentieth centuries, when the town and its landmarks were shaped. I also experienced a further longing to understand how these places shaped my family.

In order to grasp the dichotomy between my family's heritage and Lincolnton I analyze the economic growth of Lincolnton and compared it to the personal and professional development of my family members. By delving into economic growth trends in rural areas one can see the correlation between rural cultural landscapes and cultural heritage, both tangible and intangible. Through the examination of the relationship between the town of Lincolnton and my family, I have cultivated a better understanding for how a sense of place can shape one's identity. This town is an example of rural North Carolina history from the early twentieth century, needing of preservation that is often lost on evolving landscapes and intangible cultural heritage.

Historic Context of Lincolnton's Rural Heritage

Lincolnton is located in Lincoln County, North Carolina, named after Benjamin Lincoln, a Major General in the Continental Army during the American Revolution. The town was founded at the site of the Battle of Ramsour's Mill after the war's end. However, the founding location of the town was not based on military history, but rather the presence of the Catawba River. The eastern coast of North Carolina which touches the Atlantic Ocean is rocky, making the water less than ideal for ship access in the late eighteenth century. Therefore, North Carolina remained sparsely inhabited in comparison to other areas of the United States. Many of those who came to North Carolina from Europe did so by entering the continent through main ports like Charleston, South Carolina as my own ancestors did, and traveled inland by either river or road.[1] This made the Catawba River a valuable asset in the founding of Lincolnton. Not only did the river allow for the initial transportation of people to the site, but it also provided a source of food and trade. Lincolnton's seat at the southern fork of the Catawba river meant it had early access to irrigation systems which would lead to agricultural growth, providing food and incomes to Lincolnton residents.

The Catawba River proved itself to be a valuable economic feature for Lincolnton once again with the boom of the textile industry in the second half of the nineteenth century, as it provided power for the first cotton mill built south of the Potomac River. This allowed the textile industry to prosper in North Carolina, along with the cotton industry that fed into textile manufacturing. However, despite the success of this new industry, Lincolnton never became highly industrialized, and instead remained a largely agricultural town. This represents a descent from the most common trend of the rapidly industrializing United States.

Census records from the nineteenth century show that in most states the majority of people were moving to urban cores, yet in North Carolina, the majority of the population elected to stay in rural areas.[2] Lincolnton is one of the town centers which attracted people. The economic stability gained from the town's agricultural and textile industries provide some people with opportunities to establish more specialized trade, yet without attracting the large corporations seen in more urban locations. By the 1850s, Lincolnton's Main Street had physician offices, drugstores, a tailor, and a jeweler, along with civic and religious centers. The town's growth was slow and organic, evolving in response to the resident's needs.

One specific area of note in terms of the town's development and historical significance is the Lincolnton Commercial Historic District. The focal point of the district is the Lincoln County Courthouse Square. The courthouse itself is the main feature of the square and was built in 1921 in the Classical Revival Style with a central three-story Doric portico. The building and its square are flanked by commercial businesses which had been placed more densely near the core of the district than the shorter and more disperse properties found on the secondary streets. The formation of this central district occurred between 1850 and 1950 and is representative of the layout of most rural North Carolina towns that saw expansions during this time period.

The century-long span of growth allowed for the different structures in the district to have been built in a plethora of different architectural styles. While surrounding residential areas sport buildings that are more vernacular in appearance and construction, the main streets of the commercial district are occupied by buildings with facades of many different formal styles. The choice to build the Lincoln County Courthouse in a Classical Revival Style was a practical choice, as many government buildings in the United States have been historically built in either Classical or Greek Revival styles. This is due to the subconscious connection between Classical architectural styles and thoughts of democracy.

Most of the buildings in the commercial district were not built with the purpose of invoking patriotism but were rather simply representative of the time. Another common style found along the main streets of the commercial district is Art Deco. This style can be seen in the Rhodes and Corriher Company and Coca-Cola Bottling Company, built and updated in 1930 and 1935 respectively. These buildings were constructed within the decade that saw Art Deco flourish in popularity in the United States. While the construction of these structures is representative of architectural trends, some facades were selected for the main enjoyment of the establishment's proprietor. For example, the Wampum Department Stores built circa 1905 were built in the Italianate style, a choice which would not necessarily be commonplace in rural twentieth century construction since it was a nineteenth-century trend more common in the northern United States. Of the 62 contributing buildings, the two which were most notably not built in a formal style were the only two residential properties in the district. There are two other historic districts in Lincolnton, West Main Street, and South Aspen Street, which contain a higher concentration of residential properties. The residential structures were added to the historic district because they exemplified rural housing development patterns in the early twentieth century.[3] This development affected the rural middle-class's relationship with the automobile.

Prior to Henry Ford's use of the assembly line in manufacturing, automobiles were usually unobtainable among the middle and working classes. In urban areas, this translated to blue-collar workers, who typically held factory jobs, living in dense housing complexes in city cores. Urban middle-class households used transportation systems such as streetcars to live outside of the city center, since they could afford transportation and desired to live away from the pollutants of the city.[4] However, rural regions established prior to the common use of the automobile were designed in a different matter. Prior to 1950, the majority of working-class people in rural areas had jobs in the agricultural industry and often lived adjacent to the land where they worked.

On the other hand, small towns had less established modes of public transportation available to its inhabitants. With the automobile still unaffordable in the early twentieth century, many town residents valued having homes closer to their places of business in the center of town.[5] This is represented by the two homes included in the Lincolnton Commercial Historic District. The Karl L. Lawing House and Frank Beal House were built prior to Ford's use of the assembly line in 1913, constructed in 1905 and 1910 respectively. They were both constructed close to the businesses where the household owners worked for more convenient commutes. When the automobile became more affordable later in the 1910s, the development of new residential areas in Lincolnton changed with more houses radiating out farther from the town's center.[6]

While Lincolnton's central business district has been established as historically significant, when entering the town's limits, the first thing one comes across is a vast expanse of agricultural land. Many of the acres are covered by white buds of cotton, as they have been for over a century. Growing up I heard many stories about these fields, specifically from my maternal grandmother's friend Bill Rudisill, who is like a grandfather to me. He recounted his childhood memories, specifically about growing up among the cotton fields. As both of his parents would work in an adjacent field, Bill would play near an oak tree. The only thing keeping him from wandering away was a piece of twine wrapped both around the tree and himself along with the prospect of getting in trouble with his parents.

While Bill's parents were picking cotton, they couldn't split their attention evenly between their work and Bill, and in order to be able to feed the family, they had to keep working. So, the rope around his waist eased their minds as they continued cultivating the harvest. A few years then passed, and Bill no longer had to sit by as his parents worked, instead he worked alongside of them. Bill went to school when he could, but his family relied on the extra pair of hands to pick cotton in order to make ends meet. Whenever truant officers came by to take the child to school, his parents would hand them a burlap sack and give them two options: they could either leave or pick cotton in the boy's place. Every time the officer would leave without the child. I heard this story many times, along with others which described Bill Rudisill's life growing up on a rural farm. I always loved his anecdotes about the chickens he kept, and Sunday lunches his family hosted for the local pastor and his family. Although not related by blood, Bill is a grandfather to me, and his heritage is intertwined with my own. His stories represent to me a life lead by many family members before me, as they all called the same rural North Carolina town their home.

A Rural Economic Landscape

In these cotton fields, many members of my maternal family spent their working lives. While Bill and his parents worked in similar fields as my other family members, they each had different experiences which are important to my family's history, Lincolnton's history, and the history of southern agricultural economies as a whole. Bill's stories are representative of typical farm life in the early-mid twentieth century, characterized by the hard work of every available family member.

There were other forms of work within the cotton industry in which my maternal family participated: specifically sharecropping. My mother's paternal grandmother, Irene Caulvard and her immediate family were sharecroppers in Lincolnton. During Reconstruction (1865-1877) sharecropping became a common mode of farming in North Carolina. Many plantation owners had used slave labor and had to make changes once slavery was abolished. However, the system which replaced it continued to take advantage of those who worked in the fields. The laborers who made up the sharecropping workforce primarily consisted of freed slaves. However, in Appalachian North Carolina, it was not uncommon for poor whites to also work as sharecroppers, as was the case in my family.

Figure 1.1: Irene Caulvard and "Smiley" Jordan, the paternal grandparents of the author's mother. Source: From the personal collection of the author.

Sharecropping came about when plantation owners were left with large expanses of land but had no workers to cultivate it. Instead of hiring employees, the landowners would divide the fields into sub-parcels and rent it to sharecroppers. This system was extremely beneficial for the landowners because instead of paying for labor, laborers paid them. Not only did sharecroppers have to pay to work the land, they were also required to rent tools directly from the landowner. Since those who entered into sharecropping did so because they needed money, they often were not in the position to rent land or tools outright and became indebted to the landowner due to borrowing. Those who owed money to the owners were often required to also give the landowner up to three-fourths of the final crop yield to pay off their debt.[7] This meant that people working in the fields often only saw one-fourth of the crops they grew. After selling the cash crops and feeding their families, there was rarely enough money to rent the land and tools for the next harvest, so once again the sharecropper would have to promise the majority of the upcoming yield in order to grow for another year. This system left many stuck in a cycle of poverty and debt. Conditions for sharecroppers worsened after crop lien regulations gave the landowners the authority to have complete control over the sale of the crop. Sharecroppers no longer had bargaining power over the value of their harvest and were left at the mercy of the landowner to get the best price for the crop. Since the landowners were not desperate for money, they often wanted to just unload the yield and would not fight for the best price. This was exacerbated in the late nineteenth century when cash crop prices began to decline, leaving families in the rural South who were dependent on sharecropping for their incomes to become impoverished and desperate.[8]

Irene Caulvard was not the only sharecropper in her generation of my family. Her brothers worked as sharecroppers too. While Irene and her brothers were in the same line of work, the lowering of the crop prices and the establishment of the crop lien affected their households in different ways. [9] Irene's husband, Smiley Jordan, also contributed to their household funds through his job as a truck driver. The dual income household gave Irene a financial stability that her brothers did not have. However, the brothers would not remain desperate for long. While their jobs were low pay, they had a talent for a pastime which would provide them with opportunities for economic advancement. This pastime was making moonshine. In the Appalachian regions of North Carolina, it was not uncommon for folks to make their own whiskey, as they had since the eighteenth century. In many instances, it was seen as a family affair, with recipes being passed down across generations. In this instance making moonshine was a family business which "meant the difference between material poverty and economic survival." [10]

As the Caulvard brothers perfected their recipes, the sharecropping industry was at its most volatile. At one point the value of cotton crashed and no one was willing to pay a fair price for their harvest. The men had to settle for corn and sugar vouchers instead of cash if they wanted to see any return on their crop's yield. The voucher they received weren't valuable enough to sell, and the corn and sugar they redeemed them for couldn't last them until the next growing season. If the sharecropping system allowed the brothers to make a living wage, they wouldn't have been left with heaps of corn, sugar and only one option. So, they heated some mash water and added the corn and sugar, turning their valueless vouchers into liquid currency.

In 1894, another legislative decision caused the cottage moonshine industry to flourish even more. The government attempted to increase tax revenue by placing high taxes on whiskey. However, the tax initiative backfired, and more people began buying illegal moonshine to avoid spending the extra money. Irene's brothers weren't the only ones to profit off the newfound patronage: the illegal liquor market in the United States increased to approximately 10 million gallons in the next year, the majority of which was made and sold in North Carolina.[11] I never met my great-grandmother's brothers, but every time I went to her house I would notice 10-gallon glass jars filled with coins which snugly fit through the neck of the jug, and whose metallic smell almost disguised the essence of moonshine shared among my family long ago. A smell which is representative of a pursuit of wealth in a rural agricultural climate.

From the Fields to the Center of Town

During my family's involvement in cotton farming, Lincolnton's economy was largely textile-based. When North Carolina's first textile mill was built in Lincolnton along the Catawba River, the town's dependence on the cotton industry was solidified. However, the introduction of new technology also allowed some to enter into specialized industries as commonly seen in urban centers. Some specialized industries particularly relevant to Lincolnton included furniture and upholstery design, hospitality related businesses and manufacturing. My maternal grandfather Max Duane Jordan, along with his brothers, deviated from employment in farming and instead started their own electrical business, Jacklegs. Jacklegs' business model primarily worked by word of mouth networking. This was emphasized by their tongue-in-cheek business cards that provided absolutely no contact information, but rather jokes about electricians where a business address or phone number would ordinarily be. However, in a small community like Lincolnton, referrals were the main way a business would grow. Although their marketing technique of not marketing may seem unorthodox, they didn't need formal advertising since their business flourished on the quality of their work alone. This business allowed the Jordan side of my family to be stewards of the cultural landscape as they worked on the majority of the buildings in Lincolnton.

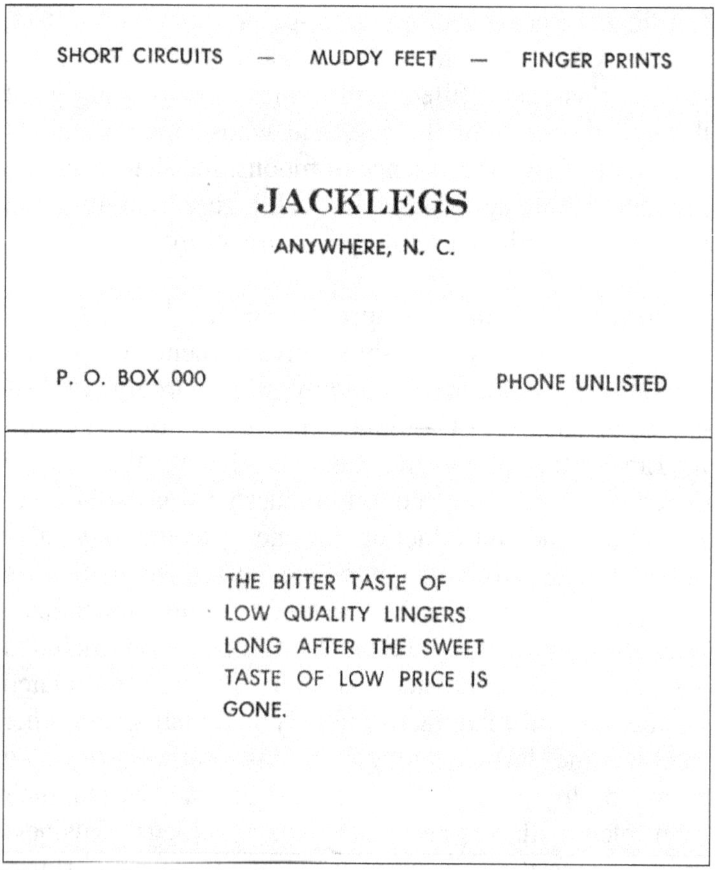

SHORT CIRCUITS — MUDDY FEET — FINGER PRINTS

JACKLEGS
ANYWHERE, N. C.

P. O. BOX 000   PHONE UNLISTED

THE BITTER TASTE OF
LOW QUALITY LINGERS
LONG AFTER THE SWEET
TASTE OF LOW PRICE IS
GONE.

Figure 1.2: The business card for Jacklegs, created by Max Jordan and his brothers. Source: From the personal collection of the author.

While their business was successful, Max wanted to break into contracting and development. However, there was a class bias which hindered his transition into the industry. Many contractors in the area were upper-middle class and did not think that there was room in the profession for a working-class electrician with no formal

20

college education. Max then carved room for himself in the industry and became a successful developer. He then married Marsha Hosey, who also made a spot for herself in the housing industry by becoming the top real estate agent in Lincolnton, serving as president of the North Carolina Real Estate Commission. The two of them both had and currently have a direct involvement in the historic landscape of Lincolnton while owning and maintaining a historic property themselves.

Figure 1.3: Jeri Lawing, Sally Freeman, and Max Jordan. Source: From the personal collection of the author.

Max and his brothers were not the only members of my maternal family who left an impact on the physical aspects of the town. Max's first wife and my grandmother, Sally Freeman, also decided not to follow in her family's agricultural footsteps and instead worked at one of the most prestigious furniture stores in Lincolnton. While it has been established that the cotton and textile industries were important to Lincolnton, the furniture industry was as well. It was easy for furniture stores to conduct business in Lincolnton since the textile industry provided a convenient source of upholstery. By working in this industry, Sally contributed to the interior design of many Lincolnton buildings and the overall material cultural of the town too.

While Max, Marsha, and Sally all left their marks on multiple buildings in Lincolnton, the paternal side of my family was also connected to the town's development. One of the most prominent buildings in Lincolnton is the courthouse, which can be found in the Lincolnton Commercial Historic District that was added to the National Register for Historic Places in 2005. Flanking large Classical Revival style building is a parking lot where a historic marker stands, crafted out of handmade brick from 1852. The marker reads:

On this site, a three-story brick building was erected in 1852 by John Motz and known as Motz Hotel, Leading hotel in western North Carolina. Fulfilling need, as Lincolnton was the most important town west of Salisbury. Purchased 1862 by Dr. Samuel Lander for Lincolnton Seminary, Female Boarding School. Toward the end of the Civil War, the hotel and the entire town received large numbers of South Carolinians fleeing the invasion of Sherman by following the railroad north to Lincolnton. 1870-71 headquarters of the Pennsylvania 7th Cavalry, Company C. In 1891 a corporation purchased the property and operated it as the North State Hotel. One member of the corporation was K.L. Lawing whose family sold the property to Lincoln County in 1966. Thomas A. Edison stayed here in 1906 seeking cobalt for a storage battery. Hand-made brick from original building used to build this marker. Building razed in January 1968 for court house [sic] parking.[12]

Unfortunately, the hotel discussed in this marker was torn down before it had a chance to be added to the National Register of Historic Places, within the central business district where it stood. However, despite its current state as a parking lot, the hotel was once of great significance to not only Lincolnton but also my family. While the building was being used as headquarters for the Union Cavalry, Dr. Samuel Lander relocated his school and expanded it into Lander University. When the war was over, he no longer had a purpose for the building and sold it to his close relative, Dr. Karl Lander Lawing, and was referred to as "grandpa" by my father, Robert Lawing. My father's paternal grandfather not only owned the hotel, but he was also a pharmacist at Costner and Lawing Drug down the road. Since he was often busy at the drugstore his wife, Beulah Philman (my father's grandmother), was in charge of the day-to-day operations at the hotel. By the time my great grandparents came to operate the hotel, the building was already old and needed many repairs. At one point, Beulah hired Luther Clyde Beam to be the head contractor for some building repairs. However, this was not a standard contract since Beulah had a son named Karl Lawing Jr who was looking for a job, so that he could pay for medical school. Beulah agreed to hire Luther on the condition that Luther employ her son Karl Jr. Luther agreed to the arrangement and gave Karl Jr. a job. One day Luther's daughter, Elizabeth Beam, came to visit him at work and was introduced to Karl Jr and the two fell in love, eventually marrying and having four children, one of which is my dad. To my family, my father and his siblings where the legacy of the North State Hotel, so it is unfortunate that the building is no longer standing. However, there are other buildings that are still standing that are of importance to my family. The historic district where the North State Hotel was located still contains two properties historically affiliated with my family.

The first is the Karl L. Lawing house, built in 1905 by the person of this name. This house is an L shaped two-story floor plan with a gable roof, a central brick chimney between the house's two junctions, and two one-story porches, one on each junction. Although the porches have been enclosed and modern updates have been made to the house so that it would be compatible with contemporary living, the main shape and structure of the house remain unaltered. Karl lived in the house until he passed in 1934, yet it remained in the family until the 1950s. While the family lived in the house in 1929, Sanborn maps show that the building was a boarding house/ hotel, although, I have found no other support of this in my research. Other family members say it was solely a residential property. Sometimes it is the case that human memory is flawed; however, Karl also owned a hotel in close proximity to the house. Therefore, it is possible that later that year the Sanborn maps were made, records could have crossed, causing the misclassification of the property. While the Karl L. Lawing house was close to the hotel, where he and his wife Beulah worked, he specifically chose the house's location so that it would be near his other place of business, the Lawing and Costner Drugstore.

Although Karl and Beulah were the ones who built their home near the drug store, it was Karl's father who established the store. When Dr. John Means Lawing built the store in 1867 it was on West Court Square, called Lawing's Drug Store. It was relocated in the late 1890s to its current location on East Main Street, close to where the Karl L. Lawing House would be built less than a decade later. When John passed, Karl inherited the business on East Main Street and sold some business interest to B. Costner, changing the name to Lawing and Costner Drug Store. This property along with the Karl L.

Lawing House is included in the Lincolnton Commercial Historic District as contributing properties.

The three historic districts in Lincolnton could be considered the central points of the town's heritage. The West Main Street and South Aspen Street Historic Districts represent the vernacular residential architecture from approximately the 1850s to the 1950s. The Lincolnton Commercial District is inclusive of commercial properties with more varying architectural styles and practical uses. This district includes the town's main street along with many government buildings and civic centers and retains heavy use today. These historic districts are all on the National Register for Historic Places; therefore, are considered to be of great historical significance to both Lincolnton and the rural South that Lincolnton represents. However, there is an important feature in Lincolnton that is also representative of the rural American South, yet is not included in the National Register, which is the agricultural land surrounding the town's core. This land, used mainly for cotton and tobacco cultivation, represents the rural South's dependence on cash crops, containing the labor history of those who worked in the fields. These cotton fields are a contributing feature not only to Lincolnton's economy but to its cultural landscape too.

Intangible Cultural Heritage

The emphasis of this study has been placed on Lincolnton's built environment. However, non-physical entities can also contribute to an area's character and cultural landscape. In Lincolnton, an important piece of intangible cultural heritage is the use of music for entertainment and life enrichment. The diversity of urban centers allowed for the emergence of various sources of amusement and social interactions. Reform efforts had gained working and middle-class people more time for leisure, and the mass production of goods allowed many leisurely activities to be more financially accessible. The invention of the Nickelodeon, in particular, provided a source of entertainment that could be consumed by families at a fairly affordable price and which also did not take too much time out of one's schedule. This was a big step towards the middle class becoming able to consume goods and services that provided enjoyment rather than simply fill a necessity. However, while leisure and self-improvement activities were becoming more widely available in urban centers, rural communities faced a different reality. Rural residents often worked longer hours than their urban counterparts, even after labor reform efforts led to a 40-hour work week in urban centers. Therefore, people who lived in rural regions such as Lincolnton often had less time for leisure despite technological progressions. That, along with the low-density population did not entice entertainment businesses to locate in these communities, and therefore many rural communities forge their own sources of entertainment and community enhancement. Fulfilling this need for leisure activities allowed rural areas to create an intangible cultural heritage.

While economic growth did not directly lead to the building of entertainment businesses in rural communities such as Lincolnton, it allowed tools for entertainment to become more widely available. One form of intangible culture which is of particular significance to my family is music. While there are a few family members on the paternal side of my family who were classically trained, the maternal side of my family was self-taught, passing on skills and instruments from one generation to another, as seen among many families in rural regions. My great-grandfather, Smiley Jordan, was one of these self-taught musicians. He could play the guitar, banjo, and violin, although he would never call it anything other than a fiddle and encouraged his children to learn how to play as well. The following are two stories about Smiley Jordan's violin and Elizabeth Beam's piano, which illustrates my argument on the significance of folk music to Southern rural culture.

My Great Grandfather's Violin

As light from the setting sun hit the divots of the golf balls, shadows concaved around the white spheres creating the protective leaves of a ripening cotton boll. The faux cotton so convincingly littered the lot, one could forgive my great-grandmother Irene for thinking she was still in the field near the town where she had just finished her day's work as a sharecropper. On the lot was a modest house where the shadows of seven pairs of children's feet echoed within the walls, a memory of the children who were once raised there. Even when the children had grown and moved into houses of their own, my great grandparents never wanted to move. So, they spent the rest of their days in that house.

Within the house itself there were empty glass jugs now filled with pecan shells but had once held moonshine shared in revelries passed. Ashtrays were scattered within reach, each lined with a couple of cigarette butts which had been rolled using tobacco grown only a few miles away. While my parents would be apprehensive about the aroma of tobacco, it never smelled like smoke to me. The air formed itself into geological layers, the recent smell of smoke lingered at the top above my head while the air I breathed smelled warm, like the crease of a book with yellowing pages, sweet, like handmade cornbread.

One year after my great-grandmother passed, my family went to visit Smiley, and although the smell of cornbread left when she did, the door was still open, and he was still smiling as we walked in. After the customary hugs and small talk, Smiley pointed out a purple bruise on the lower right side of my neck. While other relatives questioned whether or not it was a sporting accident, he asked knowingly: When did you start playing the fiddle? I told him I had only been playing since the beginning of the school year and my mom jumped in to brag about my progress, the way moms love to do. Smiley then left the room for no more than five minutes and came back with an apology; he had wanted to show me his violin but since he had a different instrument under each bed in the house, he couldn't remember where he hid it. At the time I was secretly relieved, I was nervous my parents would have wanted me to play even though I was still struggling to learn the most basic version of Greensleeves. Now I wish I had offered to help him find it. I would have loved to see him hold the violin he cared so much for even though he could no longer play.

When he passed a few years ago, as the only other violinist in the family, he left the instrument to me. As my mother told me stories about Smiley playing for all of his children and grandchildren, I was overwhelmed that I would finally see the instrument he had so much love for. He had played for the family he loved above all else. I placed the black-stained wooden case on my parent's kitchen table and unlatched the two metal hooks on either side of the handle to reveal a three-quarter size violin, which looked a little too large for his slight frame. The instrument was cradled by the case, half lined in a faux red velvet, and the other half with floral paper. While a small amount of rosin had melted into the floral lining, the strings were free of any damaging residue, the wood looked freshly cleaned, and the bows had been separated from their hairs to prevent snapping.

Smiley's income and location not only influenced the type of violin he used but also the style of music he played on his violin and other instruments. His musical style of choice clearly represents the intangible cultural heritage of music in Lincolnton, along with the rest of rural North Carolina. Smiley was particularly partial to Appalachian Folk music, which originated in western

North Carolina. Every instrument he owned could be found used by a musician in an Appalachian folk band. This music style is rich in heritage of its own. Many of the tunes were inspired by traditional Irish music, which had been brought over to North America when immigrants from Ireland settled not far from Lincolnton in the Appalachian Mountains. Traditional Irish music was also convenient for self-taught musicians to learn, which made it more accessible to members of the working class who could not afford formal lessons.

Although traditional Irish music does require a lot of precision and speed, many of the classical techniques, such as *vibrato*, which is typically only learned through formal training and was considered vulgar among traditional Irish musicians in the nineteenth century.[13] Therefore, traditional Irish music was an accessible base for Appalachian folk. Due to the lack of formal entertainment in rural communities these songs were unadulterated by popular urban music and reflected the moods of the rural South. Therefore, it was folk music that he played on his violin. Even though Smiley's violin is too small for me to play, I care for it the way my great-grandfather did. When I tune it, I apply the folk variations that he used. The *pizzicato* of the A and the D string together recreate the sound of the case's latch opening for the first time, while the A and the E string in harmony recreate the pitch of his light-hearted laugh that earned him the nickname "Smiley."

The Piano Parlor

On the top of a hill in Lincolnton, with a large cherry blossom tree in front, is the house that was my father's childhood home. There were two entrances into the house, one leads directly into a well-furnished kitchen and another which led into the piano parlor. In this particular room, it felt as if you had been dropped into a movie set in the nineteenth century. The furniture was proper and detailed: an old church pew rested underneath a picturesque mural on the wall exuding the smells of soft lake water and fresh grass it depicted. This mural sat opposite of a window which looked out on a tree I had climbed hundreds of times as a child. Between the mural and the window sat two grand pianos establishing their dominance in the space, seemingly saying that this room was built for them. Whenever my family would visit my grandparents, my older sister Margaret would always go straight towards this room pulling me behind her. My parents ensured that she and I took piano lessons as soon as we could reach the keys, so every time we set foot in this room we were excited to each have our own piano to play on instead of having to take turns like we did at home. My sister had inherited my grandma's, Elizabeth Beam, talent for the instrument. Every time she would play, grandma would complement her on her technique and give her a proper piano lesson. However, while I love the piano, I could never sit still long enough when I was a child to practice it properly and eventually took up the violin, an instrument I could practice while standing up. Even though I couldn't properly play more than scales on the piano, I would still splash my fingers against the keys while I waited for grandma to finish her lesson with Margaret and move on to me. When she would sit beside me, she would be my hands and play whatever I hummed and would even write it out for me to practice on my violin later. She was one of the main reasons I became so passionate about music. She would never chastise my clumsy movements against the keys but would rather foster an interest in the creativity behind the sounds.

My grandma had a lot of practice teaching music, as she had decided at a young age to turn her passion for music into a teaching career. Music provided her with a profession and it allowed her to become deeply ingrained into the fabric of Lincolnton society.

Figure 1.4: Elizabeth Beam presenting her senior thesis.
Source: From the personal collection of the author.

She first studied it at Winthrop University and then
Columbia University where she got her Master of Fine
Arts. It was at Columbia University where she studied
under the renowned arranger, Dr. Edwin Hughes who
could trace his teacher's linages back to Beethoven and
Czerny. [14] Elizabeth was deeply inspired by these
dedicated artists who spent their lives passing on their
craft, so she decided to teach and spent 64 years of her

life doing so. Elizabeth also had the honor of being a member of the National Federation of Music and was a presiding festival judge for more than 40 years. She had a natural talent and passion for music which earned her a lot of respect in the community as "increased importance was placed on musical proficiency as a hallmark of good taste and moral reputability."[15]

However, Elizabeth did not use music to gain financial status, for she was genuinely passionate about educating the next generation of musicians. Elizabeth used her talents for enhancing other important facets of her life such as her relationship with the church. Like many rural communities in the early twentieth century, Lincolnton had a strong traditional religious following, mostly of the Protestant Christian persuasion. Particularly important to my heritage is the Lutheran church. Since my paternal ancestor Johann Boehm came to America from Germany to establish churches in Lincolnton, the paternal side of my family has been devout Lutheran. While the building he resurrected in 1801 now houses a different denomination, the intangible Lutheran heritage in my family continues. My grandmother intertwined her musical abilities with the Lutheran church by playing during services and special church events.

While the music Smiley played was deeply influenced by his rural roots, Elizabeth's music was influenced by her background as well. She came from an upper-middle-class household which meant not only was she was able to take formal lessons as a child, but it was also expected of her. This allowed her to gain classical technique which would eventually earn her admission into Columbia University. While the pedigree of her instructor has been previously discussed, one should also note that at the time Elizabeth was a pupil herself, most curriculums were based on religious classical music. Therefore, not only was she raised in a devout Lutheran household, but she was learning music by devout Lutherans, such as Bach, combining two important aspects of her life. My grandmother used her passion for music as a career and a way to connect with the community and her faith. My great-grandfather also has a deep connection with music which lead him to cultivate his passion. While rural entertainment may have been much different than urban entertainment in post-industrial America, my family found a way to enrich their lives with music.

Preserving Lincolnton's Cultural Landscape

In the past decade, Lincolnton has had a strong showing of preservation initiatives, focusing mainly on individual structures and historic districts. However, there is still much more that is deserving of preservation beyond the typical scope of architectural prowess. I am not contesting the fact that the aforementioned historic districts are unimportant, but rather call to expand the scope of research and preservation beyond the physical boundaries of the town. For example, the surrounding cotton fields contribute to the history of the Lincolnton and the current state of the town's development. This is because it was the cotton and textile industries which allowed for the economic stability that facilitated the town's growth. Not only are the white spotted fields relevant in regard to the economic history and development of the town, they are also important to the personal histories of the people who lived there. Nonphysical aspects of the town are also worthy of preservation, such as the intangible cultural heritage linked with the practice of rural music is invaluable to the people affected by it and as a topic of research.

One of the main issues facing cultural landscape preservation is the constantly changing nature of working landscapes. As an agricultural center, Lincolnton is still reliant on the economic benefit gained from the cultivation of the fields. However, those who work the land have adapted and changed the nature of the crops they grow in order to make a living wage. As demand for tobacco decreases, industries which utilize crops such as lavender flourish. Thus, lavender buds now accompany the cotton as opposed to tobacco. This does not necessarily have to be something preservationists fight. Heritage cannot be a static a landscape frozen in time for the sake of preservation. Heritage also comes from actions and practices, besides place. So, by continuing to grow crops on the land the practice of farming can be continued, and farmers are unintentionally perpetuating heritage practices by enacting adaptive reuse on a tradition that may otherwise be neglected. As David Lowenthal observes, "[m]arks of age and decay integral to every object need to be seen not just as losses but as gains." [16] Landscapes are not static paintings because they are constantly changing and being used to better a community. Landscapes adapt in response to human needs and environmental changes. So, in order to preserve cultural heritage, we cannot expect to stop the use of the land. There is a specific rural historic landscape category for National Register nominations and this is the Historic American Landscapes Survey as a means for documenting cultural landscapes. [17]

Moreover, the United States has not ratified the UNESCO Convention for the Safeguarding of Intangible Cultural Heritage of 2003, so there is little within a legal framework on what can be done for this type of preservation. [18] Countries like Japan have specific laws to safeguard intangible heritage. Therefore, Americans must work to preserve it themselves. I will personally continue to use specialized rural tuning technique taught to me by Smiley; however, more must be done to preserve the plethora of intangible cultural heritages found across the United States. If more interest is shown in this field of study, perhaps government agencies will recognize the public's desire for preservation and will push for more ways to preserve.

Conclusion

Lincolnton is still surrounded by many of the cotton fields that my family members cultivated between the mid nineteenth and twentieth centuries. Within the border of these fields is the house where my mother grew up, and where her mother and her mother's mother grew as well. The same can be said for my forefathers, dating back to 1767 when my ancestors John Teeter Beam (Johann Dietrich Boehm) and Rebecca Reynolds came to North America from Hamburg, Germany. John and Rebecca came through Charleston harbor and traveled to Lincolnton, where many of the family still live today. Although I never lived in Lincolnton myself, traveling to the town meant getting a chance to hear about my family member's lives in a place that was important for them. Visiting my parent's hometown meant passing by the high school where my mom and dad first met and started dating, running around the track my dad trained on during his football days, and visiting his childhood home on the top of a hill where he and I both skinned our knees as children. Visiting my parents' hometown meant stopping by their favorite lunch spot from when they were younger, which still serves the same menu and clientele. My mother loves pointing out the dilapidated house she once dreamed of living in and looking at the old cars her dad had repaired and maintained from when she was a child. Therefore, when I think of my heritage in terms of a physical entity deserving of preservation, I can't pinpoint a single building or object. I see a cultural landscape of cotton fields and an old cotton mill, rows of vernacular storefronts and homes, and the intangible experiences which are dear to my family.

While I have always been fascinated by my family's history, before conducting this research I didn't realize the profound effects, certain moments in history could have on one's development. I had expected to learn about some connections between my family and a couple of buildings, but I would never have guessed that by learning about the history of an old demolished hotel I would hear about how my grandparents met through a series of nuanced events. While I had heard hushed-toned stories about my family's involvement in moonshine production in the past, had I not conducted this research I would never have known it was primarily driven by economic hardships and legislative missteps. If I had not looked into the history of Appalachian music, I would have never learned that my great-grandad Smiley's favorite genre was influenced by class, the mass production of string instruments, and Irish settler's preference for a lack of vibrato. Since he was a major inspiration for me to play the violin, in a way those things influenced my relationship with music as well. While this all may seem very personal, it is also important on a broader scale. Often times preservation efforts focus on protecting buildings designed by gentleman architects, overlooking rural vernacular structures and landscapes. This could also be due to the difficulty in preserving landscapes since they are ever changing. Cultural heritage is sometimes intangible, so there are unique and abstract challenges in preserving these specific carriers of heritage. These challenges cause a shortage of preservation in these areas which makes further preservation and research even more important. This is not to say that every place needs to be frozen in time, but if cultural landscapes like Lincolnton are not studied or documented now, opportunities could be lost for understanding and appreciating the past.

Chapter 2: What's in a Name: Establishing My Heritage through the Perpetuation of a Neglected Surname

By Flannery Wood

When asked to consider your heritage and what is important to your family a name associated with such is often called to mind. Acting as a unifying factor, an identifier, and primary connection to the people and places of your past, a surname can be the very core of what you regard as your heritage. Prior to this research assignment, I knew very little about my surname, Wood. The name Wood had been adopted by my paternal grandfather and replaced the family name Minich which was replaced and soon after forgotten. The secrecy that surrounded this occurrence is one that was kept until my father was seventeen and his paternal grandmother passed away. Upon her death, he was informed that she was not his biological grandmother but instead the sister of his true grandmother and adoptive mother to his father and aunt. By casting aside his family name and associating himself and his children with another, my grandfather made it very challenging for future generations to investigate their original surname patrimony. This change resulted in confusion and ultimately a lack of knowledge about my patrilineal family's roots. Using family histories and personal interviews I was able to begin to establish the lives and genealogy of the members of both the Wood and Minich families and ultimately the places and communities important to them. Throughout this project it became apparent that as the primary investigator into the past, I was responsible for identifying these people and places and passing along their importance and role in my past and ultimate need for preservation to my family members. Recognition of this fracture in my family's past and genealogy led me to understand that the likelihood of the preservation of a true historical material object, site, or event of my family had dwindled significantly. With the change of my last name, the potential to recognize and preserve valuable parts of my father's family heritage has become more difficult. Through the investigation of my forgotten patrilineal family surname, I have provided the potential to uncover and preserve significant parts of my heritage.

Figure 2.1: Wedding of Francis Xavier Minich Sr. and Anna Louise Lyons. Source: From the personal collection of the author.

By perpetuating my family name and the extended family surrounding it, I will expose the places, people, and stories critical in establishing my family's identity and preserving it for years to come. For a large portion of my father's childhood his family history remained unknown. The grandmother that he knew and loved was the "adoptive" parent of his father and his mother's elder sister. My paternal grandfather, Francis Xavier Minich Jr., was born the first and only son of Francis Xavier Minich Sr. and Anna Louise Lyons on July 5, 1932. When Francis Jr. was 4 his mother passed away due to complications related to the birth of his sister, Louise.[1] As was customary of the time, Louise's elder sister Mary Elizabeth Lyons and her husband Thomas Henry Wood, took the children so my great grandfather could grieve. With this decision, the Minich children became members of the Wood family. Though never legally adopted, they eventually left their name and the history associated with it, behind.

The subject of this arrangement between the two families is a conflicting account. As there was no legal adoption or written records of the arrangement, the details surrounding the situation remain uncertain. I have employed the oral accounts of multiple family members in an effort to eliminate as much ambiguity as possible. The interviews I have conducted were with surviving family members with recollections or perspectives of this event, though they differ drastically. Following the death of his first wife, Francis Minich Sr. married Virginia Anne Folsom in May of 1940.[2] In 1953, after a miscarriage and several failed attempts to become pregnant, Francis and Virginia adopted a two-year-old girl, Kathy. Kathy's accounts of Francis Sr. and Virginia depict a couple who desperately wished to regain custody of Francis Jr. and baby Louise after their marriage was in order.

Figure 2.2: Francis Minich Wood Jr. and Louise Minich. Source: From the personal collection of the author.

These efforts were halted as Mary Elizabeth and Thomas Henry, who were unable to have children of their own, refused to return the children amid claims that they had been legally adopted by the family. Unwilling to submit the children to any strife, Francis Sr. and Virginia conceded. Francis Sr. assumed a role similar to that of an uncle and visited his children once a year around Christmas. Directly refuting this account is Louise. Taken in by Mary Elizabeth and Thomas Henry as an infant, the Lyons family became the only family she ever knew. Louise recalls the situation as not one of secrecy or malice but where everyone was pleased with the "arrangement," including her birth father.[3]

Role of Intangible and Oral Histories

Oral histories such as the accounts surrounding my family's change in name are not a new phenomenon.[4] Such storytelling, and narrative has existed long before the use of written word. It was not until the mid-twentieth century that oral histories became a widely accepted resource and supplement to written archival records.[5] Slowly acknowledged in academia, oral testimonies are often neglected as a resource and frequently considered easily altered by the passage of time or the changing perspective of the interviewee. This results in general distrust stemming from the fallibility of human memory or the varying ability of individuals to recall the past.[6] Over time guidelines and methods of gathering this information have emerged in an effort to protect the historic integrity of interviews.[7] These handicaps have been outweighed by the historical richness of these previously "untapped sources" and the unique perspectives they provide into family histories and genealogical research. [8]

A prime example of the fruitfulness of these sources lies in Jacquelyn Dowd Hall's work *Like a Family*, which details the experience of individuals in the mills and mill villages of the rural South. This literary work originated from 200 interviews with former mill laborers as well as owners and managers whose oral testimonies were combined with additional historical documents in order to fully paint a picture of the time and environment surrounding mill life. [9] Reliance on these oral testimonies came with the customary limitations surrounding concerns of in accounts. Accordingly, this data was supplemented and compared to written records in order to establish the most unaffected illustration of the past as possible. Such oral accounts have become increasingly invaluable as the primary source for the investigation of family histories, as it was not "the common man nor the common practice that was recorded for posterity". [10]

Oral accounts are especially significant for marginalized or oppressed groups that have been neglected from the written historical record. [11] Gathering this information orally "produced histories for those groups which lacked documentary records" of their own. [12] While my family was neither oppressed nor marginalized, oral interviews provided information regarding the everyday interaction of family members or more importantly family events that were not documented. Often these oral versions were categorized and remembered by family name. While investigating my own heritage the family members that I have spoken to contain discrepancies in their accounts of what transpired in the past due to perspective, differences in experience, and familial influence. It is important to recognize and record these histories as the contributors will not be around forever. The preservation of the memories and oral narratives associated with my family name are in jeopardy of being forgotten and with them important insights and details not found elsewhere. These oral accounts are part of my heritage that must be perpetuated for future generations.

Importance and Meaning of Surnames

Nearly every European and consequently every North American family finds themselves identified with a surname or family name with which they associate their past.[13] Typically these names descended via a patrilineal line [14] and originated from a byname or descriptive nickname, reflected a place of residence or an occupation, or stemmed from the name of parent, usually the father.[15] Though popular now, for a large portion of history it was not common practice to utilize a surname.[16] Family names first came into use in the British Isles following the Norman conquest in 1066. Possibly originating with the formation of bureaucracies, noble men and women were the first to begin to take surnames replacing their identifying by-names that stemmed from a physical attribute or nickname.[17] It was not uncommon for these new family names to reflect the nobles primary place of residence. Over the next century the practice of taking surnames slowly trickled down into the lower classes and by the end of the fourteenth century most family names in use were hereditary.[18] This increase in popularity is possibly attributed to the increase in written records, or a need to distinguish between an increasingly slim variety in Christian personal names. [19] Surnames helped distinguish one individual from another acting as descriptive identifiers.[20] The easiest surnames to identify are place names, which were often an indicator of where a family originated.

During my research into my family's surnames (both patrilineal and adopted), I was prompted to research the historical origins and meanings of these names and the identity they may lend. The surname "Wood" has both Scottish and English origins, primarily coming from a "topographic name" or indicative of a place.[21] In this case Wood most commonly referred someone who lived in or near a forest. It could also stem from an occupational name for a "woodcutter" or "forester." [22] My paternal grandfather's surname Minich is distinctly German origin. Originally spelled Minnich, with two N's, one N was dropped at an unknown time in my family's history.[23] Over the course of history many spellings and pronunciations of surnames have been altered. Such changes could have been involuntary and a result of clerical error or an issue of pronunciation.[24] This was a common result of immigrants traveling to America who passed through Ellis Island. The name changes via clerical errors that occurred here at the hands of immigration officials were of prolific proportions and legendary in the "Americanization" of names.[25] According to a dictionary of American family names, Minich stems from the high German form of the word "Munich," or "Monk." This likely denoted someone who worked for the monks in a local monastery. [26] The third name I examined, Lyons, became prevalent in my study when looking into my grandfather's matrilineal lineage and their ties to South Carolina's textile industry. The name Lyons has both English and Irish origins and has several possible meanings and spellings depending on where the name originated. English variations of Lyons typically refer to a nickname of a particularly brave warrior stemming from the middle English "lion." It could also refer to an individual who lived in a house distinguished by the sign of a lion.[27] In the case of my paternal great grandmother's maiden name, Lyons is an Irish variant of Lyon and is an anglicized form of the Gaelic "O'Laighin," or descendent of "Laighean". This indicates a by-name meaning "spear" or "javelin."[28]

In addition to offering insight into places of origin, surnames hold significant power of recognition throughout oral and recorded history. Often a last name can be traced back for generations to a specific famed or significant person or place. This can be seen in the latter part of the sixteenth century as nobles bestowed their names upon their offspring in an effort to perpetuate their family name. Generations later, many of these names we now recognize as historically significant to a certain time or location. Names have the capacity to hold secondary meanings and associations and can be associated with disposition or relation to a person ultimately influence attitudes and relationships between people.[29] Surnames have long echoed in the minds of Americans as the driving symbol of family identity.[30] The process of understanding or researching a family name is to know the customs and circumstances that existed at the time they were implemented. Investigating a family surname can offer a connection to the past for many families, as surnames act as primary lineage identifiers and connection to a nationality or language of origin. This identity can be achieved by kinship through a name, not necessarily blood, in turn generating a connection to a community, place, structure, or other material object that otherwise would have contained no significant association.

The Forgotten Minich Genealogy

My great-grandfather, Francis Xavier Minich Sr., was born August 14, 1906 in Roslyn Pennsylvania.[31] His parents were Daniel Carl Minich and Elizabeth Louise Sauerland. My paternal great-great-grandfather, Daniel Carl Minich, was born to William and Lena Minnich. William came from Germany and his wife from Alsace Lorraine, France.[32] One of six children Daniel had two brothers, Harry and Charles and three sisters, Violet, Emma, and Gertrude. William worked as a maintenance engineer for Baldwin Locomotive works and subsequently owned a machine shop in Kensington, now a neighborhood of Philadelphia.[33] All three of his sons worked in the machine shop after school and became experts in mechanical and electrical matters. Daniel's brother, Harry, owned a grocery store and subsequently an automobile repair shop. He and his wife died young, leaving their eldest son Harry and seven daughters. Harry attended high school and seminary simultaneously later in his life and entered the priesthood. Daniel's second brother, Charles, was superintendent of Philadelphia operations of White Motor Company in Cleveland, Ohio.[34] Daniel worked practically all his life as an examiner for the John B. Stetson Hat company in Philadelphia, at the corner of Germanton and Columbia avenues.[35] According to my great-grandfather, Daniel earned a very good living for his family here.[36]

Francis Sr.'s mother, Elizabeth, passed away in 1909 when Francis was just three years old.[37] His father married Elizabeth's younger sister, Gertrude, in 1911.[38] Elizabeth and Gertrude's father, Maximilian Von Sauerland, was Prussian and hailed from northern Germany, where he served as an army officer in the Franco-Prussian War (1870-1871). How or when he emigrated to the United States remains unknown, but it is possible he journeyed here around 1872 where he then installed parquet floors for a living.[39] Anna Ansetett, Elizabeth's mother, was also born in Germany. She married Maximillian after her first husband, Barth, died shortly after their marriage. Max and Anna went on to have nine children, eight daughters including Elizabeth and Gertrude, and one son, Max. As a child, Francis lived in the same neighborhood as his maternal grandparents and remained close to them his entire childhood. In his family history, Francis recalled that grandfather Maximilian sported a large, bushy handlebar mustache and was a good Catholic who attended church regularly. He would attend German masses in his "morning formal" that included a grey-striped-jacket and trousers, complete with a black fedora top hat. At Maximilian's death in 1920, at age 72, young Francis Sr. had moved and was completing his first year of high school and regrettably was unable to attend the funeral. Though also Catholic, his grandmother Anna did not attend mass with her husband. Following her husband's death, grandmother Anna lived the last decade of her life with young Francis until she passed away in 1932.[40]

In 1916 Francis Sr.'s family moved to Burholme, Pennsylvania, where he attended Frankford High School in 1920.[41] In 1924 Francis graduated as Valedictorian from high school with a 3.96 grade point average. He proudly recorded receiving a scholarship from the Wharton School of Business at the University of Pennsylvania where he specialized in accounting.[42] After completing his education in 1927 Francis entered the textile manufacturing industry, where he worked the rest of this life. Francis Sr. was sent by his employer, La France Textile Company a manufacturer of upholstery fabrics, to Autun, South Carolina to help build a plant there. Eventually, he was elected corporate officer and began his work at Autun Mill, installing business systems and controls at the plant.

Francis Sr. detailed his work experience at La France Industries in a history he transcribed for his daughter Louise in 1994. Though he was never actually placed in charge of factory operations, Francis was extremely successful at his young age. His role in the business led to a large involvement in La France community affairs. Francis was consulted in matters regarding La France Schools by its board of trustees and once used this position to help a family member gain a job within the school system. In 1936, La France Industries, though solvent, began reorganization to prevent the intrusion of banks. Francis was named Assistant General Manager of la France Industries.[43] In this position, Francis Sr. received some responsibility for plant operation. In April 1942, following what was described as "years of pressure politics against him" with changes in leadership, Francis along with several other individuals were fired.

In December 1942, Francis Sr. joined the U.S. Army doing special work in textiles. He remained "with Uncle Sam" until August 1945 and was stationed in Washington DC, New York City, and Greenville, South Carolina.[44] Soon after he met Virginia Anne Folsom on a blind date, and they married a year later. Francis and Virginia struggled with infertility and in 1953, following several devastating miscarriages, adopted a two-year-old girl, Kathy.[45] Even with a new wife and child, Francis continued to reach out to his biological children. Francis Jr. and Francis Sr. maintained correspondence over the years, and many of these letters were kept by Francis. Louise's correspondence was less frequent than her brother's, primarily thanking Francis Sr. and Virginia for gifts around Christmas. Their adopted daughter, Kathy, remembers my grandfather coming to visit his father and staying the weekend with the family when she was very young. She does not remember Louise coming to visit but did attend her wedding when she was a child. My father and his siblings saw Francis Sr., their birth grandfather, under the guise of a family friend occasionally when they were children. These visits became less frequent over time before ending entirely, perhaps at the insistence of their grandmother Mary Elizabeth. Mary Elizabeth's death finally revealed to my father and his siblings that Mary Elizabeth was not their paternal grandmother.[46] Mary Anna Wood recalled being shocked and angry by this news and questioned if her grandfather purposely separated himself from the family. Mary Anna remained in communication with Francis Sr. and took her first child to meet him.[47] My father also established a relationship with Francis Sr. after my sisters and I were born. He apologized for losing touch and began to visit Francis on his business trips to Atlanta. Eventually the rest of my family was introduced and visited Francis Sr. and Virginia regularly several times a year until their deaths. We established a relationship with their daughter, Kathy, and continued to visit her and her husband even after Francis Sr. and Virginia's passing.

Lyons and Wood Family Genealogy

Louise and Mary Elizabeth Lyons were sisters; hence this family makes up a pertinent part of my paternal family tree. John Lyons Sr. was born in Tipperary County, Ireland in 1844. Fleeing poverty and starvation during the potato blight, John joined the British Army and was one of 8,000 troops sent to Canada at the height of the American Civil War. Soon after, John deserted the British Army and crossed the Canadian border into Elmira, New York where he eventually enrolled as a private in the United States Army.[48] John participated in the Battle of Hatcher's Run and was present for the cease fire at Appomattox Courthouse. Following his discharge, John Lyons made his way to New York City, where subsequently he met Elizabeth Diamond. John Lyons and Elizabeth Diamond Lyons moved south from New York to work in textiles. Their son, John Andrew Lyons, was raised in Greenville, South Carolina where he met and married Anna McNeill from Abbeville, South Carolina. Anna and John Andrew had six children including Mary Elizabeth, and Anna Louise. John Andrew Lyons served many years as the superintendent of the Orr-Lyons Mill in Anderson, South Carolina from the 1890s until 1946.[49]

In most mills, daily operations fell to the responsibility of superintendents or supervisors. Owners rarely concerned themselves with day-to-day tasks, primarily directing the financial dealings of the organization. Some owners maintained contact and friendly relationships with their workers resulting in loyalty and respect, while other's aloof interaction could lead to animosity towards the owner. Prior to World War I, superintendents like John Andrew Lyons, were known and respected for their ability to manage the workforce, as well as repair machinery and work alongside their subordinates if necessary. As superintendent, John Andrew Lyons was also responsible for recruiting laborers to work in the mill. This included traveling to North Carolina and enlisting German immigrants to man the machines. Beginning as a sweeper at Piedmont Manufacturing at age 10, John Andrew Lyons took school lessons at night when he was 18 and eventually worked his way up to a second-hand position in a weaving room.[50]

Figure 2.3: John Andrew Lyons and Family.
Source: From the personal collection of the author.

In 1900, he was approached by Colonel Orr and asked to take a position as superintendent at a new mill he was building in Anderson.[51] As the family of the superintendent, John Andrew and

Anna had more luxuries than their neighbors. Anna and John Andrew's home had the only telephone in the village and consequently the doctor seemed to always be there after being called to tend to an illness, injury, or new baby.[52] The women in the family of a superintendent also had greater responsibilities within their community. Elizabeth Diamond and Anna hosted the annual stockholders' meeting for Colonel Orr and Colonel Hammet, which included a grand dinner at their home in the village. Additionally, the Lyons women fed and cared for ill members of the mill community during the Spanish Flu Epidemic of 1917-1918.

Mary Elizabeth Lyon's husband, Thomas Henry Wood, like her father John Andrew Lyons and brother, was a "big mill man" according to my grandfather's cousin, Eddy Lyons.[53] My great-grandfather, Thomas Henry, was heavily involved in textiles his entire life. Thomas Henry's life and character had remained somewhat of a mystery as he tragically passed away before my father or any of his siblings were born. While he never met Thomas Henry, my father was told stories his entire life of what an influential and legendary man his namesake was. Described by a posthumous document as "Westminster's man for all seasons," Thomas Henry played an important role in the small upstate community of Westminster, South Carolina.

Born in Laurens County, South Carolina Thomas Henry was the fifth son of nine boys born to Thomas Turner and Alma Dobson Wood.[54] Both Thomas and Alma were third generation South Carolinians. As a child Thomas Henry attended Poplar Spring County School and helped with the

Figure 2.4: Thomas Henry Wood. Source: From the personal collection of the author.

family farm. With the onset of World War I, Thomas Henry volunteered with the Laurens Home Guard and eventually served in France as a member of the notorious Rainbow Division under General Douglas Macarthur, which remained a lifelong pride of his.[55] After completing his tour of service Thomas Henry returned home and attended Georgia Institute of Technology where he studied textile engineering. His summer vacations were spent working at Gossett Mill in Anderson, South Carolina. Post-graduation he was hired by the Gossett Mills chain and over his life would serve as superintendent in five Gossett Mill plants.[56]

In 1937, Thomas Henry left Gossett Mill in Calhoun Falls, South Carolina and was hired by Charles Dexter Owens Sr. of Beacon Manufacturing Company, based out of Swannanoa, North Carolina.[57] Thomas Henry was tasked with expanding and modernizing the financially failing Westminster Mill. At that time, the town of Westminster was in the throes of the Great Depression, highlighted by a lack of jobs, failing banks, and general poverty.[58] Under Thomas Henry's guidance, expansion of the old Westminster Mill continued despite material shortages during World War II, with lumber recycled from other Beacon Mills in Massachusetts and transported to South Carolina. Re-branded Oconee Mills Inc. this plant's new machinery facilitated the manufacture of the well-known Beacon Blanket at these facilities. The workforce of Oconee Mills Inc. gradually tripled in size from 150 to nearly 850 employees.[59] Thomas Henry served as superintendent and bought much of the cotton used in manufacturing at the mill visiting cotton markets all over the Southeast and as far west as Texas and California. In addition to his work with Oconee

Mills Inc, Henry assisted in the reorganization of the Winder Mills Corp located in Windsor, Georgia to Sachem Mills Inc. He also aided in the building plans and inspection of another Beacon Mills facility located in San Juan, Puerto Rico. Thomas Henry remained involved in this operation until the mill was sold to Textron Corporation, as well as aided in management of Beacon Mills located in Granby, Canada.[60]

In addition to his large role in the textile industry, Thomas Henry utilized his many talents to serve multiple roles in the Westminster community leaving behind an undeniably impressive life of service. Most notably he served as mayor of Westminster for three terms.[61] Two of these terms were served consecutively as Commander of the Civilian Defense Corps as they fell during World War II. While Mayor, Thomas Henry was responsible for the paving of the first sidewalks and streets in the town, as well as the passage of the first public health laws.[62] Thomas Henry represented the community by serving on multiple boards of local institutions. He served on the School Board of Trustees for a dozen years, three of which were spent as a member of the County Board of Education, responsible for reassigning school districts and consolidating the local county schools. Besides these roles, he also served as a member of the Board of Directors at Westminster Bank and the Oconee Memorial Hospital for 18 years where he served on the building committee over an addition to the current hospital building.[63]

Other community work performed by Thomas Henry included projects that improved the quality of everyday life for the citizens of Westminster. His influence was used to build the first modern baseball field for the county, complete with a grandstand and lights. It served as the home field for the Oconee Mills Baseball team, the "Mountaineers." Eddie Lyon's father worked under Thomas Henry at the mill and was the umpire for these games.[64] The lights also allowed the field to be dually used as the football field for Westminster High School's night games during the fall season. With the assistance of other influential community members, Thomas Henry presented the local Boy Scout group, Troop 108 with a rustic lodge for meetings and activities, as well as initiated the first school lunch program in the area, feeding 500 students daily at Westminster school. His participation in civic programs also included serving as president of the Westminster Lions, Rotary, and American Legion clubs. An avid golfer, he helped organize the Oconee Country Club and assisted in the design of the course in 1954. Eddie Lyons remembers caddying for Thomas Henry when he was 9 or 10 years old.[65]

After nearly 25 years as a leader in the South Carolina textile Industry, Thomas Henry retired from his management position but remained deeply entrenched in the surrounding community. After his retirement Thomas Henry opened a car dealership in Westminster. After selling his car dealership, Thomas Henry worked as a Gulf Oil distributor which he eventually bequeathed to my grandfather. On May 24, 1961 Thomas Henry died suddenly of a heart attack on golf course at the Oconee Country Club. While my knowledge of the extended Wood family remains minimal due to a lack of documents or offspring, I am comforted by the detailed account of Thomas Henry's life and work history that present his as a man above men. A philanthropic, civil servant dedicated to the betterment and advancement of his community.

Places of Preservation Interest

During this study multiple buildings and companies that served as places of employment of my ancestors have established themselves as significant due to their impact in the community as well as historic role in the economy and society of the upstate. The significance of my great-great-grandfather's employment for the Stetson Hat Company is substantial. As an employee of this company, my great-grandfather would have been part of one of the largest and most benevolent progressive industries in Philadelphia. John B. Stetson was hailed as a revolutionary business owner and benefactor in labor relations. Working in his 1,000,000 square foot facility included a library, a Sunday school for children of employees, and a fully staffed hospital with 75 beds and a qualified staff.[66] John B Stetson was born in Orange County, New Jersey in 1830. In 1865 after learning the trade from his father, he brought a small-scale hat operation to Philadelphia. Thriving, this business expanded and continued to do so until 1906.[67] Stetson's company established programs in interest savings plans and assisted its employees in the procurement of homes near their factory.[68] Workers received Christmas gifts from the owner and were even given common stock in the company.[69] The most notable product produced by Stetson Company was the "Boss of the Plains" line of western hats. Extremely popular these hats became iconic and evoked the lore and narrative of the American Wild West. Following this largely successful line and several other dress hat lines "the name Stetson became almost synonymous with "Hat".[70]

Figure 2.5: Clock Tower and Bay, John B. Stetson Factory in Philadelphia, PA. Source: Library of Congress Prints and Photographs Division.

By the 1920s the John B. Stetson Hat Company was the largest hat company in the world and employed over 5,000 people. The Stetson Company plant was comprised of twenty industrial buildings by the architect George T. Pearson between 1880 and 1930.[71] Most notable of these building included a copper topped clock tower situated at the tip of a triangular arrangement of buildings. The buildings were constructed of brick or concrete and were connected by bridges or openings in the walls.[72] Changes were made to the site over its years of operation. Following a decline in business due to the Great Depression, a number of the older buildings on the site were demolished.[73] Subsequently the reconditioning of the building to facilitate parachute manufacturing in World War II led to a reduction in the size of several of the buildings.[74] By 1965, the company proved too large an operation and ceased production in 1971. In May 1977 the Stetson Company donated the site and its remaining structures in Philadelphia with plans to rehabilitate and preserve the building. Unfortunately, the site was destroyed by a fire in 1980 leaving no remaining fabric.[75]

While preservation of these building is now impossible because of their demolition and unfortunate burning, I am saddened that these buildings do not exist today. The humanitarian efforts of John B. Stetson left behind a larger legacy than simply a manufacturing empire. Because my great-great grandfather was part of this operation made me feel proud. Being a part of an industry like the Stetson Company, my family was able to establish a decent living for themselves. The programs implemented by Stetson at his massive facilities would have assisted families like my own in becoming financially stable and secure. Perhaps working in a company with benefits such as these allowed my grandfather the opportunity to finish school and obtain a degree, ultimately gaining a position in upper management in the textile industry.

As an employer to nearly 5,000 individuals during the height of production, this company and its associated facilities impacted many lives. If the buildings associated with this legacy remained standing today, I feel that they would be significant to the descendants of many laboring families that lived and worked in the Philadelphia area in the early twentieth century. The benevolent and community programs associated with the company would have affected many of these families positively and improved their quality of life. In a Historical American Building Survey, the site of these operations is recognized as being significant because of its historical association with John B. Stetson Hat Company and the impact of said operations on the community until 1971. Due to its large place in history, including the impact made on many families in their history, and the implications it left for industry work in the future, this site deserves recognition despite is demolition. The placement of a marker is necessary for this site with a description of its role in the industry in late nineteenth and early twentieth century Philadelphia.

Another site of preservation interest that employed a member of the Minich Family was Autun Mill in Anderson County, South Carolina. Autun Mill is the oldest continuously operating textile mill in the state. The textile industry played a large role in the economic development of the upstate of South Carolina.[76] The abundant water power and cheap non-union labor brought many mill owners to the area. These industries began to appear in the late nineteenth century as the state's Appalachian rail lines were developed providing a network of this region to the rest of the South. Mills arose as a direct effect of the invention of the cotton gin that allowed huge increases in the production of cotton on southern plantations. The construction of the surrounding housing to support the workforce of these ventures led to the creation of mill villages. The cheap rent of these homes and close location to the factory were often used to lure workers to relocate to the communities. Made up of small, identically framed houses, these neighborhoods contained large homes for supervisors as well as churches, stores, and recreational amenities.[77]

Originally Pendleton Manufacturing Company, operations at Autun began in 1836 as a wool carding plant.[78] The original mill was two stories tall, one hundred and fifty feet long, fifty feet wide, and housed 10 cards and 960 spindles used for the assembly of yarn. Purchased in 1879 by Augustus Sitton, a prominent resident of Pendleton, the mill was renamed Autun.[79] In 1927 the property again changed hands and was sold to La France Industries, whose name was eventually adopted by the community. Save for a short period during the Civil War, the Pendleton Manufacturing Company Mill was and still is in operation. Though this mill remains standing and operational, the surrounding mill village and its historic fabric has been drastically altered over time. The building my ancestor, Francis Minich Sr., worked in has been altered for new machinery and augmented to over time. It no longer resembles the two-story brick building from the early twentieth century.

A very small portion of the building remains brick, metal apparatus and yellow siding has been used for the building's expansion.[80] Located across the railroad tracks from the mill is a sprawling cluster of small homes. It is apparent that the adjacent neighborhood was at one time the Mill Village associated with Pendleton Manufacturing Company. Upon a visit to the community this winter, it became apparent that, while some of the homes in the village retain their identical framework, many have been altered to include unsuitable embellishments such as decorative ironwork on the porches. Siding has been added, and original porches have been enclosed as additions to the small homes. Infill growth of new homes and mobile homes have been added to the area over the years breaking up the traditional organized lot lines and streetscape.[81] Main Street in La France runs behind the local elementary school and contains several larger homes that may have belonged to plant supervisors or managers. Due to these alterations, the Old Pendleton Manufacturing Company Mill and its surrounding village have not been deemed eligible for recognition on the National Register of Historic Places.

Not very far down the road, the Orr-Lyons Mill was the second factory to be built in Anderson County in 1899 by Colonel James Orr Jr. First constructed to manufacture narrow heavy goods for the China trade, Orr Mill quickly expanded and became very profitable. By 1909, a Chamber of Commerce Brochure described Orr Mill to have $800,000 of capital stock and to employ 600 people operating 57,496 spindles on 1,504 looms.[82] It was the first mill in the state that utilized electric power only. Orr Mill primarily manufactured sheeting, shirting, and after World War II, print cloths. Throughout the Great Depression Orr Mills helped create jobs in Anderson County as many southerners made the transition from farmer to millhand during this time. In 1964, Orr Mill was purchased by the M. Lowenstein Textile Chain and subsequently the name was changed to Orr-Lyons Mill in honor of the service of superintendent John Andrew Lyons. He was followed by his eldest son John Joseph Lyons, who became president of the Grey Goods Division in 1946.[83]

A Historical and Architectural Survey of Anderson County published in 2002 describes the current condition and fabric remaining at this site. In the early twentieth century the dwelling structures in the Orr Mill village could be categorized into two main groups, including homes constructed when the Mill was built, and additional homes that were constructed several decades later.[84] Two main styles built at the onset of the Mill could be seen in this village. This included a small one-story, frame home with a saltbox gable roof, a central chimney, and a shed porch all balanced on brick pier foundations.[85] This style was common to mill villages in the South Carolina Upstate. A second early mill style included one-story frame homes with lateral gable roofs, slightly larger than the first that also utilized a central chimney, shed porches, and six-over-six windows, but also had a gabled ell on the rear of the home.[86] The homes constructed later located across State Highway 81 from the main village can also be separated into two styles of building.[87] These include single-story homes with a front gable roof, six-over-six windows, two inner chimneys, and an offset engaged porch on the front of the home. These houses appear more decorative and have craftsman elements with exposed rafter tails beneath the eaves, as well as diamond-shaped attic vents. The second set of homes were distinguished by a lateral gable roof with a central brick chimney through the front slope, six-over-six windows, a shed porch, and diamond vents in the gables. All four styles of mill house that appeared in this village had weatherboard exteriors and brick pier foundations.[88] Like the mill village in La France, the homes in the Orr Village have undergone significant alterations over time. The mill itself still stands, but its surrounding village has been punctuated by empty lots, new development and the placement of mobile homes. Other inappropriate additions such as chain link fences, and alterations of the siding, porches, doors, and windows of homes in the village. According to national standards, the loss of integrity and amount of change in the Orr Mill village have determined that the Orr Mill and Village are ineligible for listing on the National Register of Historic Places.

Written Family Histories

While researching my heritage I realized that many of the physical buildings or landmarks associated with my family have been demolished or destroyed by fire. Therefore, these buildings have been absent from the landscape for quite some time. The textile mills my forebears were employed in are gone or have been altered significantly to fit and operate in a modern landscape. Similarly, the homes and businesses of the surrounding mill villages have also been modernized and now resemble many other small neighborhoods in the Carolina upstate. For example, the John B. Stetson Company of Philadelphia that employed my great-great grandfather was also lost as a result of arson in 1971. While these buildings are no longer extant today to tell their stories, I am comforted in the fact that my research has allowed me to establish the significance of these places to my family and the surrounding communities. Most notably the information surrounding these places was gathered via oral histories and accounts of family members.

These oral history accounts lend valuable insights that have facilitated additional research and discovery about my family's history. Most specifically my contact with family members regarding these lifestyles and careers have led to the discovery of written family histories. One such history I was given by family members was a genealogy written by my great-grandfather, Francis Minich Sr. Recorded in 1994 this history, written in his long hand cursive, details my great grandfather's family history and includes his paternal ancestors, his father and his siblings and their families, his own childhood and detailed work history, as well as both his marriages and a brief maternal history. This history has proved extremely invaluable in its inclusion of important dates, and names of family members from previous generations. These descriptions have allowed me to effectively research these individuals, which I can then validate with birth and marriage certificates, census data depicting family members and occupations, and death certificates. The comparison of these documents to a written family history provides a sense of authentication of these family documents.

While this family history provides connection to important documents, it also provides descriptions that would only be available via oral or written histories. Everyday observations that would not be recorded in historic documents are provided via these sources. One such instance is a physical description of my great-great-great grandfather, grandfather Sauerland, and what he wore to church daily. While this written family history has proven to contain valuable information, it, like oral histories, can be influenced by the perspective of the author or the audience for which it was written. In this case, this family history was written for Francis Sr.'s daughter, my great-aunt Louise. While I hoped this history would contain details of Francis' decision to allow his children to live with his sister in-law, or how these events transpired it did no such thing. Presumably written in such a way to appeal to Louise, this document mentions dates surrounding Francis Sr.'s first marriage to Louise Lyon and does not mention his second wife Virginia, though he mentions his employment history while he was married to her. Though accurate, this family history contains variations to cater to its intended audience.

Mary Lyons Wood also provided a written family history of the Lyons family. While Francis Sr.'s document contained many facts including dates and locations, Mary's document was more of a narrative, written in descriptive language and seemed to impose emotions and attitudes on the "characters" or family members included in the narrative. The Lyons family history focused mainly on the very early generations of the family in Ireland, specifically her great-great-grandfather, John Lyons, and his immigration to the United States from Ireland, as well as dates and details John's service in the United States Army.

Other written documents I came across during my research included a skit of the Lyons family history written to be performed at a family reunion. While less formal, this document still provided a unique perspective into the Lyons family history, and it was interesting to see this history personified and written in the first person. Research into the Wood family also yielded an unpublished written document that detailed accomplishments and work history of my adoptive great grandfather.

While my knowledge of the extended Wood family remains minimal due to a lack of genealogical documents or offspring, I am comforted by the detailed account of Thomas Henry's life and work history that present him as a man above men: a philanthropic, civil servant dedicated to the betterment and advancement of his community. Furthermore, I learned valuable information about Thomas Henry's role in the community and his hand in the inner workings of multiple textile mills in the South as well as internationally and am able to relate this past to the heritage of other extended family members in the upstate.

Additional Special Items

In addition to these written family histories, my great-grandfather Francis Minich Sr. kept a scrapbook filled with various items that has made its way into my family's hands. This scrapbook is extremely special in that it provides a unique look into what Francis considered significant and worthy of preserving for future generations. Among them is a wide assortment of documents that include, telegrams, letters, newspaper clippings, and textile manufacturing pamphlets. The telegrams are extremely interesting and exhibit correspondence between business partners. There are also several telegrams between family, including one announcing the death of Francis' grandmother, from his father on August 30, 1932. These are a testament to what news telegrams were often used to convey in the early and mid-twentieth century.

Many of the telegrams came from the Western Union Telegram Company and cost between 25 and 35 cents to send as advertised on the envelopes. [89] Newspaper clippings from *The Anderson Daily Mail*, a local paper contained an obituary for the owner of a men's store in Anderson, Francis must have known. Another clipping from the *Textile Herald* on December 11, 1941 paper recognizes Francis Sr. for his "various and valuable services" as general manager of Pendleton

Manufacturing Company and mentions his "integrity and faithfulness as a business man."[90] Documents in the scrapbook also revealed Francis strong involvement in his community Lions Club while he lived in Anderson and Greenville. A small Lions Club directory published July 1, 1945 lists Francis Minich Sr. as Negotiator Quartermaster, armed services and contain asterisk identifying him as a past president of the club, and the only president to ever serve two terms. Another Lions Club document includes a letter transferring Francis Sr.'s Lions Club membership from Greenville, South Carolina, to Ware Shoals, South Carolina where he moved and began work for Riegel Textile Corporation in 1947. Company publications entitled "La France at a Glance are also included in the scrapbook and were published by La France Industries for their workforce and the surrounding community. These magazines include articles for their workers and advertisements for their upholstery manufacturing.

One magazine includes an article questioning the future of the upholstery business after World War I ends detailing what to expect and how to encourage good business during those challenging times. [91] The documents help communicate the sentiments of the manufacturing field during the 1940s and give context to the environment in which Francis would have worked a general manager of the company. Francis Sr.'s scrapbook also contains newspaper headlines of nationally relevant news events, most notably the bombing of pearl harbor and the death of Franklin D. Roosevelt. To see and hold primary source documents from such important events in history is surreal. My great-grandfather's decision to preserve these documents has provided my family with a rare glimpse into the past.

Perhaps some of the most pertinent documents in this scrapbook include letters dating from 1942 until 1949 from both my grandfather Francis Jr. and his sister, Louise. Most of these letters are from Francis Jr. and were typically short, and discussed a recent visit, a thank you note for a gift, or requested a gift for a special occasion like Christmas. The postmarks on the letters change frequently, with the majority originating from Westminster, South Carolina where Francis Jr. and Louise lived with their adoptive parents Thomas Henry and Mary Elizabeth. Several others come from Saint Genevieve of the Pines in Ashville, North Carolina where Louise attended boarding school and Saint Leo's boarding school in Florida where Francis Jr. attended.[92]

One of the most notable letters from Francis Jr. is postmarked October 20, 1948 and addressed to Francis and Virginia. This letter details my young grandfather's decision to abandon his birth surname and take the name of his adoptive father and mother: "I received your other letters under my real name. I am registered under both names, but I go by Mickey Wood [instead of Francis Jr.]. I don't want you to think that I am forgetting my real "old man", but as you know I must pay all due respect to Uncle Henry for he has been awful nice to Sister and I."[93] From then on Francis Jr. went by his preferred named of Mickey Wood.

Figure 2.6: A young Francis Minich Wood (a.k.a "Mickey"). Source: From the personal collection of the author.

This correspondence verifies the arrangement between Francis Sr. and his sister-in-law in the care of his children. It also reveals the reasoning behind my grandfather's decision to change his name. In a matter of loyalty to the man who raised him, my grandfather abandoned his birth name and assumed the surname Wood in honor of his adopted father. The discovery of these written accounts and documents has brought to light many aspects of their lives. Where oral histories have deviated, and deceased family members have left gaps, these written histories have provided unique perspective and information in what would otherwise be lost.

Now that I am aware of their existence, I plan to preserve these documents (or copies of them) for future generations, and to educate my immediate family on their own heritage, which has been neglected for many years. These family histories, accompanied by the oral accounts my family have provided, paint a wonderful picture and assist in establishing the significance of many of the physical places in the South Carolina Upstate that tie closely to my family. I feel like these documents have become part of the heritage that I wish to preserve for future generations. Such papers are increasingly rare as we move into the digital age and are extremely valuable pieces of information.

Larger Implications of a Surname: Adoption
While conducting my research, I realized my plight of a substituted surname paled in comparison to individuals who truly know nothing about their heritage. A surname has much larger implications when it begins to facilitate the process of conducting genealogical research and eventual development of ethnic ties, lineage, and a family tree. Individuals who have no knowledge of a family name run into many obstacles when

attempting to research family narratives or genealogy. This is most often the case for the 5 million individuals in the United States who have no knowledge of their birth families or family histories.[94] While my grandfather and great aunt were adopted, their case was unique in that they remained with extended family, were aware of their biological ties to their adoptive family, and of what a change in name would bring. While many adoptees love their adoptive families, it is common for them at some point in their life to pursue genealogical research about their own biological past. It is not uncommon for most adoptees to feel a sense of "genealogical bewilderment" in their lack of knowledge regarding their own pasts.[95]

The main reason for Kathy Minich's "search," who was adopted by Francis Sr., and Virginia Minich, was to an attempt to answer the bewilderment later in her adult life. Adopted when she was two-year old, Francis Sr. and Virginia are the only parents Kathy has ever known, yet this did not prevent her from doing the research that she could to discover her biological family's history. Unfortunately, her search was unfruitful due to South Carolina's practice of sealing adoption records, preventing her from learning anything about her biological family, including a surname. This has left Kathy speculative if people she encountered in her search are relatives or not due to similarities in significant dates and locations.[96]

Knowledge of family histories and backgrounds can be instrumental in providing a sense of identity. This "knowledge of one's heritage and the people and places associated with it is a necessary part of identity formation."[97] Often a search for information about an adoptee's family begins with a principal search for birth parents. While the primary reason adoptees feel the need to search is attributed to "the need to understand why they were abandoned," additionally adoptees feel the need for "continuity of their own history,"[98] as well as need to connect pieces of their background to establish community and a sense of belonging.

Perhaps this misconception emerged in that I had been fortunate enough to establish a relationship with Francis Minich Sr. and Virginia, and felt they served a larger role in my life than their Lyons counterparts. They had, after all, passed decades before my birth. My only association with them resided in my father's family name and stories communicated to me from Mary Elizabeth Lyons. Reaching out and speaking to my family members while gathering oral accounts proved to be an eye-opening experience. Strangely, I found myself surprised that my great-aunt provided me with information about the Lyons when questioned about her family history. Rather abashed, I realized that the very family I attempted to ignore was the most significant to my great aunt, my father, and his siblings. This awareness allowed me to discover similarities between both sides of my family and the strong contributions and influences both contribute to my identity and familial connections.

Constructing Identity

Throughout this thesis I worked to develop a narrative for the Minich side of the family that remained in the dark for many years. Utilizing family histories and documents, building family trees, and even including the Wood branch of the family in my research helped to fill a knowledge gap about my relatives spanning several generations. During this process I uncovered buildings, family documents rich in details, and a deep connection to the textile industry of the South Carolina Upstate, all seemingly fitting of the theme "What is your Heritage and the State of its Preservation?". The preservation efforts at places like the Pendleton Manufacturing Company, Orr-Lyons Mills, Oconee Mills Inc., John B. Stetson Company and their respective remaining facilities and villages will only become increasingly difficult as these places and their remaining fabric continue to change and deteriorate. Today, several of these buildings do not exist, and have been lost from the landscape forever, as seen with the John B. Stetson Company facilities in Philadelphia. Similarly, the Oconee Mills Inc, located in the old Westminster Mill has also been demolished. Others have been rebranded and altered beyond recognition. The Orr-Lyons Mill now operates as a Wamsutta Plant in West Anderson.

Pendleton Manufacturing Company, now La France Industries remains in operation today as the oldest continually operating cotton mill in South Carolina but no longer resembles its former structure due to renovation and expansion. However, in considering what was deserving of memory preservation I concluded it was not only these buildings, their remains, or pieces of paper that require attentive and dedicated protection. While some buildings no longer stand, identifying my family's names and their stories or associations with these places has been a critical first step in ensuring some sort of preservation. My responsibility moving forward is to continue to act as a steward of both the Minich and Wood family names, sharing their origins, stories, and identity made up of a history anchored in the textile culture of the South Carolina upstate, specifically Oconee and Anderson counties. Ultimately, my research has helped establish the significance of these places to my family, encouraging their preservation through the perpetuation of our family name, and hopefully to other individuals who may feel a connection to the narrative of these places.

Chapter 3: New Orleans Mardi Gras: More Than Just a Wild Party[1]

By Ellen Feringa

As you mature, the things that you once looked forward to change. I left New Orleans to attend the College of Charleston where I was a Historic Preservation and Community Planning major and run Cross Country and Track. Nowhere else besides New Orleans gets off for Mardi Gras. To everyone outside of Louisiana, Mardi Gras is simply a big party. The history and traditions of Carnival are unknown to them. The more time I spent away from New Orleans, the more I began to affiliate Mardi Gras with outsider perceptions. I forgot the history, the family traditions, the artistry of the floats, gowns, pins, and other Carnival heirlooms. I forgot how important Mardi Gras is to this place. For this thesis, I define the cultural, political, and economic significance of Mardi Gras throughout the years. This thesis explores Mardi Gras with a focus on the Rex Organization and my related family's history.

I begin my thesis with the reason I chose to write about my family's Mardi Gras heritage, the debutante season. I then dive into the formation of Carnival and the significance of the School of Design, who is responsible for producing many Mardi Gras traditions, and continues to embody its motto, Pro Bono Publico, "for the public good" (*Pro Bono Publico Foundation*). The Cabildo, a museum and historic landmark and building, preserves and documents Mardi Gras's history, artifacts, and cultural heritage. The Cabildo's warehouse houses my great-great grandfather's Rex King costume and my great-grandmother's Queen's gown and Mardi Gras regalia. Through oral stories, interviews, newspaper articles, and pictures. I animate Carnival, the Rex Organization, and my family's history. While Mardi Gras is not on UNESCO's Representative List of the Intangible Cultural Heritage of Humanity, I compare it to other festivals that are go into detail about past, present, and future threats. I then conclude the thesis with my family's history.

Mardi Gras is no different than any other holiday in the calendar year. As a child born and raised in a New Orleans family, it surprised me that nowhere else in the United States do people celebrate the Carnival season as they do in New Orleans. Schools and businesses shut down, families come together, king cakes line the grocery store aisles, and jazz music and merriment fill the air ("Local Intelligence"). There is a different ambiance during the Carnival season that cannot be fully explained unless one experiences it first-hand. Hundreds of thousands of people come to the city to participate in the weeklong festivities. Neither rain, cold weather, hail, nor blazing heat can steer people away or dampen their spirits. For many New Orleanians, the Carnival celebration starts much earlier than most would expect. Costume and dressmakers, float artists, and all the many Krewes and Mardi Gras organizations must start planning for the next Mardi Gras as early as Ash Wednesday, the very next day that follows Mardi Gras Day.

Family traditions reveal what is important to understand within a cultural heritage (Stenning). If traditions are not passed down the cultural heritage can disappear. Whether it is tangible or intangible, heritage gives people a sense of identity and the feeling of belonging. The city's centuries-old Mardi Gras tradition demonstrate New Orleans' commitment to preserving its past. The most widely-known customs of parade watching, catching throws, drinking, and eating traditional New Orleans cuisine are only a fraction of the celebration. Of all the visitors that flood to the city every year, very few receive the opportunity to partake in the organizations and Krewes' traditions. Each Krewe and organization contains their own unique attire, symbols, parades, balls, ceremonies, court, and several other rituals (Ettinger; Hales). The identities of their members and locations are kept a secret to preserve the Krewes' heritage and customs. Certain Mardi Gras Krewes and societies are regarded as more significant than others. One of the oldest and most prestigious organizations is the School of Design, informally known as the Krewe of Rex (Brown).

The culture and traditions of the Rex Organization have been immersed in my family for generations. Fathers, daughters, sons, and cousins have served as riders, maids, lieutenants, and even the King and Queen of Carnival. Writing about my family's Mardi Gras heritage and the Rex Organization's traditions was influenced by my own return to New Orleans in 2018 in order to make my debut. As part of my research I listened to my grandmother's debutante stories and flipped through old newspaper clippings and photographs of her time in the balls. I struggled to explain to some of my professors the importance of Mardi Gras and making your debut while having to withhold many of our cultural secrets. Many of the original intentions for forming the Mardi Gras Krewes have been overshadowed by the superficial materialism that encompasses the twenty-first century. Pictures from the Library of Congress illustrating Mardi Gras in the 1900s depict the different ambiance and behavior of the crowd as well as the collective transformation and progression of Mardi Gras.

Debutantes

As a child, I treasured the music, time spent with family, and seeing my father hurl beads from the float, towards my siblings and me. There was always a king cake in the house, and every morning we would anxiously try to select the piece with the baby hidden inside. I remember attending the Rex Den the Sunday before Mardi Gras Tuesday, where all the floats, costumes, and regalia of the Krewe of Rex are held. My siblings and I would rush to admire the beautifully crafted floats, especially the float my father would ride. He would bring us into a purple, velvety-floored room filled with memoirs and historic, glittering court costumes displayed behind glass. Images of former Kings and Queens hung on a royal green and gold gilded wall.

We would quickly skim through the names to find our family members. On Fat Tuesday, my mother would take us to the Pickwick Club to watch the day parades. The Queen of Comus and her court would stand on the balcony of the Pickwick Club and Rex, the King of Carnival, would toast her and her court. The highlight of Mardi Gras day was seeing a tall, masked figure lean over the papier-mâché float hollering and waving spears and bags of shiny, pearl-sized, plastic beads in our direction. More floats would pass by until the sounds of firetruck sirens filled the air, signifying the end of the parade and the public Carnival celebration.

For Mardi Gras 2018 I had the opportunity to be one of the debutantes, who are daughters of members that belong to Carnival organizations like Rex and are in their junior year of college (age 21), where we are presented to society at a ball. It is a tradition that demarks a rite of passage in a young women's life. The number of events a debutante partakes in is based on her father's membership in various organizations, the donations he has made, his ranking, and economic standing. Debutantes can receive from one to as many as thirteen invitations. My father has two sisters, Barbara and Lisa Feringa, who did not make their debut for financial and personal reasons. Their decisions created a break in our family's tradition. My sister and I have revived the tradition by accepting invitations to be honored in the Carnival organizations and making our debut this past Mardi Gras season.

The Twelfth Night Revelers, a Mardi Gras Krewe founded in 1870, commences the official Mardi Gras season with a ball held twelve days after Christmas. The significance of January 6th predates the second century B.C.E., before Christmas was celebrated. The date is recognized as the Feast of the Epiphany marking the day the Magi visited Christ and an end to the holiday season ("Louisiana's Biggest Annual Celebration: Mardi Gras;" Branley). In New Orleans, the Carnival season continues until Ash Wednesday and is comprised of public and private events. The events held prior to January 6th are private and revolve around a group of women known as debutantes. A majority of the balls following January 6 remain private though. The parades are the most well-known and popular public event and begin after January 6 ("Louisiana's Biggest Annual Celebration"). Elaborate floats roll the streets with marching bands, flambeau carriers, and troops of masked dancers of all ages go on parade.

Debutantes are selected from families who have ties to select New Orleans Mardi Gras organizations. Originally, debutantes took off from school and any other obligations for many months to partake in the festivities. It was and continues to be a social event—retelling memories, forming and rekindling friendships, and passing down heirlooms. These private events are restricted to the debutantes and their families, beginning the previous June with *Le Début des Jeunes Filles de la Nouvelle Orléans*, continuing until the grand ball on Fat Tuesday ("Meet the Debs"). The families and friends of these debutantes host extravagant parties, luncheons, and brunches. The debutantes may receive gifts and continue to be presented throughout the Carnival season at elegant balls and by the secret societies and social clubs.

Birth of Carnival in New Orleans

The Carnival celebration traces back to Roman Catholicism and continues to this day to serve as a prelude to Lent (Bookhardt). The Carnival season during the seventeenth century included lavish banquets, masked balls, parades, and other boisterous *éclat* events (O' Neil 19). In 1699 the French introduced the Carnival celebration to the New World. Fat Tuesday included a parade with an extravagant procession led by a *Boeuf Gras*, a fatted ox signifying the last meat eaten before *Smo* (O'Neil 20). French aristocrats sponsored parades displaying paper-mâché creatures from Greek and Roman mythology (O' Neil 21). These Carnival pageantries are still displayed along with themes depicting social and political satire (Bookhardt).

New Orleans has been rooted in Mardi Gras since its founding when Jean-Baptiste Le Moyne de Bienville and Pierre Le Moyne d'Iberville explored the Mississippi River on Lundi Gras, the day before Mardi Gras (Hardy, 2018a). On Fat Tuesday, they named a point located 60 miles south of present-day New Orleans Point du Mardi Gras (*Mardi Gras in New Orleans and Louisiana*; Hardy, 2018a). Under French rule, New Orleans held festivals, operas, and masked balls preceding Lent. When Spain acquired Louisiana after the Seven Year's War, the Spanish governor banned all Carnival events (Hardy and O'Neil 24). Carnival celebrations were restored by 1823 under American rule, and the public celebration or "street masking" was allowed in 1827 (Hardy, 2018a).

The public Mardi Gras celebrations were predominantly composed of maskers wandering the streets either by foot, pulled in carriages, or riding horses until 1837. These were the earliest documented parades where maskers collectively gathered and wore costumes. However, the revelers' barbarous behavior put Mardi Gras in danger over the next two decades (Ettinger; Hardy, 2018a). The formation of the Mistick Krewe of Comus in 1857 safeguarded the Mardi Gras celebration by holding a safe, yet boisterous Mardi Gras event. The Mistick Krewe of Comus, the oldest Carnival organization and first secret Mardi Gras society, established several traditions, such as themed parades followed by a ball with a tableau corresponding to the theme. The parade was comprised of male, costumed and masked revelers riding floats (Hardy, 2018a). Comus inspired other Mardi Gras revelers to establish their own Krewes. The Krewes drew their names from Greco and Latin titles (O' Neil 33). Not until 1872 did the School of Design formalized the Carnival season by establishing organizing a daytime parade, and selecting purple, gold, and green as the official colors. The School of Design elected their King, Rex, to reign over the celebration (Hardy, 2018a).

Carnival Becomes a Formal Affair

Elements of the origins of the Krewe of Rex are shrouded in mystery (Brown). One speculation involves the arrival of the Russian Grand Duke, Alexis in New Orleans (Laborde, 1999). Since his journey to America was a turning point for the Mardi Gras culture and led to the birth of Rex. The Grand Duke witnessed the Krewe of Rex's first parade on Fat Tuesday (Farrow 5).

The Grand Duke's journey to America was prompted by his father, Alexander II, to break up his forbidden romance with Alexandra Zhukouskaya and as a "good-will tour" to strengthen the relationship between the United

States and Russia (Farrow 4). Legend has it that while traveling, the Grand Duke became enamored with a British burlesque performer after watching her show, and he followed her to New Orleans. Merchants took this rumor and his royal arrival was used as a marketing and advertising opportunity. As Mardi Gras approached, local newspapers published articles expressing their concern about the lack of grand display for the Grand Duke's arrival. According to the *Times* on January 31, 1872, a group of "bankers, educators, and business men" met at the St. Charles Hotel lobby to make the Carnival festivities a formally organized event (Hales 34). Within two weeks, "Rex," or the King of Carnival, was announced. Rex issued proclamations and edicts declaring all others who wished to partake in the Carnival celebration to report to his Marshalls. In addition, their motto, *Pro Bono Publico,* was selected (Hales 34).

Prior to Rex, Mardi Gras took place only at night and was described as "Individuals and small bands of masked revelers wandered the streets to celebrate the last hurrah before Lent..." (Farrow 185). The Twelfth Night Revelers kicked off the Carnival celebration by parading in the evening and holding a ball that same night. Comus concluded the Carnival festivities with a grand parade and a ball on the evening of Fat Tuesday (Dufour and Huber 17). *The New Orleans Bee,* a bilingual newspaper that ran from 1827 to 1923, described the maskers as: "rarely with any design and with but little sign of wit or humor, showing nothing but unmeaning grotesqueness, used to move through the streets, singly, in couples or in threes or fours, and the day light spectacle was simply an exhibition of the vulgarest buffoonery" (1).

Figure 3.1: Mistick Krewe of Comus's Night Procession. Source: Library of Congress Prints and Photographs Division.

In the days leading up to Mardi Gras, Rex issued proclamations to all Louisiana officials and governmental bodies requesting their support, cooperation, and participation on Mardi Gras day (Hales 36; "City Intelligence"; "Local Intelligence"; "Notice"). Rex sent a letter to the St. Charles Hotel, where the Grand Duke was staying, welcoming him to the city and describing the event held in his honor on Mardi Gras day (Farrow 193). On Fat Tuesday at precisely 3 o'clock, the Royal Salute of Thirteen Guns fired to commence the Rex Procession (The King of Carnival). The Order of Procession went as followed: Squadron of Mounted Police. Chief Marshal of the Empire. H.R.H THE KING OF THE CARNIVAL, With Attendants. Music. Lord of the Yeomanry. First Division. Music. Lord of the Carriages. Second Division. Music. Lord of the Vans. Third Division. Music. Lord of the House. Fourth Division. Music. Lord of the Unattached. Fifth Division. Platoon of Police (Grand Marshal of the Empire).

The Grand Duke's story causes debate amongst historians since the edicts Rex issued never referred to Alexis as the focal point for the Carnival season. The *Times-Picayune* described the organization's objectives as providing amusement for the people, promoting the "prosperity of New Orleans," and making New Orleans "the grand center of attraction during the Carnival season, thereby bringing tens of thousands of people and millions of dollars here" ("The King of Carnival"). Nonetheless, the Grand Duke's arrival in New Orleans is still intertwined in Rex's history. Historians agree that the group of civic leaders served as the catalyst for the formation of Rex (Laborde, 1999, n.pg.). The Civil War left New Orleans desperate to draw visitors to the city to revive the economy (Brown). Coincidentally, the Grand Duke Alexis visited New Orleans at the same time these civic leaders were creating the Krewe of Rex. The main driver to restore the economy through Mardi Gras was tourism and unification (Farrow 230; Laborde, 1999, n.pg.).

The group of civic leaders, including Rex himself, gathered in the lobby of the St. Charles Hotel to plan the first Rex parade, entice visitors to the city, and establish order amongst the chaotic Mardi Gras groups (Brown; Laborde, 1999, 5). The men included "Bob Rivers, Albert Baldwin, E.B. Wheelock, W.E. Pike, Chris Mehle, William Mehle, C.H. Hyams, C.T. Howard, Durant Dupante, and E.C. Hancock" (Brown). Since Carnival's net value showed a continuous decline in the past years, the Rex Captain and his predecessors paid for the Carnival bill. Lewis J. Salomon raised funds to pay and reigned as the first King of Carnival (Laborde, 1999, 5). Regardless of whether Carnival was thrown in the Grand Duke's honor or to attract tourists to New Orleans, or both, Rex became Mardi Gras's international emblem (Hardy, 2018a). The *New Orleans Bee* noted on February 14, 1872: Considering that King Carnival so lately broached the idea of organizing the maskers and presenting them, in all their heterogeneous conceptions, methodically in a continuous line, his effort was successful beyond what could have been expected.

In obedience to his orders, many, on the route of his progress, … and otherwise decorated their houses and shops, and the… which followed him was the largest number of merry makers that ever turned out in New Orleans (1). This demonstrates the respect the citizens of New Orleans had for the Krewe of Rex, the King of Carnival's role as a "prominent civic leader," and the community's desire to cultivate their Mardi Gras roots (Brown). The passage exemplifies the word "Leadership" which is a key principle of the School of Design's civic background. The formation of the Rex Organization helped establish the New Orleans' Mardi Gras culture we see today, and still remains the cynosure of Mardi Gras (Laborde, 1999, n.pg.).

Preserving Traditions with the Appearance of Super-Krewes

From the very beginning, New Orleans was a tourist destination, and throughout the 1960s New Orleans was pushing tourism as a new industry. This was at the same time that the Super-Krewes started to appear in the Mardi Gras celebrations (Philips). Local businessmen founded the first Super-Krewe, Bacchus, in 1969 followed by Endymion in 1974 and Orpheus in 1998 (Philips and Capo 24). The investments from businesses and corporations transformed Mardi Gras into a marketing industry and started a new era of tourism for Mardi Gras and New Orleans (Capo 21; Gotham 175). Tourism, materialism, entertainment, and consumer culture drove the Super-Krewes. They are characterized by containing hundreds of members, mile-long parades, double-decker and tandem floats, over the top balls, celebrities reigning as Kings and Queens, and excessive spending on their events (O'Neil 86; Capo 24). In order to preserve Mardi Gras's origins and prevent over-commercialization, the city placed a ban on branding floats, beads, cups, trinkets, floats, and throws (Peter Feringa).

Bacchus and Endymion had the same motives as Rex, to attract tourists, but they went even further: "'But Endymion did more than attract tourists and provide jobs; it played a major role in the democratization of Mardi Gras, opening its doors to some who had been barred from the old-line clubs'" (Gotham 174). Membership into the old-line Krewes was strictly limited to New Orleans natives of specific social and economic status. In 1877, Rex's parade established three rules for those who wished to join the School of Design: 'First— No promiscuous maskers will be allowed to join or participate in the Royal pageant...Second— Organized bodies of Maskers will be gladly received and assigned positions...Third—No advertising van, or any designs of such character, will be allowed in the Parades' (Laborde, 1999, 38). Super Krewes opened up their membership to everyone across the United States, including California and New York, as long as they paid the admission cost (Gotham 174; Capo 24). Only five krewes—Krewe of Rex, the Twelfth Night Revelers, the Krewe of Comus, Krewe of Proteus, and Krewe of Momus—paraded before 1900 (Rothman). Super-Krewes such as Endymion and Bacchus ride at night starting on the Saturday before Mardi Gras day, providing an incentive for tourists stay from Saturday to Tuesday (Gotham 175). Kevin Gotham states that the tourism sparked by Bacchus, Endymion, and Orpheus transformed Mardi Gras into the "world's greatest free show" (178).

The core values of the Super-Krewes differ drastically from the old-line organizations. Endymion's motto, "Token of Youth" and "Throw until it hurts," epitomizes the new Mardi Gras— promoting tourism, entertainment, and consumer culture ("Endymion"). Endymion boasts over 15 million throws and being the "finest entertainment in Mardi Gras" ("Endymion"). Using celebrities as the Kings, Queens, and Marshals encapsulate the idea of entertainment. Celebrities including Will

Ferrell, Sandra Bullock, John C. Reilly, and Britney Spears have reigned as Kings, Queens, and Grand Marshals of the parades. The School of Design upholds their motto, *Pro Bono Publico,* meaning "for the public good," and stands by their traditions, owning their own floats, designing original themes, and performing civic projects. As described by the current Captain of Rex:

Our membership is comprised of community leaders, who work on a volunteer basis together each year to maintain the traditions of the organization and stage the preeminent parade and ball of the Mardi Gras season. This all is done under the organization's motto [which] took on special significance in the aftermath of Hurricane Katrina when the members formed the Pro Bono Publico Foundation to help support the rebuilding of our city's public schools (Brown). Since 1872 the Rex Organization has chosen its King based on civic duty. Unlike other old-line Carnival Krewes, who keep the King's identity a secret from the public, the identity of Rex is publicly announced (Brown). This lack of secrecy in the city allows crowds to form a relationship with the Krewe of Rex, unlike other organizations.

The Rex Organization has abandoned certain traditions and introduced new ones throughout its history. Rex's floats now contain animation, and over half of the floats have abandoned the original, wooden cotton wagon chassis in favor of steel-framed ones (Brown). The props, figures, and decorative pieces are still handcrafted using traditional materials *(Rex: King of Carnival)*. The School of Design has abstained from implementing typical Super-Krewe contraptions, such as fiber optics, double-deckers, and high-tech lighting. The School of Design has continued its traditional Carnival style of gold and silver tensile, historic colors, and papier-mâché figures, flowers, and ornamentation (Ettinger 73-74).

Besides the traditional costumes and floats debuted each year, such as the Boeuf Gras float and the riders' butcher costume, the rest of the Carnival costumes and floats are designed new each year (74). Bill Grace, Krewe of Rex representative says, "we made decision years ago to stay with a traditional papier-mâché look…. It fits the scale of the floats, it's the right size for what we're trying to represent" (Ettinger 73). Traditional Rex floats carry anywhere from eight to twenty riders while the Super-Krewes' floats carry anywhere from fifty to 200 riders. Endymion carries at least 150 members on each float, totaling 2,000 members in the entire parade ("Endymion"; Ettinger 73). Rex is very strict on what their riders are able to throw. Throws are strictly limited to Rex items only. The Krewe of Rex one-ups other parades by having each float throw emblem beads, imprinted cups, and items with the float's specific theme rather than the Krewe's overall parade theme (Brown).

In 1969, the Krewe of Bacchus completely changed the nature of Mardi Gras when they presented the largest floats in the history of Mardi Gras (Hardy, 2018a). The Krewe of Bacchus and the Krewe of Endymion continue to debut some of the largest floats, attracting thousands of visitors each year and changing the atmosphere of Carnival (Gotham 174-175; Ettinger 73). Hundreds of thousands flock to the city to see the celebrities and ornate, double-decker tandem floats and catch the colorful plastic beads, boas, and trinkets (Gotham 174-175). Since the Super-Krewes and the new era of culture, Mardi Gras has received a reputation for being an "orgy in the streets" (Foster). Arthur Hardy, a Mardi Gras historian, states in Brian Ettinger's article "Rex Appeal," "Getting past the image is hard. I find that I have to spend more time educating them, telling them what the real Mardi Gras is like." However, Carnival organizations, such as Rex, are committed to preserving and reviving the original Mardi Gras heritage and culture (Foster). The Super-Krewes are important to the transformation of Mardi Gras. The innovations established by the Super-Krewes continue to be popular among locals and visitors. They started a new era for Mardi Gras and several organizations have copied their innovations, such as the large floats, the celebrity rides, and the replacement of the traditional ball with an extravaganza ball for anyone able to purchase a ticket. They brought life to the "static" parade and made Carnival accessible to everyone (Hardy, 2018a).

The Artistry of the Rex Organization

Mardi Gras has always been driven by history and an artistic expression of the past, as seen with the Krewes' depiction of the rich local history and creative and chaotic myths and mysteries on the floats (Bookhardt). Carnival Krewes draw from history, ancient cultures, and artistic movements such as surrealism and literature work to create glimmering and mystical pageants (*Rex: King of*

Carnival; Bookhardt). The "simple conceptual sketches" completed by the talented artists and designers are masterpieces (*Rex: King of Carnival*). In the mid-1870s, newspapers began to feature black and white illustrations of the float designs with a short description or no illustration and a lengthy explanation (Schindler, 2001, 111). Henri Schindler's book, *Mardi Gras Treasures: Float Designs of the Golden Age*, displays and explains the surviving watercolor sketches and lithographs of Carnival Krewes from the 1870s through World War I (Hales 102).

The School of Design's classic pageantry and traditional construction separates them from the rest of the parades, especially the Super-Krewes (Bookhardt). Their pageantry is fused with mystery, beauty, exotic fantasies, and opulence to display the artistry of New Orleans Carnival (Schindler, 2000, 7-9). Their floats are all hand-painted, and all of the elaborate props and decorations are hand-crafted to fit the float's scale (Ettinger 73). Henri Schindler, Carnival historian and Rex's Artistic Director, and the artisans and craftsman at Kern Studios preserve the traditional design process and artistry of float building for Rex (73). The School of Design's floats feature highly stylized, handcrafted flowers and lots of gold and silver foil that glimmer in the sunlight. The glittering and floral decorations add an element of elegance and motion under the sun (*Rex: King of Carnival*; Ettinger 73). The handcrafted figures and props serve as the focal points for each float and illustrate each float's individual theme (*Rex: King of Carnival*).

Figure 3.2: "2018 Rex Proclamation." Source: From the personal collection of the author.

The School of Design sent Blaine Kern, founder of Blaine Kern Artists, to Europe to study the Italian, German, and French Carnival float design and construction, so he could understand and recreate the traditional Carnival spirit and artistry (Ettinger 74; Bookhardt). The design process today only differs slightly from the original design process. The ideas and sketches are miraculously transformed into works of art. The sketches guide the construction of the floats, and the sketches are transformed into colorful illustrations, resembling the watercolors and lithographs from the Golden Age (*Rex: King of Carnival*). Invitations, admit cards, dance cards, scrolls, and posters reflect the opulent Carnival pageants each year.

The members of the Krewes and their families save these pieces of art and frame them in their household or bind them together in volumes (Schindler, 2000, n.pg.). During the late nineteenth century, technological advances in colored printing and lithography enabled invitations and edicts to become more extravagant and complex. Instead of using the postal system, special messengers hand delivered the beautiful Carnival masterpieces (9). The invitations, posters, and other Carnival cards have become valuable collectibles and remembrances of the New Orleans Carnival (*Rex: King of Carnival*). Many of the centuries-old Carnival traditions and culture found in New Orleans during the eighteenth and nineteenth century are reflections of the Old World European pagan celebrations, including Roman festivals such as Saturnalia and Lupercalia ("Mardi Gras 2018"). In the 1540s, *carnival* in French meant "time of merrymaking before Lent;" in Italian, *Carnevale* meant "Shrove Tuesday" (*Online Etymology Dictionary*). The folk etymology of Carnival is from the Medieval Latin word, *carne vale,* meaning, "farewell flesh!" (Brown; *Online Etymology Dictionary*). Historically, the Rex Procession included a live ox decorated with garlands. The live ox was either lead on foot or placed on a wagon and pulled through the parade (Hardy; "L'Ancienne Nouvelle-Orleans"). The Krewe of Rex adopted the symbol in their early years; since 1959, a float features an enormous papier- mâché sculpture of the Boeuf Gras float with men dressed in butcher costumes ("L'Ancienne Nouvelle-Orleans"). The fattened ox remains an important part of the Carnival celebration today and a symbol of the last meat eaten before Lent (Brown and Hales 100).

Figure 3.3: The Boeuf Gras Float at Mardi Gras. Photograph by Carol M Highsmith. Source: Library of Congress Prints and Photographs Division.

The Mardi Gras symbols and festivities hold their same purpose as the prelude to Lent. Locals and tourists participate in the Mardi Gras life of debauchery and excessive indulgence of alcohol and New Orleans traditional cuisine of king cake, crawfish, po'boys, beignets, and gumbo before fasting and starting their religious obligations.

Today, ancient Greek mythology and medieval symbols take on modern twists, but the traditions are still linked to their historic Carnival origins (Hales 100). Certain symbols—the Carnival's signature colors, golden doubloons, and their theme song—cannot be traced back to European capitals (Hales; Ettinger 72).

The history of the Krewe of Rex selecting the Carnival colors—purple, gold, and green—is unclear. Errol Laborde, Historian and author of *Marched the Day God*, believes Rex chose the colors for their heraldry symbolism (Brown). According to heraldry, there are only five acceptable choices. In the context of Rex, they are startling. The acceptable colors are: red, blue, purple, green and black. With purple being a logical choice and with gold as the metal, the final choice came down to two combinations; purple, gold and green or purple, gold and black, and so the combination with green was decided upon. For centuries, purple has been associated with royalty, and the color of the flag's metal was either white or gold (Brown). The Rex flag arrays the Carnival colors diagonally with a royal crown placed in the center of the yellow diagonal. Former Carnival Kings and Queens hang the flags outside of their home during Mardi Gras (*Rex: King of Carnival*). In 1892, Rex's parade theme, "The Symbolism of Colors," explained the symbolism of the Carnival colors (Dufour and Huber 43). The parade featured nineteen floats with purple meaning justice, gold meaning power, and green meaning faith (Schindler, 2001, 60-61). Dufour and Huber stress that the explanation suggested in the theme does not explain the selection for the colors two decades earlier in 1872 (43). Nonetheless, the colors have served as the School of Design and Mardi Gras' signature colors ever since 1872 (Brown; Hales 100).

The 1870 hit song, "If Ever I Cease to Love," can be heard all along the Big Easy's streets (Hales 100). On November 6, 1871, a poem called "A Song for Sentimentalists" written by Hancock, one of the young men who gathered in the St. Charles Hotel lobby, was published in the *Times* (Brown; Laborde, 1999, 5, 32). According to Laborde, "the song's popularity in New Orleans months before either Lydia or Alexis arrived was made evident in [this] poem...suggest[ing] a familiarity with the published version of the song" (1999, 32).

> *If never I cease to love,*
> *The moon may change her hue,*
> *And 'mid the stars above*
> *The sun no more burn blue,*
> *Among the Woodland trees,*
> *The whales their song may cease,*
> *And oysters at their ease,*
> *May keep their beds in peace...*

The burlesque performer, Lydia Thompson, sang the song in the musical *Blue Beard* while Alexis was visiting New Orleans in 1872 (Brown; "Tuesday Evening, Mardi Gras Night"). According to legend, locals amplified his infatuation for her and the song (Brown; Hales 101). Laborde states that the Russian National Anthem was played specifically for the Grand Duke at the Rex parade, and the popular tune was played for Rex at the viewing stand (1999, 32). Rex later adopted the song as their anthem. Since then, the Grand Duke Alexis has been linked to Rex's anthem, "If Ever I Cease to Love." The song is played whenever the King of Carnival is present (Brown; Farrow 229).

The 1921 Rex parade marked the popular tradition of throwing beads, but as years passed, the crowds became apathetic to catching beads (Hales 102). The golden doubloon was introduced in 1960 to excite the crowds. It was introduced at the same time the Super-Krewes began emerging. Rex members would throw "His Majesty's golden coins" to the paraders (Brown). The doubloons were inexpensive and made out of aluminum. The golden coins bore His Majesty's face and seal (Hales 102). Paraders must pay close attention for Rex riders who toss these gold coins into the air. It is an easy throw to catch, but also an easy throw to get a small bruise from. Unfortunately, many of the Krewes' emblemed throws grew in popularity and began to outshine the historic doubloons (Hardy, 2018a).

Important Places: The Cabildo
The Great New Orleans Fire of 1788 destroyed 856 buildings, including the structure that stood before the Cabildo ("The Great New Orleans Fire"). From 1795 to 1799, the Spanish government hired Gilberto Guillemard to design the Cabildo to serve as the headquarters for the New Orleans' government. In 1853, the Cabildo, a French timber-framed building, became the headquarters of the Louisiana State Supreme Court. In 1908, it became the Louisiana State Museum and continues to educate the public and visitors about Louisiana's

history and heritage. That same year, a blazing fire severely damaged the Cabildo. It took five years to completely restore the historic building. In 1994, the building was reopened with exhibits about Louisiana's history, Hurricane Katrina, and Mardi Gras culture (*Cabildo*).

Ever since 1906, the Cabildo has been collecting Carnival material and artifacts. Mardi Gras has always been a huge part of the New Orleans' culture and history, and it is important that this history and culture is documented. Since the founding of Louisiana in 1699, Mardi Gras Day has been integrated in its history. However, Mardi Gras was not a celebration at all in 1699. It was simply a day in the calendar that was recorded in the journals of Bienville and Iberville (*Cabildo*; Philips). This all changed by the 1720s when people wore elaborate, colorful costumes and wandered the streets, making this "event" the first documented Mardi Gras. The Cabildo is the only museum that actively collects costumes and gowns for preservation as artifacts (Philips). There is always a Mardi Gras exhibit displaying the general history with a separate room used solely to depict the extravagant balls.

New Orleans has a unique artistic community, so museums and curators have the responsibility of preserving the work of these artists. Unlike other places, New Orleans's artistic community can make a living designing floats, gowns, costumes, and other Mardi Gras artifacts. For some, careers have lasted 30 to 40 years (Philips). Wayne Philips, the Curator of Costumes and Textiles and Curator of Carnival Collections, said, Mardi Gras at its core is an artistic event, and there is so much design and so much skill that goes into the creation of Mardi Gras whether its ball gowns, debutante gowns, king costumes, the floats, the sets for the balls, and there is so much artistry that goes into creating Mardi Gras.

The Presbytère, an architecturally significant building neighboring the Cabildo, contains a permanent Mardi Gras exhibit, and the condition of the costumes and artifacts determine whether they go on display (Philips; Parks). The goal is to showcase a variety of Carnival costumes and artifacts—Rex and Comus, Zulu, Mardi Gras Indians, and street costumes. However, out of the 5,000 pieces in the Cabildo's Carnival collection, only a small percentage of the costumes and pieces are actually displayed. A majority of the costumes from the early 1900s need restoration, stabilization, repair, or cleaning before being displayed (Philips).

A French Quarter warehouse, located two blocks down from the Cabildo, serves as the storage facility for the Louisiana State Museum (Parks). The warehouse is filled with rows of acid-free boxes holding the hidden treasures from the Carnival celebration, including royal gowns and costumes, crowns and scepters, street costumes, proclamations, family paintings, books, and other historic artifacts (Parks). The warehouse is not regularly open to the public. A "Hidden Treasures" tour is offered annually with a limited number of guests for each tour, and the funds raised go to a nonprofit group, known as the Friends of the Cabildo (Parks).

Prior to 1960s, both the museum and warehouse were not air-conditioned; few large institutions were air conditioned before the mid-twentieth century (Philips). The 1970s served as the era when museum standards and practices became universal, and the importance of consistent humidity and the consistent temperature was realized. During Hurricane Katrina, the Cabildo lost power; fortunately, the warehouse had no water damage. The loss of electricity for a long period of time caused temperature and humidity levels to fluctuate. As museum science as evolved, preservationists have discovered that drastic fluctuations in humidity and temperature are more destructive than a gradual drop or rise in temperature and humidity. Gradual change allows for artifacts and costumes to slowly adapt (Philips).

The Rex Den, where the floats, costumes, and artifacts of the Rex Organization are held, was severely flooded during Katrina. The flooding from Hurricane Katrina severely damaged the floats for the 2006 Mardi Gras parade and a set of costumes Elaine Hartmann made for Rex in the early 1980s (Philips; Hales 148-151). The floats were sent away for repair to be used in the upcoming parade, but the costumes were damaged beyond repair (Hales 148-151). The Rex Organization decided to preserve the costumes and donated them to the Cabildo. With Rex's understanding, the Cabildo has kept the costumes in the condition that they were donated since Hurricane Katrina is a part of the history of Louisiana (Philips).

On February 6, 2018 I went to the warehouse to see Barbara Bouden's, my great-grandmother, Rex Queen's gown, and Charles Whitney Bouden's, my great-great-grandfather, Rex King's costume. I spoke with Wayne Philips about the details of the costumes and preservation. He informed me that Lillian Gaylord Urquhart, my great-great-grandmother, wife of Charles Whitney Bouden, and mother of Barbara Bouden, donated her daughter's Queen of Carnival gown, scepter, and mantle and her husband's King costume to the Cabildo in 1943. Everything Lillian donated has been at the Cabildo since 1943 (Linda Feringa; Philips). Barbara Bouden's gown was once on display, but the dates are unknown. All that is left is a picture, but the picture shows a variety of costumes from different periods, making the date hard to decipher. The museum world in the 1950s was not exactly accurate, as illustrated by the photograph. The Mardi Gras display was arranged to resemble a throne and show off the costumes. The exhibit featured costumes from the early to the mid-1900s, which would never occur today. The way the Cabildo and other museums display costumes and artifacts has changed over the years. They do not want to create a false impression and avoid showcasing a hodgepodge of pieces. Her father's crown and scepter are on display at the Presbytère, while his costume has never been exhibited because of its poor condition (Philips).

King and Queen of Carnival: Charles Whitney Bouden and Barbara Bouden

Until the 1930s Rex was not supposed to spend any money. The expense of reigning as King is meager compared to what the Queen of Rex has to spend. Reigning as Rex remains an honor; thus, the crew honors Rex on their behalf since Rex is a member of the Rex Organization and pays annual dues. Each King used to have a custom costume made, but today, the Rex costume is reused every year. Charles Whitney Bouden's, my great-great-grandfather and King of Carnival in 1934, King costume is in poor condition and would cost $10,000 to restore. His gold, rhinestone covered costume was very complex and flamboyant—false sleeves, delicate lace cuffs, lace trim collar, and glass-bead fringe attached to the hem of the tunic. The costume is missing a few more rhinestones than his daughter's Queen gown, and the rhinestones on the false sleeves caught the lace and tore the sleeves over the years. The glass bead fringe has not been seen on any Rex costume in fifty years. In order to save money, only one costume is created to last roughly 20 to 25 years. The next King's costume will be created in 2019. The costume would either be taken in or taken out based on the King's height and weight (Philips; Royal Design House).

It was uncommon for a father and daughter to reign so closely as King and Queen of Carnival. Barbara Bouden, Queen of Carnival in 1935, happened to be the right age, but it could have also been because of the Great Depression. The Boudens were one of the few families who had money and could afford for their daughter to make her debut. Debutantes needs multiple dresses, one for each presentation and ball. If the daughter is Queen, it is the family's responsibility to purchase the gown, mantel, and scepter and pay for the post-ball entertainment (Philips).

Figure 3.4: Charles Whitney Bouden's Rex costume.
Source: Photograph by the author.

Barbara Bouden's gown is characterized as being very complex, fashionable, "sleek…very body conscious, [and] very Hollywood-esque in a way…" (Philips). The silk satin gown is covered with rhinestones and glass beads made to resemble pearls. The back of the dress contains a lot of back exposure that was atypical of the 1930s but not completely out of the ordinary. The Medici collar covered most of her back, so this could explain why the designer allowed for so much back exposure. The gown contains rhinestone and pearl covered shoulder panels with slits where the mantel would hook. Since this was during the Great Depression, the gown probably cost between $3,000 and $5,000 (Philips). She also served as Queen of Twelfth night that year and as a maid in Comus the next year. This was a major expense for the family. This was possibly allowed since no other family had enough money to do so (Linda Feringa; Philips).

Wayne Philips believes Barbara Bouden's gown was designed by the Liberty Shop based on the characteristics and style of other dresses by them. Bonny Broel bought out the Liberty Shop, located on St. Charles Avenue, in the early 1970s. The business is now known as the House of Broel and still located on St. Charles Avenue. The Liberty Shop was opened as a high-end establishment in 1910, where they originally designed hats, but later expanded in the 1920s into a house on St. Charles to design Queen's gowns (Philips). The gown also features a long scallop-like train which is not allowed anymore in the design of Carnival gowns.

The beadwork on the train made the train extremely heavy, especially while wearing the Medici collar and pulling the hundred-pound mantle (Philips; Royal Design House). In order to carry the weight of the mantle and the Medici collar, the Queen wears a special corset and harness under her gown (Royal Design House). The corset bears most of the mantel's weight and must be laced tightly. However, the young women's ribs would break

Figure 3.5: Barbara Bouden's Queen of Rex gown.
Source: Photograph by the author.

from the corset being laced too tight. Queens still go through extensive training in preparation for the ball, which includes pulling a mantel twice as heavy as the original one, stacking a pile of books or chairs on the end of the mantel, or having people sit on it (Peter Feringa and Philips). When the time came to serve as Queen, the mantel would feel light, and the Queen would effortlessly glide across the ballroom. Past Queens have said they were always grateful to have gone through the grueling training (Philips). Barbara Bouden's scepter is a classic style of the 1920s and 1940s and features amber colored stones, which were regularly used to decorate scepters and crowns, but this type of ornamentation was discontinued in the 1950s. Sometime after Barbara Bouden wore the crown, and before it was donated to the Cabildo, it broke into pieces. It appears that someone attempted to solder the rhinestones onto the metal, but the attempt caused more damage. The crown could be restored, but it would be extremely difficult because of the number of rhinestones attached to the soft metal (Philips).

Over the years the gown's glass pearls have tarnished, and the silk satin has mellowed, turning from a pure white to an eggshell color. Since the gown was only worn once and then put away, this may be why the gown is in good condition, unlike her father's Rex costume. The gown is free of any tears and is only missing a couple of rhinestones. The only restoration needed would be cleaning the gown in order to minimize scuffing. If the gown would ever be re-displayed, an inner structure would need to be sewn inside the gown to prevent gravity from pulling it down due to the weight of the dress (Philips). Currently, Linda Feringa, Barbara Bouden's daughter, is attempting to raise money to clean the gown and minimize scuffing. The few missing rhinestones can no longer be purchased or found (Philips).

Megan Feringa, my sister, used Barbara Bouden's Queen gown as inspiration for her Achaeans Queen gown. The Feringa Family has now had two women reign as Queen for the Achaeans Organization, a non-parading organization founded in 1948. Linda Feringa, my grandmother, reined as Queen in 1960 with Megan following in 2018. Megan states that she chose to model her dress after her great-grandmother's gown "because of the history and tradition. To use something so pure to my family made the tradition of Mardi Gras come alive." Megan and the Royal Design House, a women-run business that designs men's costumes, royal mantles, Medici collars, and dresses and gowns for debutantes, Queens, and the old-line Mardi Gras Krewes, visited the Louisiana State Museums' Mardi Gras collection to see the Rex gown. The Royal Design House modernized the beaded motif and mimicked the "fitted trumpet shape and the long train" (Royal Design House; "Stars Align for"). The bodice featured "contrasting pale silver appliqué that played off of the shape of the lace [dimensional] flowers on the skirt, contoured over the hip and plunged down into a "V of rhinestone trim at the center" ("Stars Align for"). Silver bugle beads, pearls, and Swarovski lochrosen and navette rhinestones enrich the bodice and flounce. Lace flowers adorned the skirt's sides and silver bugle beads and pearls form elegant serpentine coils ("Stars Align for"). She adorned her gown with her Queen's Achaeans' pin, a gold gilded drawn bow. Megan is donating her dress to the Cabildo where an exhibition will be held on the progression of Mardi Gras tradition spanning generations.

Figure 3.6: Megan Feringa, Queen of Achaeans 2018. Photograph by Josh Brasted. Source: From the personal collection of the author.

Material Culture: Pins, Medals, and Paintings

As early as I can remember, my grandmother, Linda Feringa, always wore a handmade necklace with a variety of antique, colorful, handcrafted Rex pins she had accumulated. Families have found other creative ways to use their pins such as decorating hats, creating festive Carnival pillows, or a string of pins in a shadow box to showcase their family's history and lineage in the Rex Organization. The pins have become a fashion statement; people pin them on suits and dresses.

The pins have been a longstanding tradition of the old-line Krewes. People not associated with the Krewes often miss these hidden jewels pinned on the members' clothing (Klusby). The pins showcase the creativity and artistry of the Carnival organizations and local craftsmen. Since 1872, the School of Design has crafted a special pin. These pins tell a story about the parade theme and the Rex Organization (Philips; Klusby). Unlike the parade which is very public, the distribution of the pins is very private and much more personal and memorable. The pins are solely for the Krewe members and their families and friends (Klusby). The pins are placed in a special box with a card describing the design of the pin.

Each year, the King of Carnival assists the extremely skilled and talented jewelers in designing the Rex pin. The pin, along with invitations, ties in with the parade theme and the Carnival traditions. The most distinguishable element of the Rex pin is the purple, gold, and green ribbon (Klusby). The School of Design's pin is crafted to model the ducal medallion that is worn specifically by Rex members

(Peter Feringa; Brown; Cusanza, 2015a). Each King and Queen also designs their own personal pin that reflects themselves and their organization. Each pin has a different personality (Megan Feringa). The maids on the court receive a special pin crafted specifically for them. Each pin contains the initials of the recipient and the year. These pins have become collector items.

The ducal medal and Mardi Gras regalia were originally imported from Europe (Hales 51). The ducal medals and pins were composed of "paste jewels, plated and enameled metal and, of course, purple, gold and green ribbons" (51). Originally, the King and Queen were allowed to keep their crown, mantel, scepter, and scepter (Philips). Today, only the pins and the ducal medals are designed new each year while the other regalia is reused to cut costs. Family members of previous Kings and Queens have donated their precious artifacts that are now on display at the Louisiana State Museum, the Cabildo, and the Rex Den.

An important tradition that has ended was showing the Mardi Gras regalia in the window displays of jewelry shops. The costumes, scepters, crowns, and other court essentials were imported from France (Hales 128). Jewelry stores located on Canal Street, such as Adler's who continues to craft trinkets for the Rex Organization, displayed the scepters, crowns, and pins in the windows in the days and weeks leading up to Carnival. Tourists and visitors would gather around the window display to see the treasures that the Queen and King would wear to the grand parades and balls. Of course, the identity of the King and Queen was kept a secret, so no one knew who the scepter and crown belonged to (Philips). Secrecy has always been a part of Carnival tradition that contributes to the anticipation of Mardi Gras. The reason behind the secrecy has changed over the years and maintaining secrecy has become more challenging due to cellphones and social media. Everyone and their mother are biting at their nails trying to figure out who the Queen and King are. As the Mardi Gras season closes, everyone knows who is in what ball and parade through the process of elimination making it easy to figure out who is Queen of Carnival, but it is a fun tradition that will hopefully continue (Philips).

According to Philips, a previous Queen, whose name was withheld, would regularly stroll past the window display to observe the curious bystanders and eavesdrop on their conversations. Unfortunately, the purchasing of the Mardi Gras regalia and medals was discontinued after World War I, and the displaying of the beautifully crafted jewels and crowns stopped in the late twentieth century (Hales 51). The year 1964 was the last time a new scepter, mantel, and crown was specifically crafted for the King and Queen (Royal Design House; Philips). Retiring the tradition of creating new Mardi Gras regalia annually and importing jewels from Europe ended because of the high cost. The Mardi Gras regalia used today is not secondary to the ones used in the 1930s and 1940s. It remains an important part of the carnival spirit and helps bring the royal court to life. Having a set of Mardi Gras regalia used over and over allows the Krewes to save money while continuing to have that splendor of royalty (Cusanza, 2015b).

Today, the School of Design is known for their gold King costume and Queen's gown while the rest of the Carnival organization's Kings and Queens wear white or silver. The gold versus the silver gowns—specifically in regard to Rex and Comus—did not emerge until the 1950s (Philips). Today, the Rex Queen's gown is a gold lace, highly beaded rhinestone gown (Royal Design House). Prior to the 1950s, the Queen of Carnival's gown, as seen in my great-grandmother's dress, was white and adorned with rhinestones and pearls or white glass beads. There was no gold element found anywhere on the dress. These color traditions are very important to the Krewes, but ironically, the Queens and maids hire the same dressmakers to design their dresses. More so now, the Queens have a degree of input in the design process, giving the dress a personal touch. After the early twentieth century, the parade theme ceased to be reflected in the design of the King costume and Queen's gown. The Queen's gown is typically reflective of the style of the time period (Philip).

Traditionally, the Royal family commissioned a talented painter or photographer to document the Carnival King or Queen in their flamboyant yet elegant royal garments. Portraits ranged from a simple headshot to life-size. Many of these pictures remain in the family while others have been donated to museums or the organizations themselves for preservation. An unknown artist completed a four-foot painting of Barbara Bouden as Queen of Carnival in 1935. Linda Feringa states that her mother loathed the painting and forbid her father from purchasing the portrait.

Figure 3.7: Barbara Bouden's portrait. Source: From the personal collection of the author.

The daughter of the painter contacted Linda Feringa after her father, the painter, passed away. The painter's daughter requested that the family purchase the painting from her. Linda bought the portrait and gave it to her daughter, Lisa Feringa, because, at the time, her house was the only one that had high enough ceilings to hang it (Linda Feringa).

The Rex Ball

The Rex Ball concludes the Mardi Gras season. The glittering celebration involves music from the Marine Band, traditional pageantry, the Royal Procession, the Meeting of the Courts, marching, and dancing. The entire ball is televised on WYES for the public to see (*Rex: King of Carnival*). The final act of Carnival is the Meeting of the Courts where Rex and his Queen visit the Comus Ball, and the King and Queen of Comus greet the Rex monarchs. Both Courts come together for a grand procession. The same procession is used each year for the Rex Ball. As a result, I walked the same procession of my forefathers. For decades, Rex's Court has consisted of Rex, the Queen of Rex, eight Maids, and eight Dukes, but this number has fluctuated throughout Rex's history (*Rex: King of Carnival*; Brown). Since Rex is not a "mystic carnival krewe," the Rex ball is unmasked, but guests are required to dress in full formal attire just as every other ball (Brown; *Rex: King of Carnival*). Unlike other balls, the School of Design follows "Rex Time," meaning if you are supposed to be dressed and ready for 7:00pm, you must be ready promptly at that time and not a minute earlier or later. The Rex Ball always begins at 8:00pm on Fat Tuesday with the New Orleans' Marine Corps Band performing. Then, Rex and his Court make their grand procession towards the Dais and Throne Area with the Maids and Dukes following. The Dais and Throne Area are off-limits to members and guests.

Presentations that follow include the presentation of a number of Debutantes and the recognition of the Fifty-Year Queen, active duty, and veterans. Special guests are also honored and adorned with Rex gifts. In accordance with the theme of the year, a "special guest" is honored (*Rex: King of Carnival*). Since New Orleans celebrated their Tricentennial this year, Rex chose the theme "L'Ancienne Nouvelle-Orléans" (Romig, 2018). The float designs, Rex Proclamation, Rex Arrival, Lundi Gras Festivities, and invitations explored the rich history and culture of New Orleans. They portray the people, places, and events that shaped New Orleans (*Rex: King of Carnival*). Rex officials honored the founder of New Orleans, Jean-Baptiste Le Moyne, Sieur de Bienville, by having a Rex member impersonate Bienville who accepted the Rex medal and a scroll ("Rex, Comus Continue"). The Grand March and the first dance of the ball occur shortly after where guests and members are allowed to curtsy and bow to the Rex monarchs and their court. Promptly at 9:40pm, the Captain of Comus enter the ballroom inviting Rex and his court to the Comus Ball to participate in the Meeting of the Courts, with the song "If Ever I Cease to Love," queuing Rex and His Queen to head over (*Rex: King of Carnival*).

Today, the Sheraton Hotel hosts the Rex Ball, and the Marriott Hotel hosts the Comus Ball. Previously, the two balls were held together in the city's Municipal Auditorium with a large curtain dividing the two balls. The large curtain would be drawn back initiating the Meeting of the Courts, making the tradition very simple and open to everyone (Hémard). Unfortunately, the Municipal Auditorium suffered severe damage from the levees breaking during Hurricane Katrina forcing the two old-line organizations to change venues to two hotels on Canal Street (Hémard). The change of venue brought about a new tradition of rolling out a red carpet on Canal Street from the Sheraton Hotel to the Marriot Hotel. The red carpet serves as the pathway for Rex, his Queen, and the court from the Rex Ball to the Comus Ball ("Rex, Comus Continue"). Those who wish to watch the Meeting of the Courts must receive a special admit card on top of the admit card for the Rex Ball. Once the Meeting of the Court ends, the Comus and Rex court go to the Sheraton Hotel for the Queens' Supper to eat, drink, and dance some more.

More than a Lavish Parade and Ball: The Pro Bono Publico Foundation

Similar to other old-line Carnival organizations, Rex chose a Latin motto to reflect the intentions of their organization. Rex Organization's public role in New Orleans and the Mardi Gras celebration is evinced by their motto, *Pro Bono Publico*. When the founders of the School of Design wished to revive the unstable city and bring order to the chaotic, public Carnival celebration, the founders approached it with *Pro Bono Publico* in mind (Hales 148). Due to Mardi Gras being both a public and private event, many law officers and city officials contemplated canceling any future carnival celebrations because of the disruptive and riotous nature of the masked revelers and the crowds. However, the city needed to attract tourists, lift the spirits of locals, revive the economy, and solve the lingering political instability brought about during the Reconstruction period (1865-1877). The Rex

Organization proposed a plan in response to city officials' potential ban and graciously received approval from the mayor and chief of police for Rex to assume control of the Carnival celebration. The civic leaders hoped to attract tourists by creating a daytime parade, strengthening the Mistick Krewe of Comus's nighttime parade (148-149).

After the successful Carnival celebration, Rex leaders have "continued to actively support Carnival's public purpose, providing an important balance to the many private celebrations of Mardi Gras" (Hales 149). The Rex Organization fulfilled their commitment to civic duty and service after Hurricane Katrina damaged the city (Brown; *Pro Bono Publico*). The post-Katrina recovery and rebuilding process was slow and devastating.

Mardi Gras organizations debated on whether to participate in the 2006 Mardi Gras parade. Many of the Mardi Gras Krewes' warehouses, where they store their floats, costumes, etc., experienced major flooding and wind damage. In addition, trash and debris were present, floodwaters severely damaged the infrastructure, and citizens were still trying to return to the city and rebuild their homes. The Rex Den, where all of Rex's costumes, floats, and historic artifacts are held, was filled with four feet of water. Almost everything was ruined and damaged beyond repair. The School of Design was determined to roll the streets and began salvaging and repairing whatever they could. The Rex floats rolled the damaged streets displaying a fresh new coat of paint that failed to hide the faint waterline mark from the dirty floodwaters (Hales 151). Nonetheless, the 2006

Mardi Gras was a historic event for New Orleans. Even though the parade route was shorter and fewer parades rolled with some Krewes merging together, Mardi Gras rose awareness, raised spirits, and showed New Orleans's strength (Burnett).

The Pro Bono Publico Foundation was launched in 2006 under Christian Brown to respond to the aftermath of Hurricane Katrina and assist in the rebuilding of New Orleans's public schools (Brown; *Pro Bono Publico*). "Operation Pro Bono Publico" contained three initiatives, each named after the Mardi Gas colors—Project Gold, Green, and Purple. The projects raised money for police officers and first-responders, mobilized over a thousand volunteers to clean the parade routes, and rebuilt many of the public schools and improved the public education system (*Pro Bono Publico*). Each project greatly exceeded their expectations. By 2010 the Foundation raised and donated over $6.5 million to the city to Charter Schools and supporting organizations (Hales 153). On January 14, 2018, the Rex Foundation donated $1 million to 63 organizations for education. For the past three years, the Pro Bono Publico's grants have reached $1 million and have supported approximately 34,000 local students (Reckdahl 2B).

Since 1872, the strong relationship between the city and the Rex Organization has continued. The city leaders who met in the St. Charles lobby to establish a formal Carnival celebration kept in mind the needs of the citizens and the city. Christian Brown, Chairman of the Pro Bono Publico Foundation states, "Founding Rex members in 1872 felt an obligation to do something special for their beloved city. We believe we have a similar duty to honor their legacy now as New Orleans faces such unprecedented challenges for recovery in its future" (Hales 155). The city leaders recognized the possibilities of the Carnival celebration to strengthen the city after the Reconstruction era, reestablish the city's commercial and cultural legacy, and serve as a civic booster (*Rex: King of Carnival*). The School of Design gave more than a parade; they fostered a tradition of service and support (Hales 150-153).

UNESCO, Festival Commemoration, and Mardi Self Reflection

In 2003 the Representative List of Intangible Cultural Heritage of Humanity and Register of Good Safeguarding Practices were created by many state parties within UNESCO for the purpose of raising awareness of cultural practices and intangible heritage expressions. Unfortunately, as of today, the United States is not part of this program. However, two festivals were nominated to the Representative List of Intangible Cultural Heritage of Humanity: The Fiesta de San Pacho and the Gion Festival (*UNESCO*). The Fiesta de San Pacho is an annual festival held from September 3 to October 4, which is both an identity marker and "a platform to promote solidarity, community and social cohesion among the people" for the twelve Franciscan districts in Quibdó, Colombia (Fav4eva). A Catholic Mass commences the festivities with a carnival parade following. Groups dress in elaborate costumes, perform traditional dances and the chirimía, and sing hymns during the parade and mass ("Festival of Saint Francis of Assisi, Quibdó").

Yamahoko, the float ceremony of Kyoto, Japan's Gion Festival is held every year on July 17 by the Gion neighborhood in the Yasake Shrine. For generations, residents of Gion's self-governing district have come together to build floats. *Yamahoko* means "moving museums" which reflects the elaborate floats that exhibit the ornamental craftwork of the city ("Yamahoko") The floats are decorated with tapestries, dyed silk, Persian rugs, umbrella ornaments, and Belgian weavings depicting scenes from Greek mythology ("The Gion Festival").

Similar to the Fiesta de San Pacho and the Gion Festival, New Orleans local artists and craftsman showcase their talent and culture through the creation and designs of the floats, costumes, gowns, invitations, court jewels, and other carnival essentials used during the parades, balls, and presentations (Fav4eva). Mardi Gras is a worldwide celebration and several countries celebrate their own versions of it including Oruro, Bolivia; Recife, Brazil, and Barranquilla, Columbia ("Carnivals around the World"). Each celebration draws from different cultures, including pre-Columbian and African traditions, to create their own Mardi Gras. Many of the pre-Christian elements and traditions seen in the Mardi Gras parades stem from pagan rituals practiced thousands of years ago ("Carnivals around the World"). Once Christianity was introduced to Rome, the pagan traditions were "Christianized" rather than abolished ("Carnivals around the World;" "The Rich Heritage of Mardi Gras in New Orleans").

During the 1980s, New Orleans' Mardi Gras gained attention from international media, including European and Latin American countries. Big Businesses began holding conventions in New Orleans during Mardi Gras at this time (Hardy, 2018a). Theme parks such as Disney World and Universal Studios recognize New Orleans's Mardi Gras as a universally popular event, when they began reproducing Mardi Gras parades and balls (Capo 30). Even popular destinations are replicating the popular event and throwing their own spin on it, like Folly Beach, South Carolina with "Folly Gras," which includes an annual parade, street festival, live music, Cajun and Creole food vendors, and art vendors. The event, similar to New Orleans, is used to promote Folly Beach and draw in tourists. ("Folly Gras 2019").

Mardi Gras Past Documented

From the archives of the Library of Congress, the photographs depicting the Rex parade from the mid to late-1900s are breathtaking. Thousands of people can be seen watching the floats pass by. Many are struggling to catch a glimpse of the magnificent pageantry. The size of the crowds watching the Rex parade may be bigger than they are today revealing how grand and important the Rex parade was. This does not mean the Rex parade loss its grandeur. The black and white photographs do not demote the mythological, whimsical, and traditional yet eccentric float designs created by the School of Design. The crowds can be seen behaving in a civilized manner unlike most of the crowds today, and the police barricades are absent. The parade-watchers on the streets are dressed in their best attire which is rarely the case today. In addition, the floats, or cotton wagons before construction, were pulled by a team of mules. Semi tractor-trailers have replaced the mule teams, and "sturdy wooden chassis and traditional wooden-spoked, iron-rimmed wheels" replaced the cotton wagons *(Rex: King of Carnival)*.

The mule teams and cotton wagons could no longer accommodate the larger floats, the number of riders and their throws, and the more extravagant and complex designs ("Mardi Gras Floats"). Riders' costumes used to impersonate the tableau characters, but the costumes remain a crucial element of the parade (Hales 131). The costumes, which are designed new each year, are created from a mix of materials including felt and satin, which are embellished with colorful sequins and colorful fabrics. Each costume comes with a mask and hat (131). As illustrated by the photographs, the School of Design is very meticulous when designing, constructing, and creating the floats and costumes, but this attention to detail and ability to bring life to their floats makes them the emblematic parade of Mardi Gras (Bookhardt; Library of Congress).

Rex has utilized New Orleans's resources— the river, the land, the infrastructure, the technology, and the culture and history—in their festivities. Within the 146-year history of Rex, the School of Design has held 137 parades. Rex did not parade due to the "political unrest in the city" in 1875, World War I in 1918 and 1919, "inclement weather"

Figure 3.8: Mardi Gras Procession on Canal Street, New Orleans. Source: Library of Congress Prints and Photographs Division.

in 1933, World War II from 1942 to 1945, the Korean War in 1951, and a police strike in 1979 (Romig). Rex has lost several traditions, but new traditions and adaptations of old ones have come about. Prior to World War I, Rex arrived on a "His Royal Navy" at a dock along the Mississippi River (Brown; *Rex: King of Carnival*). The mayor greeted Rex, and visitors gathered along Canal Street to catch a glimpse of Rex. The mayor then handed Rex the keys to the city (*Rex: King of Carnival*; Brown). The 1874 tradition of arriving by river was recreated in 1987 to celebrate the Centennial of Rex (Hardy, 2018c). The new tradition included a meeting of the King of Carnival and the King of Zulu, along with the mayor.

From 1987 to 2014, Rex used several vessels including a U.S. Coast Guard Cutter and Robert E. Lee's steamship to the Spanish Plaza (Hardy, 2018c). Three years ago, Rex began taking a different form of passage, "His Royal Train," but this was only used a few times (Brown; Hardy, 2018c). The 2015, Lundi Gras arrival of Rex used historical sounds and imagery to recreate the grand event: "Fireworks will burst over the Mississippi River, a noisy reminder of the deafening sounds of steamboat whistles and cannon salutes celebrating Rex's arrival more than a century ago" (*Rex: King of Carnival*). All of these traditions have turned Lundi Gras into its own celebration (Hardy, 2018c). In 1877, Rex ceased to lead the parade on horseback and rode on his moving throne, the King's Float. The King's float has been a permanent float since 1877 (Brown). Today, the King's float is a torch-lit throne topped with a glittering, royal red, papier-mâché crown and adorned with papier-mâché jewels. A gold mantle drapes down from the crown.

Other permanent floats include the Jester, *Boeuf Gras*, Desire the Streetcar, Royal Calliope, Royal Barge, and His Majesty's Bandwagon (Romig). Each float contains their own history and origins (Brown). In 2012, an animated float known as the Butterfly King was introduced to carry 24 masked riders (see fig. 34). This was the first float to become permanent since 1985 (Pope). According to Christian Brown, former Captain of Rex and creator of the float, "Much of the artistry of the early invitations and ducals also disappeared. I have worked with members to revive some of that artistry" (2018). The Butterfly King Float revives some of that artistry and "has become a new symbol of Carnival" (Brown). The 1882 Rex Ball invitation was the source of inspiration for the float design, and the Butterfly King is a recurring theme that symbolizes "the transient nature of [Rex's] annual celebration" (Brown).

The floats, the costumes, and the attire of the Mardi Gras monarchs and court are works of art. Due to the tradition of secrecy, many costumes are never exposed to the public (Royal Design House). However, Rex's public position in the city and the nation separates Rex from the other Carnival Krewes. Royal Design House states that since a majority of the custom costumes designed are for the private events during Carnival, their designs are only seen by Carnival Krewes and the small group of people who attend the balls (Royal Design House). However, Rex's visibility allows Royal Design House to present their designs and creations to a bigger audience. The designs and creations by Katie Johnson, Ashley Sehorn, and their team can be seen all along the parade routes, during the ball, and on television. As stated by Katie Johnson and Ashley Sehorn: "Rex often represents the face of Carnival and New Orleans to the world so it's so special to be a part of that" (2018).

Threats to New Orleans's Mardi Gras

The Carnival season is continuing to evolve and address potential threats. New Orleans has had a constant issue with flooding and drainage. In addition to the hurricane-prone location below sea-level, Mardi Gras beads have been proving to be a challenge in keeping the storm drains clog-free. The shiny, plastic beads, or "throws," have been indicative of Mardi Gras since the 1970s but have become a major hazard to the entire city (Redmon; Delzo). Revelers will do anything to catch the beads—flinging themselves in crowds, screaming "Throw me something, mister!" and flashing their breasts. Many revelers can be seen walking through the streets with stacks of beads hanging around their necks. Children stuff their Mardi Gras bags to the brim and anxiously wait to sort through their throws at home. However, a majority of the beads end up in a landfill shortly after Mardi Gras ends (Fausset).

Approximately 25 million plastic beads are imported to New Orleans every year for Mardi Gras (Delzo, Fausset). During this past Carnival season, approximately 93,000 pounds of petroleum-based beads were dug up from drains on only five of New Orleans' downtown blocks (Delzo). The numbers rise from there; over 7 million pounds of Mardi Gras throws, and debris was pulled from the city drains that resulted in city-wide clogged drains, environmental hazards, and potential health risks (Delzo). When the Mardi Gras season ended this year, approximately 150 tons of waste was produced (Redmon). David Redmon, a Criminology lecturer at the University of Kent, says that Tulane University's Department of Pharmacology has found the total number of beads thrown each year to convert to roughly 4,000 pounds of lead being potentially exposed to the public once it hits the streets. Recently, a Louisiana State University professor, Naohiro Kato, developed an ingredient that could be used in beads and doubloons to make them biodegradable. Over time, the biodegradable beads would disintegrate in the soil, making the Carnival celebration more sustainable for the environment (Satake).

The ritual of throwing beads is not going to go away according to Mardi Gras historian, Henri Schindler. It is a part of the culture, but many environmentally conscious locals want New Orleans to start taking initiative (Faussett). The city can place conservation restraints on Mardi Gras, create beads that are environmentally friendly, or have beads and throws locally produced (Fausset). Recycling programs have been proposed with some plans implemented. Some parades have started to include an empty float at the very end of their parades for revelers to throw beads on. The Arc of Greater New Orleans, a nonprofit organization, attached the slogan "Catch and release" (Fausset). One proposal involved allowing revelers to use beads as a form of currency. Revelers would cash in their "token" at a business who in exchange would allow the revelers to use a clean bathroom, a luxury during Mardi Gras (Fausset). Not all of the throws are imported or simply discarded after the Carnival festivities come to an end. The Krewe of Zulu's, primarily an all African American parade, is known for throwing hand-painted coconuts. The Krewe of Muses, an all-female Krewe who began parading in 2001, takes used shoes and transforms them into glittering works of art (Cornish; "Shoes"). Of all the throws, the Zulu coconut is probably, if not the, most prized one during Mardi Gras (Fausset; Cornish). Both the coconuts and the shoes are one of a kind, and riders spend months preparing these throws (Cornish; "Shoes").

Mardi Gras is a festive yet historic event. It is a legal holiday in Louisiana where schools shut down and hundreds of thousands of tourists arrive. Second lines, parades, colorful beads, extravagant balls, and an array of costumes, king cakes, Cajun food, and jazz music are just a fraction of what occurs. Mardi Gras is reflective of New Orleans' rich heritage and draws from European, African, and Native American cultures (Melancon). The Cajun French saying "Laissez Les Bon Temps Rouler" meaning "let the good times roll" reflects the spirit of the people during the Mardi Gras season before Lent begins. However, this culture does not hide the racial, social, and gender hierarchies prevalent during Mardi Gras (Melancon).

The Carnival celebration started off as a rowdy party for and thrown by the lower class, but the parades and some of the balls are not limited to a specific class today. Not too long ago, the Carnival celebration was only for the city's elites (Gotham; Rothman). *Time* magazine published an article on February 9, 1948 revealing the exclusivity of the Mardi Gras Krewes and balls that were solely for New Orleans's upper class; and only people with "money, blue blood, or both" were allowed to join the Krewes (Rothman). Prior to 1900, only the daughters of the members belonging to the five Krewes, Comus, Momus, Twelfth Night, Rex, and Proteus, could serve as debutantes with the "fairest" reigning as Queens. The guest lists were carefully chosen and very selective. People outside of this social class were determined to enter into this social group and began creating their own. From 1928 to 1946, the number of Mardi Gras Krewes grew from

16 to 36. In 2015, the number rose to 49 (Rothman). Since the 1940s and specifically after, there have been a number of Krewe options for people of all backgrounds, income class, gender, ethnicity, and race to join, but the exclusivity and separation of Krewes in regard to race and gender is still prevalent today (B. Nolan).

The exclusivity of the Carnival Krewes has caused much controversy since the 1990s when the New Orleans City Council passed a law requiring all Carnival Krewes to integrate by 1994 (Melancon; Gotham). A lot of mixed reactions arose from the law. Three old-line organizations, Comus, Momus, and Proteus, protested the law and canceled their parades (Melancon; Gotham). Rex opened their membership to all, making them the oldest parading organization (Hardy, 2018a). Proteus returned to the parades in 2000 and agreed not to discriminate, but Comus and Momus never returned to the parade scene (Hardy, 2018b; B. Nolan). Regardless of being private clubs, the city holds jurisdiction of the streets and can strip their rights of holding parades.

The article in the *TIMES* accurately describes this elite part of Mardi Gras. This social group has existed and will continue to exist. The exclusivity of the balls, selective guest list, and lavish debutante season remains, but this particular part of Mardi Gras would not be the way it is without it. Many of my friends, whose families were not members of Krewes, described it as a different world, and they are correct. However, this element of exclusivity and secrecy is not supposed to debar or make anyone feel belittled for not being a part of it. It is important to remember the Krewes' heritage, especially since they are responsible for the Mardi Gras traditions and culture we have today. The non-discriminatory pledge is not an issue today. The Krewes are diversified today with memberships open to all if you can afford the dues. Regardless, Mardi Gras will continue to change every year (Peter Feringa). New Krewes will form, and inevitably, some may disappear.

Continuing a Mardi Gras Tradition in the Feringa Family

My family's membership in the Rex Organization began with Harry T. Howard, my father's godfather's, great-grandfather. He reigned as King in 1888 with Genevieve Cottraux as his Queen. Harry Howard kicked Mardi Gras off in an unconventional way. He failed to make his arrival for the Lundi Gras activities. Even though the typical crowds came to see his arrival, the pre-Mardi Gras festivities never occurred, but the Rex parade rolled the streets as usual on Fat Tuesday (Dufour and Huber 39). On February 14, 1888, the Rex parade's pageantry depicted "The Realm of Flowers." Floats were adorned with the Roman Goddess Flora's blossoming and blooming flowers from her garden. His Majesty's Ball and Reception was held at Washington Artillery Hall (Huber 140). It was not until the early 1900s when my maternal great-great-great-grandfather, John Edward Bouden Jr., joined the School of Design and re-established my family's presence in the Rex Organization.

John Bouden Jr. was born in New York in 1869 and married Lilian Belle Hojer on January 24,

1889 in New York City. Their first child, Dorothy, was born on January 12, 1890 and died 15 days later. On October 6, 1893, Lilian gave birth to Charles Whitney Bouden (Linda Feringa). Around 1911, they moved to New Orleans. J. E. Bouden became Vice President, soon to be president, of the Whitney Bank in 1918. During the Great Depression, he was immersed in restoring New Orleans' economy (Peter Feringa). According to Linda Feringa, his great-granddaughter, many people said that his leadership kept the Whitney Bank afloat during the Great Depression. He supposedly predicted that "there would be hell to pay" and put the bank in a financially stable position to prevent a run from occurring (Linda Feringa). His role as bank president likely led him to be becoming a member of the old-line organization. On February 22, 1927; J. E. Bouden was appointed to the Board of Directors at the Rice Export Company ("Rice Export Co. is Formed…").

His son, Charles Whitney Bouden, stayed in New Orleans and attended Tulane University. On January 28, 1915, Charles Whitney Bouden married Lillian Gaylord Urquhart in New Orleans and they had one child, Barbara Bouden, born on December 19, 1916 (Linda Feringa). Charles Bouden worked as a cotton broker, was a member of the Whitney Bank Board of Directors and held a seat on the Cotton Exchange Company. On February 13, 1934, C. W. Bouden was proclaimed as King of Carnival ("New Orleans Brings Mardi Gras to Brilliant Close;" *1935 Rex Court*).

Since the Carnival season occurred during the Great Depression, every organization felt obliged to halt the Carnival festivities. However, Charles Whitney Bouden ruled as his Majesty presumably because he was one of the few families that had money at the time (Barbara Feringa). The weeks leading up to Fat Tuesday were filled with "chill rains," but the sun shone brightly on Mardi Gras Day ("New Orleans Brings Mardi Gras to Brilliant Close"). The Pageantry of Rex, "The Conquest of the Air," drew inspiration from Pegasus to depict man's victory in the air (Huber and Dufour 145). The *Shreveport Times* described the Mardi Gras celebration as "... the most brilliant Mardi Gras celebration since the World war [and] Rex, ruler of the revel, impersonated this year by Whitney Bouden, banker, headed one of the most elaborate parades in the long history of the carnival" ("New Orleans Brings Mardi Gras to Brilliant Close"). The ratification of the 21st Amendment in 1933 re-legalizing liquor (repealing the 18th Amendment on Prohibition), undoubtedly contributed to the merrymaking of the Carnival celebration in that year ("Prohibition ends"). The reception and the ball were held at the Athenaeum (Dufour and Huber 145).

A year after he reigned as Ruler of the Reveler, his daughter, Barbara Bouden, reigned as Queen of two old-line organizations and almost a third—the Krewe of Rex, Twelfth Night Revelers, and the Mistick Krewe of Comus. Unfortunately, she could not reign as Queen of Carnival and Comus since both occurred on Mardi Gras (*Rex: King of Carnival*). On March 5, 1935, she reigned as Queen of Rex (*1935 Rex Court*). The weather on Mardi Gras day was overcast with light showers, but this did not stop the crowds in any way ("Care-Free New Orleans Celebrates Mardi Gras;" Dufour and Huber 96). Rex's theme was "Nature's Workshop" depicting "the wonders of the original characteristics of the universe were displayed by indigenous scenes of splendor" (145). Her reception and ball were held at the same place as her father (145). A year later, she was a Maid of Comus, making your debut "twice" was inconceivable (Barbara Feringa). Barbara Bouden's debutante season was not as wonderful as pictured by the photographs. She was determined to pursue an education, play golf, and make her debut. Her teachers made it very difficult for her. She was beaten as a child for being left-handed. She learned to play golf right-handed but later developed polio in her right-hand. When she was diagnosed with polio, she was forced to switch back to her left hand. When she switched back to her left hand, she ended up becoming New Orleans' City Champion in golf. When she reigned as Queen of Carnival, she held her scepter in her left hand (Peter Feringa).

On January of 1937, Barbara Bouden married Markham Deweese Kostmayer who served as Lieutenant of Rex in the 1950s and 1960s. They had two daughters. Barbara "Linda" Kostmayer, my grandmother, was born on September 2, 1940. Their second daughter, Joan Bouden Kostmayer, was born on August 4, 1949 (Linda Feringa). The Rex Court announced Linda as Maid in 1960 and Joan as Maid in 1970 (*1960 Rex Court; 1970 Rex Court*). In 1960, the Pageantry of Rex depicted the "Wonderful World of Let's Pretend" with floats portraying fairy tales and tall tales from the East and the West

(Dufour and Huber 147). In 1970, twenty-two floats, three bandwagons, a calliope, and a streetcar portrayed the theme "Classics, Cartoons, and Comics" (148). Both of the balls and receptions were held at the Auditorium (148-149). That same year, Linda Kostmayer also reigned as Queen of Achaeans, a newer Carnival organization compared to the School of Design, but just as important. Linda Kostmayer married Peter Anthony Feringa Jr. who was born in the Netherlands in 1933. He had no connection to the Mardi Gras Krewes, so Linda Feringa helped him join the necessary organizations. They had four children, Peter, Matthew, Barbara, and Lisa, between 1961 and 1969.

The debutante and carnival traditions came to a halt with Barbara and Lisa. Due to personal, financial, and certain high-society social-norms during the 1980s, they both decided to not make their debut. Barbara and Lisa Feringa were never pushed to make their debuts by their parents. According to Lisa Feringa, her father pushed them to travel and being a debutante appeared stressful. Many of her friends' families suffered from family strains and struggled financially after the debutante season, reinforcing her decision to study abroad. Debutantes were expected to take the entire semester off as well, which did not appeal to either of them. As for Barbara Feringa, making a debut was never emphasized and a negative connotation was associated with it. Sadly, Linda Feringa's debutante experience was greatly affected by her mother. Barbara Bouden saw her debutante season as her peak in life and that life never improved after that. She suffered from alcoholism and depression and was institutionalized the day Linda Feringa reigned as Queen of Achaeans (Peter Feringa). This may explain why Linda Feringa never urged her daughters to continue the Mardi Gras tradition.

Peter Anthony Feringa III, my father, married Kara Lynn Garbo, my mother, on July 9, 1988, and they moved to California. On July 18, 1996, Kara gave birth to triplets, Megan, Brett, and me, Ellen Feringa. In January 2002, we moved back to Louisiana. Family was the main driver for returning home but participating in the Mardi Gras traditions influenced my father's decision to some degree. Within a year of moving back, Peter Feringa III joined the Rex Organization and started riding in the Rex parades. In 2006 and 2008, Brett Feringa, my brother, rode as an animator at age 8 and 10. An animator is in charge of moving the float's animations and is one of the members' young sons.

In 2006 and 2009, Shelley Blair Scanlon and Kathryn Lane Scanlon, my second cousins on my father's side, were honored as Maids on the Rex Court (*2006 Rex Court; 2009 Rex Court*). This year, my sister and I followed in our grandmother's footsteps. Megan Feringa was presented as a debutante in Rex, and I, as a Maid in Rex. The theme of the parade was "L'Ancienne Nouvelle-Orléans" to honor the 300th anniversary of New Orleans. The floats illustrated New Orleans' rich history by starting with New Orleans' indigenous people. The last float depicts Andrew Jackson and the Battle of New Orleans (*Rex: King of Carnival*). My father, brother, and uncle all rode as riders in the parade. Peter Feringa rode on the "Chitimacha Indians" float which depicted the indigenous

Indians who inhabited the Mississippi River delta area ("L'Ancienne Nouvelle-Orléans"). A papier-mâché Chitimacha Indian was the focal point of the float with native flowers and plants decorating the sides of the float. Brett Feringa rode on the "Good Friday Fire" float, which depicted the Great Fire of New Orleans. The float featured a papier-mâché shotgun house on the front of the float with fiery, blossoming flowers coming out of the windows and doors. The fiery, blossoming flowers decorated the rest of the float, making it appear on fire.

Conclusion

Mardi Gras is culturally important to the city of New Orleans, the state of Louisiana, and the nation. My family's history in Mardi Gras contributes to telling the story of the Rex Organization, Mardi Gras, and New Orleans. New Orleanians will continue to add to the Carnival celebration and bring cultural heritage to life. As it continues to evolve, I hope the next generations have that nostalgia for Mardi Gras and their family's history and work towards preserving, cultivating, and bringing more awareness to their cultural heritage. This thesis explores a small fraction of Mardi Gras and Rex's history. There are many traditions, historical events, people, places, and artifacts that are crucial to telling the stories of Mardi Gras, the Rex Organization, and my family.

Writing my senior thesis on my family's heritage and the Mardi Gras traditions and culture has made me appreciate New Orleans's rich history, culture, and traditions and reminisce about my family's and my experience. To many outside of

Louisiana, Mardi Gras is a huge party. The history and traditions of Carnival are neglected or unknown. The more time I spent away from it, the more I began to affiliate it with these perceptions. I forgot the history, the family traditions, the artistry of the floats, gowns, pins, and other Carnival heirlooms. I forgot how important Mardi Gras was to the city and the state. In addition, most of the debutante season is misunderstood and obscured by public intoxication, food, and expensive and over-the-top, parties. Even though this is part of the Mardi Gras and debutante culture today, the Carnival celebration and debutante season is also about different generations coming together, passing down traditions, forming and rekindling relationships, listening and sharing relative's stories, and participating in the same carnival and debutante rituals your ancestors participated in.

I believe the repurposing and reviving of Mardi Gras and family' cultural materials, artistry and traditions make the debutante and Mardi Gras season all the more memorable. It increases the sentimentality of the heritage. As humans, we crave developing close associations with our past. As seen in Rex's history, Rex has found inspiration and revived many of the old invitations, sketches, and events. This allows the people to connect and form a relationship with Rex. With all the Krewes, parades, balls, and other carnival activities, people of all backgrounds can find a connection.

From my own research, the creation and cultivation of Mardi Gras cannot be linked to a specific organization or time in New Orleans' history. Every event, person, and place has shaped

Mardi Gras. The public and rowdy Mardi Gras celebration during the nineteenth century was beautified with the birth of the Mistick Krewe of Comus in 1857. The Carnival celebration shook when the School of Design formed in response to the city's unstable political and economic system and the arrival of the Russian Grand Duke. The five old-line organizations, especially Rex, established several Mardi Gras traditions (Hardy, 2018a). The birth of the Krewe of Zulu and parades based upon neighborhoods, Krewe of Thoth and Krewe of Mid-City, were highlights of Carnival (Peter Feringa, Hardy, 2018b).

In addition to the cancelation of Mardi Gras during World War I, it barely survived the Great Depression and World War II. The sharp drop in consumer spending and investment from the Great Depression and World War II severely impacted New Orleans (Peter Feringa). The Mardi Gras celebrations of the 1960s experienced drastic changes. Super-Krewes emerged, and Rex introduced the doubloon. During the 1970s, 18 Krewes formed, but the same number died. During the 1990s, growth began with 28 new Krewes and the death of 17 Krewes. In addition, many Carnival traditions were revived. Rex revived their Lundi Gras celebration. The 1990s were a significant moment in Mardi Gras. The annual economic impact of Mardi Gras exceeds a half-billion dollars. The changing values of the 1990s were reflected in the non-discriminatory ordinance issued by the city requiring all Krewes to integrate. The death of some of the oldest organizations reflects the change in socio-cultural values (Hardy, 2018a; B. Nolan).

Mardi Gras will continue to evolve and reflect contemporary society; some traditions will disappear, others resurrected, and new ones created.

When Hurricane Katrina hit, New Orleans' community was in a vulnerable state. Mardi Gras served a different purpose; locals used Mardi Gras to express their frustration with the government in an artistic, creative, and inventive way. Costumes, floats, signs, throws, etc. were designed and created to illustrate what was going on in New Orleans and mock anything and everything including local and national government figures and levee inspectors (Barber). For many New Orleanians, Mardi Gras was not about the alcohol, partying, or reviving the economy; the battered-city and citizens needed a way to uplift their spirits, feel a sense of community, and find reassurance (Laborde, 2016). Mardi Gras has been shaped by the historical, political, and social events and will continue to change as the world changes (B. Nolan).

Chapter 4: Landscapes of Memory: Exploring Family Heritage Through Place and Travel

By Madison Alspector

On Thanksgiving night, any given year during my childhood, a fairly typical scene occurred: the meal is over, and everyone is stuffed either of turkey or fried plantains and the evening is creeping towards us. As my family is spread across the living room of our condo watching a movie, probably *Pirates of the Caribbean*, I'll have a glance across the room and out the patio French doors that are open, letting in salty air and a lingering smell of mangrove trees. We got really lucky that our old condo faces the ocean and is not blocked by any buildings or tall ships. The sun has started to descend, and I know my mom's about to hit pause on the VCR, so we can all get down to the docks for the show.

Though usually we try to watch the sunsets that have made Key West famous from Mallory Square a few blocks down the road, on Thanksgiving we like to watch it alone as a family on our own dock. Hurrying to grab sweaters and binoculars, my cousin, sister and I race out the door first, trying to steal the elevator before the rest of the family can catch up. We succeed and as we near the bottom, my cousin counts to five, letting my sister and I know when to jump. We've been doing this since Reese was old enough to walk on her own. How we haven't broken the already-aged elevators, I don't know. The door opens, and we race out again, this time through the pool and Tiki bar area to get to the docks. Eventually everyone else catches up and we all sit together, watching the sky change colors before our eyes.

Figure 4.1: Sunset at Key West, Florida. Source: From the personal collection of the author.

First the change is soft, introducing shades of pink and peach into the clouds. A couple minutes later the colors become more dramatic and now the whole sky is lit up as peach turns to burnt ocher and pink becomes crimson. By this point the horizon is a blur of hot, deep reds around a dark orange epicenter, sandwiched between the darkening twilight blue and the endless indigo ocean slowly swallowing the sun. Reese and I frantically grab for the binoculars my grandpa has been holding, trying to see the green flash. The green flash at the end of the sunset is a local Key West legend, and as kids it was all we cared about, as my mom laughingly recalls "that green flash was always so serious to you and your sister!" Disputes over whether one of us had seen it were constant, and pictorial evidence was the top goal. Though I was always angry when I was younger that I never captured it on camera, now I get to enjoy hundreds of sunset photographs that instantly pull me back into these nights spent on the dock, surrounded by family. Everyone I talked to about favorite Key West moments agreed watching the sunsets was on the list. The consensus for the whole family seemed to be that whatever problems were happening in our lives at that point were always left at home on the mainland, at least for a week. When in Key West, it was all fun, adventure and memories like this; sitting on a beach chair leaning against my mom, listening to water lap against the wooden posts of the dock, light music, and clapping coming from Mallory Square. I always remember feeling a faint shiver as the sun went down and took away the last of the day's heat, and most importantly eagerly awaiting the trip to Ben and Jerry's I came to expect after the sunset.

Growing up, certain events stick with you. These memories go on to shape who you'll become as an adult and help define what is meaningful to you and your family. The most significant memories our grandparents and parents pass down to us are traditions, which is what makes up our cultural heritage. This patrimony can be both tangible and intangible; such as heirlooms from generations past, or songs and stories told about ancestors to us in the present. Heritage can be as simple as a favorite recipe or as complex as an archaeological site. Sometimes heritage might not even be obvious, like trying to identify an established characteristic of one's family and what makes them and their combined histories important. Though not every family has a special artifact or long held tradition to leave for future generations, one thing everyone does is construct shared memories. Memories are key in developing one's identity and are helpful in defining one's relationship within a group. The family heritage I chose to write about is relatively young, beginning with my grandparents, and is based on shared and honored experiences catalyzed by place.

For my case study on family heritage I am focusing on the tradition of traveling to two specific locations; Key West, Florida and New England, around coastal Maine. These two locations are more than just dots on a map or a vacation destination. They have been significant parts of my life as well as places of appreciation and importance to my parents and grandparents. It is in these two places that my family has grown and developed, and the cultural landscapes of each have had lasting impacts on all of our lives, both individually and as a whole. Stemming from a divide within the family, the tradition of traveling to these separate places came about. However, through the blending of the two sides of the divided family, the formation of a cohesive family heritage has occurred over the years. For this reason, I am focusing on the effects of continued family travel and the influences of certain place-based locations on creating a family's sub-culture. The connection of landscape and memory is one that has allowed generations to connect to one another and create a special lifestyle uniquely their own. Through this case study, can be seen how certain landscapes serve as a stimulus of memory and in turn, how those memories define who we are as an individual family unit as well as how families are perceived within society at large.

When you think about family vacations as a kid, what comes to mind? Do you picture cramped cars, fighting with siblings over what song you get to listen to? Maybe you think of activities like going to sports games, visiting amusement parks, even participating in an outdoor activity you didn't usually get to do. Sometimes it can be hard to recall exact details of where you were, and maybe the place wasn't even that significant for you. Rather, what stands out most are times spent together as a family and the actual travel experience. When asked about family vacations, or even any specific family event I experienced, I can immediately smell salty ocean air and feel the stickiness of humidity curling and my tangled hair. Depending on the time of year I'm remembering, the air is either chilly and crisp or warm and muggy. Though I was lucky enough to go on many family trips growing up, Key West and Maine are the two places I remember and cherish the most and are places we return to year after year.

Having a family split and separate traditions developed among different grandparents, I guess you could say I formed double the practices. It was easy to draw a line between my different relatives. When I was younger I associated different activities and ideas with different sets of grandparents. Though everyone lived in South Florida for most of my childhood, and all my grandparents were greatly involved in my and my sister's lives, I had interests and activities I did with each separate relative.

When thinking about my three grandmas and my two grandpas growing up, I immediately associate certain things. I knew if I was going to my Bubba's house, I could count on climbing her backyard tree with my cousin and going to McDonald's for breakfast in pajamas. If my Mimi and Poppo were picking up my sister and I from school, I got excited for the tacos we always made and playing outside on their golf course. If we were going to grandma Carole's for dinner, I prepared myself for an overload of crisp chocolate chip cookies and her talking parrot, Laura-Bird.

Figure 4.2: My three grandmas at a family celebration. Source: From the personal collection of the author.

I even associated different holidays with specific grandparents and knew when I would see certain relatives depending on what family gathering we were attending. Hanukkah and Christmas were always with Bubba and Papa, where we would all sit in a circle in her living room, watching each other open presents. Easter was at Mimi and Poppo's, where we would terrorize their condo building searching for eggs, even though the chocolate was usually melted by the time we found them. Passover, which is my favorite holiday, was spent at Grandma Carole's. To this day, eating her signature matzo ball soup in dainty crystal bowls brings me back to sitting at the kids table, apprehensively getting ready to recite the Four Questions. I realize now that geographically the places of significance for different parts of my past are very far apart, but the cultural attitudes, activities and things we appreciate from each spot aren't so different after all. So, though Key West and Maine are literally at opposite ends of the United States, physically as well as culturally, what my family loves about both places are very similar. And even the things that make them different from one another have metamorphized over time and combined in the melting pot that is our family's heritage. As my mom said during a discussion of why those two places are where we keep returning to, she pointed out to me the "traditions are the same in a way as we do the same type things- just in a new location and with different grandparents."[1]

Memories have power that illustrate draw an image in one's head. Recollections can bring you back to a specific time in your life, or even a specific place. They can remind you of all the emotions you once felt, and they allow you a small

150

glimpse of traveling back in time. Besides nostalgia for where you've been, they can also allow you to see friends and family who are no longer in your life. In this way, the power of memory is something special and precious to people and it serves as a means to define ourselves in an ever-changing world. [2] For example, the sight of a palm tree immediately draws up an image of my cousin, sister, and I sitting on a curb under the shade of a Sabal palm, eating sticky-sweet plantains, with the sound of chatter and cameras clicking coming from a line of tourists admiring the views of a crystal blue ocean stretching before them. On the other hand, the mention of blueberry pancakes brings me back to sitting in an Art Deco diner much older than myself, wearing a red, white, and blue dress; laughing as my grandma drenches my breakfast with fresh-made syrup and trying to get a glimpse of the upcoming July Fourth parade. There are many things that can trigger memories, but the most vivid ones – the ones I will pass down to my children – are all tied directly to these landscapes because of the impact they had on my life.

After identifying the two most important places for my family's heritage, I had to try to understand why they were so influential. Why did we begin the tradition of going to Key West and Maine? Why did these places rub off on us and how we have adopted various customs from each place? What makes them special, and in turn how they make my family's sub-culture special? Both Key West and the towns we visited in Maine (and the rest of New England) are relatively small, historic places with a long maritime tradition. The coastal landscapes are what originally drew my family to the Florida Keys and Maine, which foster our love for the water. Though both of my grandparent's families are from communities far from an ocean, over time seaside towns were what they were attracted to. Living near the beach and participating in water-related activities was very important to my parents growing up, and later became a huge part of mine and my sister's lives.

In addition to coastal settings, another influence I observed from family interviews was the frequent mentioning of food. Both of my parents are into cuisine, including fine dining at nice restaurants, trying new places, and having favorite spots that we go to regularly. Cooking is also important to my family, and the recipes we use now are heavily influenced from previous generations and the places we hold dear to our hearts. For example, instead of ham for Christmas dinner at my grandpa's, the rest of my family gets to eat stone crabs, fresh from South Florida thanks to a family connection in the fishing industry. Over Thanksgiving or any fall dinners, there's always an apple, a pumpkin, and a key lime pie present for dessert. Every summer, my mom and grandpa enjoy opening a seasonal Sam Adams on the front porch. My mom makes amazing meals inspired from Caribbean and Cuban roots. My dad loves a good Cuban or mahi-mahi sandwich, and my cousin believes rum and coconut water is a cure for everything.

Though the Florida and New England fair is something special for me, my family has additional food traditions, particularly relating to my Dad's side and his Eastern European-Jewish customs.

Coming from a larger and better-connected family than my mom, food was a big part of his life, and both he and my mom make a point that many of the recipes he enjoyed as a child are still made for special occasions. While food is a great way to show the influence and effects of other's culture on our family unit, it is also used to create a connection to those who have passed on. For example, every time my mom attempts to recreate my paternal grandmother's famous brisket for holiday meals, it brings with it a flood of memories and a sweet nostalgia for those that have passed. My dad teaching Reese and I to grill steak and lamb-chops (or vegetables in my case) is something special we get to share, something I know his dad did with him. In these ways, the food and the memories bring to us the activity and customs of cooking as a family tradition to uphold.

These are just a few examples of the many things I feel make up my family's sub-culture. Most importantly however, before you can describe a family heritage, you need to be able to define yourself and who is included in your family. Thinking back, there are many times I've felt the comfort, safety and content that comes from being surrounded by loved ones. Being twelve years old, dealing with the drama of life as a pre-teen girl, but getting one week off of middle school to be with my parents, grandparents, and cousin in my favorite place in the world, Key West. Spending the week swimming in our condo's pool, exploring the beach and snorkeling under docks, walking the streets lined with "conch cottages" and enjoying the happiness everyone felt. People often call the

Caribbean islands and the Keys a "paradise" and I have got to say, it's hard to disagree. Something about the place just puts you at ease and opens your heart to all the beauty, making it an escape from the monotonous stress of daily life. The easygoing attitude of locals is infectious, and the eclecticism makes it okay to just be yourself, and really be free to embrace what you want. Both my mom and grandma continually expressed the idea of simple happiness and enjoyment, as well as learning to be open minded to those unlike us throughout our conversations of life on the Keys. It is through the sentimental attachment to place that keeps my family returning to the place. I am grateful for the time spent on these family trips.

Summers in Maine with family always gave me peace of mind – an opportunity to enjoy serenity. For example, the months before I began at the College of Charleston were a time of apprehension and bitter-sweetness, but for a few weeks in July I got to forget about all the upcoming change and just enjoy time with my family. Bar Harbor, a coastal town on Maine's southeast coast, has long been the place we like to spend the Fourth of July. Thinking back to that summer, I'm flooded with memories of sweaty hikes through Acadia National Park, hearing my grandpa lecture on about survival skills and showing us where to find the ripest blueberry bushes. I remember one night visiting the lobster pound and waiting outside because I couldn't stand to see the lobsters sitting in tanks waiting to be cooked. As I wandered along the rocky shore outside of the shack-like building covered with weatherboarding that housed the pound, cold and damp breezes whipped against me. The clearness of the air and the fleetingness of that moment made me stand still and embrace it all. When we got back to the rental house we always stayed in, my sister and grandparents were waiting at the door, excitedly pulling us inside to show the makeshift track designed for our annual lobster race (another inhumane lobster related activity I usually skip).

These two landscapes not only provide a backdrop to fun and exciting memories, but are also places of comfort, joy, and reassurance. The Keys and Maine are been locations my family has come together and appreciate who and where we are, without worrying about all the other facets of life. Florida and Maine are where I have learned very important life lessons, where I have explored myself, and had the freedom to examine my family and our dynamic. Obviously, I know what Key West and Maine mean to me, but there is much that I have learned from the interviews conducted for this assignment is like working through a puzzle. Putting together my family's stories with my own introspection, I've been able to create an image of each place; one that demonstrates the character and importance of each. In this way, these two places become what I would call "home".

Who I am and where I come from is largely based on who raised me, but also deeply connected to the places I spent my childhood and formative years. In defining family, it is helpful to look at those who I can relate to, regardless if we are blood relatives, because we have shared experiences. Family is one of the most important aspects of human life. Who you relate to, whom you confide in, where you come from, and how you define yourself are all linked to the idea of family. Family, however, can have many different meanings depending on your experiences and point of view. Familial ties, though usually defined through genetics or marital connections, can be much deeper and more tangled than they might seem. Everyone has some crazy family story, or something that they consider unique when it comes to those they are closest to. Also, family does not have to be your blood relatives, as many consider close friends as part of their chosen tribe. There are also different levels of family, separated by closeness and emotional attachment. Loved ones, relatives, kinship... how do you define who is your family and why they are important to you?

Family for me is who you grew up with, who you feel safe and comfortable around, and who has had the most impact and active role within your life. I used to think of my family as a relatively small and tight-knit group that included my parents, sister, cousin, grandparents, and aunt. Of course, there are many more people biologically related to me, but growing up, this was the extent of my family tree. These were the people who raised me, who were always around and who I did special things with. As I have gotten older and realized my scope of family was inaccurate from the reality of whom I was actually related to, my ideas of family and heritage evolved. It is no secret among us that I am stubborn and strong-willed when it comes to my opinions on many things. This can also translate into being closed off towards those who I don't trust, particularly to blood-related family members. If new people arrive, or I learn of some far distant cousin, I feel a sense of hesitation and the need to protect my idea of who is defined as family. I have come to realize that this is not the best quality characteristic because I have had to get over it a lot in the last several years as I grew up and we grew into new family forms.

Now I try to be more welcoming to those I have never met, or new people coming into our little clan. I have had to deal with the reality of losing significant family members, either through death or unexpected life events that have taken people away. With relatives coming and going, I have had to search my conceptualization of family and who I am among them, which is something many people go through as they get older. Though the physical nature and geographic proximity of my family has greatly changed since my childhood, the traditions and cultural heritage that I grew up with has remained. In this way, though the family may grow or shrink, and the dynamics change over time, I can still look at someone special and know we have a connection through our shared memories and traditions from either Key West or Maine. This is something unique to us and something we continue giving to one another. It has become harder to keep up with one another in our family and to continue doing the things the exact way we always have. But the effort is there and when we do participate in these traditions, it's like no time has passed.

Because of limited knowledge on the matter of family lineage it can be difficult to find something historically significant that has been passed down through multiple generations. Since my known family history does not extend far beyond my grandparents, my personal heritage is relatively young and based off the traditions created by my grandparents and parents. These are the things I consider sacred and invaluable. Traditions that have shaped who I am today due to the way I was raised. A lack of recorded ancestors going back several generations signifies a need to acknowledge and preserve the traditions we have in the present for future generations, and to continue practicing them so that descendants will understand who their ancestors were and what was significant to us.

Our heritage is directly connected to memories and emotions and is what unite us. Culture guides our values and occasionally serves as a reminder to love one another, even when we may be struggling to. No family is perfect, and mine comes with its fair share of familial drama and emotional baggage. However, if there is ever a time I'm feeling confused about who I am and where I come from, or what is important, all I need to do is think about a place and time when things made sense and felt right in my life. As things change and kids grow up, it's not easy to be that tight-knit group who is always right by your side. Preserving our heritage and keeping memories and traditions alive however is what keeps this family strong.

When delving into family research or doing a study on traditions, it is typical to think back to long ago generations and finding the connecting ties that explain why one's family believes, celebrates, and acts the way it does. That was my first thought when beginning this process. I originally hoped to find my long-lost ancestors and use their lives to help explain mine. Though this would have been an interesting path to take, and I certainly would have learned a lot from it, I don't know about my distant family. Long forgotten relatives don't always make sense when regarding the topic of heritage. Of course, where I come from and the people who worked to get my family to where we are today are important, but those stories don't resonate in my life today. When I think of what has shaped me and which stories or traditions I consider significant and will pass down to my children and grandchildren, I can easily point to where they began, as it wasn't too long before I was born.

The characteristics and traits I think of when I see my family has little connection to our ancestors and where they came from in Europe. Rather, it has been the practices, beliefs, and customs cultivated from lives spent in America, particularly in South Florida. The complicated make up of my family also didn't help the matter, because with divorces, deaths, estrangements, and relocations, whose ancestral heritage would I choose to claim as mine? Since the most important cultural make up and influence for my family is based on the different places that are significant to each set of my grandparents, that is what I have chosen to focus on documenting.

My family is not the kind that has many meaningful heirlooms or that has tracked their ancestors back hundreds of years. We don't come from a long line of war heroes or have a far related royal ancestor to draw our sense of family pride. Though there are certainly material objects we keep that have been passed on, they are not the type of heirlooms you can paint a picture of heritage around. These weren't the kind of things that were considered important when my parents and (later) I was growing up, and the history of my great-great-grandparents remain unknown to me. Our view of who we were came directly from the relatives I saw almost every day, and the lives they had carefully constructed. Though my parents have a vague idea about where their ancestors came from, there has been little research done on the subject. Because of this, my heritage and sense of connection to the past is through more contemporary social practices and informal cultural expressions.

For example, my dad is familiar with his great-grandparents and their emigration from a small town near Kiev, in what is now the Ukraine, and another town near St. Petersburg, Russia, but for the most part, his biggest tie to that part of his past is a love for Russian vodka and pierogis. And that's only one side. Another branch is documented in family research as from German descent, with many relatives going to Canada. My mom's family history is even fuzzier to me. My maternal grandma, Jane, never talked to us about her parents growing up. Most of what I know about her comes from her life in Florida, while I was young. She has a strong connection to Boston and New England, and claims to be Irish, but no one has confirmed this story.

My maternal grandfather, Wayne, on the other hand is an endless source for stories of his childhood and his large family growing up in rural New England. Wayne is probably the family member most interested in our past and has gone the farthest by signing up for Ancestry.com and keeping family tree records to the best of his ability. His own theories and stories though are what are most significant to him, and therefore me, in regard to his heritage. I have heard him say we are French, English, Canadian, Spanish, and even part Native American. I am unsure whether any of this is accurate, but it is what he has been going on for years, and honestly what has influenced my opinions of our cultural heritage. My mom's parents are also divorced and both remarried, which brought in new customs and traditions from those new grandparents as well. With a significant divide in the family, two separate traditions of travel developed- one going North and the other South.

The cultural heritage and family values my parents have created is probably partly due to their distinct yet similar pasts. Issues with siblings, not always steady or traditional home lives, and childhoods with a lot of deeply affecting changes for them transcended into the ways they chose to parent my sister and me. That is why the traditions that connect us now are ever the most important and special, as they were created by my grandparents and parents to give us the strong and steady family they didn't always have and the ability to remain connected to one another as time has gone on. Though both of my parents were born in different states, their families moved them to South Florida at very young ages, so Broward/Dade County is really where they grew up and felt the most impact on their characters and memories. My dad grew up traveling with his family a lot, to many different places. My mom's parents also liked to travel, though she was often left at home. Their two experiences have blended into a shared appreciation for travel, which the past onto their children.

My mom's side of the family is from a small town in New England, where my distant relatives still live today. My maternal grandpa is Wayne Phoenix, and he was born in 1936 and raised in South Hadley, a rural town in western Massachusetts. My maternal grandmother, Jane Cohen, was born in 1940 in Boston, but also spent a large part of her life in South Hadley. They were married in 1956 and soon started a family. My mom is the youngest by eleven years out of three girls, and she was born in South Hadley in 1969. Her family left Massachusetts when she was still a baby and lived in Winston-Salem, North Carolina for four years. After this, they returned to South Hadley for another year, before finally settling in Plantation, Florida. At this point, my mom was seven years old, and her sisters were all out of the house. My maternal grandparents divorced after they moved to Florida, and my grandma Jane remarried Howard Klubik, who became my mom's stepfather and played a large role in her life growing up.

With my grandpa Wayne often out of the state working, the biggest influencers on my mom's early life were her mother Jane and stepfather Howard. Welcoming a new side of relatives, she also had to adjust some aspects of her life. For example, my grandparents had previously belonged to a Congregational Church in South Hadley, though my mom never had a formal education or active practice of any religion. However, after marrying Howard, who came from an Orthodox Jewish family, Jane converted to Judaism and my mom was introduced to that new world. Many of her friends in South Florida were also Jewish, including her best friend Lori, with whom my mom would sometimes go to Sunday School with at the synagogue that later became where my sister and I went to elementary school. My mom's childhood and teenage years in South Florida have definitely shaped who she is, and the many things she has passed on to Reese and me. Though we were also raised in suburban South Florida, Plantation was much more rustic when my mom was growing up. During the 1970s and 1980s Florida was still undergoing the beginnings of its urban development, meaning she had a lot of freedom to explore woods, marshes, and other open lands that were not-yet built on. Florida also used to be a relatively safe place for kids to run around all day, biking to one another's houses and through neighborhoods. Beginning in middle school my mom even used to take the bus alone to get to the beach.

Jane and Howard would often go on trips or cruises, leaving my mom alone at their house. This freedom led to her developing close relationships with several friends, who would stay at the house with her for weekends or with whom she learned a lot from. Her childhood was very "outdoorsy", and she spent a lot of time at the beach. My mom enjoyed playing softball, surfing, swimming, and frisbee in the many parks South Florida has. On the trips she did get to go on, many were to Key West. Howard introduced my grandma to Key West in 1979, and a year later they bought a condo there, called the Galleon (which we still own, as it was given to my parents when Reese and I were young).

Once they had the Galleon, my mom started joining them, usually two or three times a year.[3] When she was in high school, she got to bring friends with her on these trips. Other places that she got to visit with my grandpa Wayne were often in North Carolina, as he had remarried my now grandma Karlene, and they had a house in Lake Lure.[4] My mom says she always wanted to go back to New England and visit Boston, which is something we have gotten to do more often now as our own family. But Key West quickly became a favorite place of hers to visit, and many of the activities and places she started going to as a kid and young adult are still some of the places we consider family traditions. Many of her favorite memories have become my favorites too.

Figure 4.3: Swimming pool at the Galleon. Source: From the personal collection of the author.

Unfortunately, Howard died when my mom was eighteen, causing another significant change in their lives. Financially and emotionally, Howard's death was difficult for my grandma. Around the same time, my cousin Andrew was born, but was unable to live with his mom Wendy. My mom's sister dealt with many substance abuse issues for most of her life, and because of this, my grandma Jane adopted Andrew. During this time, my grandmother remarried again, to my now grandpa Stan Cohen. By this point my mom was away in college, so Jane and Stan raised Andrew like a son. Because of this, my mom and cousin have a very close relationship, as he was still very young when he went to live with my grandparents. When a couple years later my parents got married, they played a large role in Andrew's life, both as friends and provisional parental figures. It is for all of these reasons he is such a big part of my life, as we both grew up spending a lot of time together. Andrew, Reese, and I have a close sibling-like relationship and his opinions and actions as well as the many experiences we have shared have been influential in how I look at the world in regard to family.

My dad's family, on the other side, is from Chicago, Illinois. He and his brother Robbie were born outside of the city in 1968. His mom, Carole Chez, and his dad, Michael Alspector, were also born and grew up in Chicago. The Alspector's and the Chez's have many relatives still living in Illinois, however my paternal grandparents moved to Hollywood, Florida shortly after my dad was born. Hollywood is another suburb in South Florida, about fifteen minutes from Plantation. Though they lived close to one another and enjoyed many of the same activities, my dad's childhood and home situation was fairly different from my mom's. Though Carole and Michael had left most of their relatives to come to Florida, my dad's paternal grandparents were already living in Hallandale, a few miles up the highway, where they had chosen to retire. With six Alspectors living near each other and away from the rest of the family, they became very close. My dad enjoyed weekly Sunday night dinners with his grandparents and lots of family time spent doing things like dining out and going to the beach. My great-grandpa even lived until I was about seven, so I have some faint memories of times with him too. When my dad was ten, his parents opened a crystal shop in Hollywood, called the Crystallerie. They both had a strong work ethic, which was instilled in my dad, and were well off for all of his childhood.

Though he had a stronger family dynamic and was raised in a different kind of household, my dad still participated in most of the activities my mom did, and he also describes his childhood as outdoorsy, with an emphasis on the beach and water. Though there was no serious religious practice in his family, he did grow up in a Jewish household, going to synagogue on occasion and celebrating holidays with his immediate family. This helped influence my mom after they got married and had kids, who chose Judaism despite growing up somewhere in between. Many of the family traditions I remember relating to my grandma Carole involve holidays at her house and the Jewish recipes brought over from her parents. Things my dad fondly remembers are her simple yet delicious matzo ball soup, kasha, sponge cake, and brisket, all of which she left to my mom and I in a cookbook she made after my parents were married. My dad also took many family trips growing up. My grandpa, Michael, is a Civil War history buff," so they toured the Old South and visited many historic and scenic sites, mostly in North Carolina and the surrounding region. While my dad was still a kid (and after) the family had opened the Crystallerie, they began taking trips to tropical locations, always right after Christmas (being a busy retail time for them). From this custom of going to Club Med and different island spots, eventually they bought a boat. This changed their family trips and weekly family gatherings, making a large impact in his life.

Indeed, it was in the Jewish section of the Key West Cemetery where I learned about the tradition of leaving stones on Jewish graves. There is a significant Jewish section inside the cemetery, marked off from the rest with an iron and stone gate inscribed with the Hebrew words "B'nai Zion." We always took time to visit this section, and on one of those days while I was leaving wild daisies and weeds on people's headstones, I became infuriated to find dozens of rocks sitting on the Jewish graves. Before my mom had time to tell me this was not a rude prank, I decided I would fix all the graves up.

While my family was out walking in the main area, seven-year-old me was swiping every last pebble from the Jewish graves, leaving the thoughtful offering of a twig with some leaves behind instead. A few minutes later my grandparents walked into the area and my grandpa stopped me and asked what I was doing. I explained the situation to them and before I could ask why they looked so confused at my good deed, my grandma started laughing hysterically. She called my mom over and continued laughing at the stones scattered around their feet. So, it was here, in the Jewish section of the cemetery, one hand holding stones and the other a handful of wildflowers, where I learned an interesting fact about my religion (stones are used to decorate graves). This is another example of the innumerous lessons I've learned from time spent on Key West. In this way, the island is more than a beautiful landscape. It is a physical map of my growing up and becoming the person I am, as well as for my father before me.

Figure 4.4: Tending to the gravestones at the Jewish section of the Key West Cemetery. Source: From the personal collection of the author.

When my dad was in middle school he would often get to take Fridays off to help his father get ready for weekend trips. They spent a lot of time on the boat *Carole Lee*, sailing throughout the Florida Keys and also to the Bahamas. It was from this experience that our family traditions of love for the ocean and water-related activities, like snorkeling, diving, windsurfing and fishing, began. When I think of my childhood in Florida, I remember many of the same activities, and how excited my dad was to show them to my sister and me. It's interesting to get a different perspective of my parents through their stories, and to see that so many of the banal things I did growing up were actually traits and hobbies passed down from things they enjoyed as kids themselves. Besides boating off to tropical vacations, my dad's family often took the boat out for dinner during the week, going to the many restaurants along the Inter-coastal Waterway. Much of this stopped however, and my dad's life changed drastically during his sophomore year of high school, when his father passed away.

After my grandpa Michael's death, they couldn't keep the boat, so along with special family time in South Florida, trips to the Keys and days out on the water stopped for my dad. At this point, he became more involved in sports, having to fill the time previously spent helping his dad on the boat or being with family in some other way. He thus spent his time doing things with friends as his brother (now estranged from the family) was always with their mom or at their house with his girlfriend. Luckily, my dad attended the same school building from kindergarten through high school, so he had some very close friends from other suburbs nearby that he could do things with. In this way, both my mom and dad had similar high school experiences of being left on their own much of the time. It is probably what helped them connect when they met, later influencing the way they parented Reese and I, making sure they are involved in our lives.

Despite losing the boat and the relationship he had with his father, my dad and grandma Carole continued on many important traditions, and so the Keys and the ocean had a special place in his heart. Unlike my mom, my dad grew up eating a lot of Cuban and Caribbean island food, which influenced a certain air of the island lifestyle in his house. Because he started visiting these places so young and his family was exposed to the culture of the Keys and the Caribbean through friends and hired help, it influenced his childhood and his own family's sub-culture (and later our own) more so than my mom. Even though my dad was already used to Caribbean culture, they both shared an immense love of the Keys that continued to grow once they met and decided to start their own family. My mom got to show him Key West and share her childhood experiences, while he got to show her the rest of the region and the inviting culture that had been transfused into his life.

Between my dad being accustomed to frequent vacations and the love of exploring distinct and historical towns, and my mom's desire for family trips that included everyone, traveling has been ever-present and important my whole life. Also, the tradition and continuation of going to the Keys was important to both of them, which is why it is a place of common ground and shared love for all of us. Their own separate traditions in the area joined as they brought together all my grandparents.

The Keys are not the only place our family enjoys visiting, and smaller trips are just as fun and a part of our family customs. Traveling the American South and appreciating the small towns, outdoor adventures, and slow-paced way of life is something I got to participate a lot in when I was growing up. Visiting family in North Carolina or New England and finding new towns and adventures to love was always something my parents were keen on and considered an important aspect to continue and pass down. They're two separate background of place-based travel and significance of certain landscapes eventually helped shape what is now our own special cultural heritage and is why the places we traveled when I was young are so valuable to me now.

Because my mom and dad both came from complicated families, with loss of loved relatives, they made sure we were always surrounded by affection, comfortability, and respect. That meant I could count on an aunt, a cousin, and all three sets of grandparents to be heavily involved in our lives. Growing up, my family all lived within thirty minutes of each other. This meant weekly family dinners, pool days at our house, beach days at Bubba and Papa's or grandma Carol's, terrorizing Mimi and Poppo's condo, and golfing with Reese and cousin Andrew, countless celebrations, and most memorably, family trips. I previously believed these activities were just a unique part of my childhood and something that began after mine and my sister's births. Hearing stories about my own parent's childhoods made me realize this behavior started before me, and the specialness I felt from it was the same my parents felt as kids, and why they worked so hard to make it a part of their children's lives. Though South Florida is where my family met and came together, the attachments and patrimony from the distinct places my distant relatives came from have been passed down through my grandparents and are now sources of pride, impact, and invaluable memory to me.

Conclusion

A city is just a place until it means something to someone, and once there is a cultural or personal significance, it becomes a part of you. The emotions, memories, and values I associate with these places are why they are important and have significantly added to my own cultural heritage. Each branch of my family has imbued in me the love and attachment to certain sites or landscapes, and further has cemented the tradition of traveling to visit these places. Though cities and places can't literally be given to someone, I do feel a sense of possessiveness towards these locations, as though I have a stake in their history and future, just as they have a stake in mine. Heritage is a shared socio-cultural bond between people. This is what I have with my family's favorite places, and the customs and rituals that have been passed down.

Our shared memories grow more important as time goes by and the family continues to change. Sickness, death, and increasing distance between people has the ability to make family feel less important, or at least less together. The traditions we hold onto keep the memories alive. Through the study of my relatives' pasts and their perceptions of what has gone into creating a family heritage, I have received an in depth look at the power of memories and stories and how they can connect people together. Furthermore, the landscapes that encourage those memories are physical catalysts and reminders of what in this world is important to us. This is what makes every family special and different from one another. It boils down to what we believe is most important; values, locations, people, and emotions. What we choose to hold onto is passed down to our children, and later to theirs, creating a cultural heritage uniquely our own. In this way, our memories serve as a construction of our identity and help us to understand our relationships with different people, like family.

Figure 4.5: Rees and Madison at the beach, Key West, Florida. Source: From the personal collection of the author.

Chapter 5: A Pilcher Tradition: The Legacy of the Elgin National Watch Company

By Madison Moga

When contemplating my heritage and the aspects in which I could conduct formal research, I was at first concerned that my family was without any real topic of interest or significance; no famous people, places, or priceless family heirlooms. Initially I was drawn to my fiancé's family history and traditions and his proud Southern roots and their two-century old homestead still owned and actively used by the family, and their Thanksgiving celebration that annually draws over ninety family members. In comparison, my roots in rural northern Illinois, with a small direct family seemed insignificant and lacking. Nevertheless, I decided to call my Papa, Jim Pilcher, my maternal grandfather, and ask him what he thought I should write about, and he immediately responded with the idea of researching and writing about his great-grandfather, George Pilcher, who worked in a prominent watch factory in Elgin, Illinois. I decided to take his advice, and I began researching this ancestor's story.

Before undertaking this project, I had always known of this family member who worked at the Elgin National Watch Company, but I had never realized how significant it was that George and his family decided to move all the way to the United States so that he could work at this factory; or just how famous and important this watch company was in the history of not only watchmaking, but also of industrialism in America during the late nineteenth and early twentieth centuries. This company became famous for its beloved pocket watches, which played an important role in American history.[1] The ironic nature of the timelessness of a watch, even watches that no longer work, is revealed in the way that they are often valued as family heirlooms that speak to family history and lineage and are readily passed down through generations in families.

Through my research I also discovered how long the family tradition of the Annual Pilcher Family Picnic in Elgin, Illinois extended back in time. I had always known of these picnics, but when I attended them as a child I had no understanding of how amazing it was that this tradition had been passed down for so long, and I had no idea where this tradition originated from until this project. As someone who is interested in historic preservation and the architectural history of the factory, the development of the surrounding residential areas, and how my family had a connection to it, however small, was most intriguing to me in my research. This focus revealed drastic concerns from a preservation standpoint, as almost the entire watch factory complex was demolished over the years of the company's decline in the twentieth century.

Literature Review

I am certainly not the first person to research the history of the Elgin National Watch Company, and also not the first to research the history of the

Pilcher family. Elgin is a town full of residents who understand and appreciate their town's rich history, and many have researched and published histories of this great historic town. The Elgin National Watch Factory was so ingrained in the town's development that anyone researching Elgin undoubtedly also came across information on the watch factory and its influence. One notable Elgin historian is E.C. Alft, former mayor of Elgin, has written numerous histories of the town including, *Elgin: An American City, 1835–1985*, and *Elgin: Days Gone By*. I used my Papa's copy of *Elgin: An American City* and on the front page found a touching note from my great-grandma Elsie to her son, "Merry Christmas Jim- To remember your 'old home town,' Mother + Dad 1984." This reinforced how important this town is in the history of my family. Luckily those who care about Elgin's history have taken efforts to preserve this history and the built environment that reflects it, through the creation of the Elgin Heritage Commission, Elgin National Watch Historic District, Elgin National Watch Company Neighborhood, The Elgin Historic Preservation Ordinance, the City's Historic Architectural Rehabilitation Grant Program, and a Historic Plaque program.

A relative, Gary Biesterfeld, is very interested in genealogy and has taken it upon himself to create a three-volume history of our family titled *Pilcher Cousins*. His books contain histories, pictures, family trees, and stories about many of those descended from my great-great-great grandparents, George and Mary Pilcher, and their nine children.

Origins of The Elgin National Watch Company

The origins of the Elgin National Watch Company, originally known at the National Watch Company, were wrought in the hard work and zeal of both management and employees who collectively made the goal of not only competing in the watch industry on an international scale, but also the goal of high standards and a streamlined approach to production for their pocket watches, which allowed them to conquer business domestically. The watch market and the history of the Elgin Watch Company forever changed when their innovators developed a more modern, streamlined approach to the manufacturing process, which led to more affordable watches and a wider consumer base.[2] Traditionally, the leading watch producers in the world were the Swiss, who were lauded for their precision and excellence. Even these giants in the watch industry; however, were eventually surpassed by the American watchmakers due to their ability to produce watches that were more efficient and more accurate than those made by the Swiss.

In the nineteenth century the traditional Swiss-model cottage industry of making watches using a guild system was still in use. This system, which required a master craftsman to both manufacture and assemble each individual unit, became obsolete by the American use of precision machinery and the assembly line. In the United States, the process of watchmaking was shortened through the introduction of machines that replaced various steps and hand tools. The machinery allowed for higher standards through less variation in the pieces, as the repetition of mechanical movements made by the manufacturing devices were more precise than a human hand and eye during the construction of creating each individual component. The introduction of interchangeable watch parts by American manufactures, like the Elgin Watch Company also increased the efficiency of the process, reducing costs, and the need for master watchmakers to make specialty parts.[3]

After 1850 the need for precise time keeping by the military, industry, and railroad transportation boost demand and sales for watches.[4] In response five new watch companies were formed by 1864. Of these five companies only one survived and grew to great prosperity, the Elgin National Watch Company.[5] Elgin, a small town about 40 miles northwest of Chicago, was founded in 1835 by James T. Gifford along the Fox River. Gifford chose the specific site for his town based on access to the river. Another benefit of the site was its central location between Chicago and Galena, which was significant as Gifford postulated the area would soon be connected by the railroad, a prediction that soon came to fruition.[6] After the new rail line's construction the town of Elgin began to flourish, as it became a shipping point, providing agricultural products to Chicago.[7] In 1864, Elgin, a town of 3,000, with an economy based in a tannery, a distillery, and four gristmills investigated how to attract more industrial growth. Accompanied with popular support, the proposition of constructing a watch company in Elgin was officially organized on August 18, 1864. Soon after on August 22, 1864, the new commercial venture was licensed as the National Watch Company of Chicago. The construction of the watch factory was set to begin in Elgin, on land provided by a number of investors who purchased twenty-five shares in the company at $1,000 each.[8]

The company's newly formed board of directors decided in a lucrative business move to begin production by recruiting already skilled workers from Massachusetts, who were employed by the leading American watch production company at the time, the Waltham Watch Factory. From the initial recruitment drive, seven highly skilled workers from Waltham agreed to move to Elgin and work at the new factory, after the appealing offer of a $5,000 signing bonus with a five-year contract at the fixed rate of $5,000 per year accompanied and a one-acre lot in close proximity to the factory in order to build a house on. The seven men became known in the company lore as the Seven Stars, as they were the key to the enterprise's initial success and lasting reputation.[9] The Seven Stars went on to build some of the most impressive homes in Elgin on the land they received.[10]

The Watch Factory

By January 1865, a temporary workspace comprised of a three-story wooden structure was constructed, providing the Seven Stars with the first factory workspace at the Elgin Company. As the men began assembling and preparing machinery for production it became evident that the makeshift workspace was insufficient as the workers discovered the wooden building shook due to the movement of heavy machinery and the constant strain of what was intended to soon become a site of mass production. The initial production and assembly of the machinery was slowed by the need to acquire steel, iron, and brass by rail from Chicago. In response to the increasing inconveniences caused by this dilemma the company constructed a private foundry and their own illuminating gas plant, which made materials necessary for production both readily available and less expensive.[11]

One of the Seven Stars, Daniel Hartwell's, brother, H.H. Hartwell, of Boston, happened to be a renowned architect and was chosen to design the company's new factory. [12] Hartwell was well equipped for the task as he also conveniently was the architect who designed Waltham's watch factory. In early 1865, equipped with the designs made by Hartwell and the steady stream of revenue made possible by the Seven Stars, construction began on the permanent factory site in Elgin. At the completion of the first phase of construction, the structure was comprised of a single story central square area, measuring 20 feet by 20 feet, with an adjacent two-story wing on the western façade and a smaller two-story wing extending from the rear of the building.[13] A matching wing was later added on the eastern façade in 1868. The factory was constructed originally of brick and limestone, complete with metal roof framing and slate shingles. The central square section of the building was used as office space, with the wings utilized primarily for factory work. These wings featured multiple large windows where workbenches were strategically placed for access to adequate light, as employees were required to work with extremely small mechanisms and components.[14]

Behind the main factory structure were a number of out buildings; one building solely used for dial making featured enameling furnaces and a special room where the dial faces were carefully hand painted. Another building was used for burning coal and distributing gas to fuel mounted light fixtures throughout the factory campus. The machinery used in production was fueled by a centralized steam engine, connected by a series of belts and pulleys, which transferred motion to the individual machines used by employees. At the time of the factory's completion, in 1867, the Elgin Watch Company not only employed the Seven Stars originally associated with the Waltham Watch Company, but also amassed the aid of Waltham's former Superintendent and fourteen foremen. These workers with already established skill sets provided the leadership necessary to train the new local workers.[15] In April of the same year, the first watches were produced and named after the company's first president, Benjamin W. Raymond. Numerous other watches by the company were named after Raymond; however, the use of his name was always reserved for premier lines.[16] In this first year of production 9,000 watch movements were sold, and by 1868, six different movement grades were in active production. By 1869 sales nearly doubled, and in 1870 the company's 525 employees were producing well above a hundred movements a day.[17]

In 1870, the factory reached maximum capacity and started working on new expansion plans, beginning with renovations on the south wing, and the following year construction on a new engine house. The company's assets produced so much revenue during this period that the board of directors came to the decision to construct a new factory in front of the original one that mirrored it in both structure and size, with the exception of an addition that included a six-story bell tower located above the center section of the front building. This new building doubled the factory's size and was connected to the original structure by a wing at the center section, giving the facility an "H" shape.[18]

By 1873, the Elgin Watch Company produced well over 100,000 movements, including fourteen different grades. Among these grades, a watch made specifically for women, aptly named the Lady Elgin was added to the fold in 1869. The company also began developing new technology previously unseen in American watches including, "quick train movements that beat 18,000 times per hour, straight line escapements and over sprung balances." [19] During this time the Elgin Watch Company was able to save money by utilizing jewelry wholesalers to ship the movements to regional distributors, who in turn sold them to local jewelers. This came as a benefit to the Elgin Watch Company, as it was no longer required to manage distribution of their products, nor the expense of employing a sales and shipping department. Likewise, the company opted to refrain from the production of watchcases during this period, saving the immense cost of financing construction of an additional production line with all new machinery and extra workers.[20] Until May 12, 1874, when the board of directors agreed to change the company's name to the Elgin National Watch Company due to local requests, the company had simply been called the National Watch Company.[21]

A devastating fire at a watch factory in Freeport, Illinois, which destroyed all of the competing company's assets within the building, acted as both a *Memento mori* and a harsh reminder to the Elgin Company that their production assets were left vulnerable to the spread of flames. In response to the tragedy, the Elgin Watch Company established a private fire department comprised solely of Elgin employees in 1875. Like any city fire department, the Elgin National Fire Extinguishing Company (NFEC) wore uniforms in parades. While the NFEC was established specifically for the protection of the watch factory, the force often came to the aid of Elgin's city fire fighters if a fire ever occurred within reach of the factory fire department.[22]

Early Employee Housing and the National House

In 1866, the Elgin Watch Company purchased a city block diagonally positioned across the street from the factory, where they constructed five small one-story cottages, all identical in design to each other. These cottages each were equipped with two bedrooms, a parlor and a dining room. They also each had a storage cellar and coal bin in the half-basements.[23] When the company no longer required the use of the cottages for the housing of factory managers, the properties were leased to employees for the price of ten dollars per month.[24]

In 1867, the company began construction on the same block as the cottages for a much larger boarding house for the use of its many employees. Despite the many expenses both managed and balanced by the company, the board understood the employee's imperative need for adequate housing, and a location for their families to live. This boarding house cost the company over $10,000 to construct, and was named the National House, with the nickname "The Nash" used lovingly by boarders. Nearby housing to the factory was important during this period due to the lack of public transportation. Elgin was still largely undeveloped during this time, requiring the factory to confront a housing shortage in the town. The National House was built as a residence for single employees; however, it did feature a few rooms for married couples and suites for the use of the company's officials when they came from Chicago to visit Elgin.[25]

The National House was a four-story building, constructed in the Second Empire style with a mansard roof, featuring other architectural embellishments such as porches. Those living in this boarding house received amenities such as steam heat, as well as hot and cold running water, which were uncommon amenities during the period. The building featured a large central dining hall, where both residents and employees not residing at the National House could enjoy affordable meals, which revolved around the factory schedule. Aside from a comfortable and affordable place to live and meal service, the National house also provided employees with a social life, where new people in town and singles could interact and find friendship and romance. In fact, many residents ended up later getting married.[26]

Economic Depression of the 1870s

After years of growth and prosperity, the Elgin Watch Company experienced its first period of decline during the Panic of 1873, a nation-wide economy business depression. As a result of the economic depression, unemployment rose, resulting in a decrease in the sale of luxury items. Soon the economic stress reached the doors of the Elgin Watch Company, as people simply were not buying as many watches as they had in previous years. This strain forced the company to shut the factory down for nine unpaid weeks during the summer, and a couple months later all wages were consequently reduced by twenty percent. As the panic reached its peak, the factory was eventually brought to such a low that it had to close down for two months in the summer of 1874, due to the decline in sales. Amidst this turmoil; however, on May 12, 1874, the company used the down time to change their official name to the Elgin National Watch Company and to install new machinery in the expanded areas of the factory.[27]

Elgin Watch Company's board decided in 1875 that it needed to make changes in response to the market as the country was still in the midst of economic depression. The company began to introduce a line of watches that were nameless, unlike all their higher priced grades, which bore the names of specific people. These nameless watches were less expensive, and only featured the company name, Elgin. These new movements featured the new technology of stem winding. Another decision made by the board was an extensive study regarding the factory's manufacturing process beginning in 1876. The improvements gained from this study contributed to the streamlining of the factory's processes and reduction in expenses. These improvements were the foundation that supported the success of the company's next venture. In May of the same year the company introduced a new plan, which dramatically decreased the prices of the higher end watches, called the "Popular Price Policy". After the implementation of this policy the price of the B.W. Raymond movement, which was one of the most expensive lines, was reduced from $67.50 down to $39.75. [28]

These decisions paid off as demand for Elgin watches began to increase due to the price cuts as the economy slowly recovered. In 1879, the company was again producing 100,000 movements a year, which was twice as much as the amount produced during the economic panic. [29] The company continued to reduce the prices of its watches, and "with the greater volume came economies of scale and the company returned to profitability."[30] The price cuts employed by Elgin weakened their competitors, but also inspired the creation of new watch companies, many of which did not succeed. The Elgin National Watch Company transformed a small town into a center of economic development based on industry.[31]

Boom Years

The Elgin National Watch Company managed to survive the recession of the 1870s, strengthened by its updated machinery and factory processes, along with a wider market of consumers who appreciated the price and quality of the watches.[32] The board's decision to lower watch prices paid off, providing widespread success and prosperity that the company enjoyed for over nearly a decade. The company was able to spend over half a million dollars on the expansions of its factory between 1879 and 1883.[33] The company employed 1,100 workers in 1880, a work force that went on to produce nearly 500 movements per day. By the end of 1889, the company employed 2,700 employees producing 1,650 over movements per day, a success that lead to Elgin's ascension in the industry, surpassing Waltham as America's leading watch producer by the end of the 1880s. Elgin and Waltham watch companies enjoyed a position that provided them with advantages over smaller firms. The companies possessed influence over the majority of watch making market from its production all the way to sales. This trend of market dominance lasted over another half century.[34] In response to the increased demand for Elgin Watches and the need for an increase in the number of workers, the factory had to expand again in 1879 with a three-story brick addition, which brought the facility's square footage for manufacturing purposes to 175,000.[35]

In addition to the factory expansion, the Elgin Watch Company also invested in an entirely new facility connected to the National House, called the National Gymnasium. This large three-story structure was state of the art, and it provided space for entertaining and physical fitness for the company employees who utilized it. The first floor was entirely dedicated to the National Watch Factory Military Band as a space for them to practice. The second floor was designated as a space to host receptions, ceremonies and various other social gatherings.[36] The third floor is where the employees could exercise and shower. Later, tennis courts were added behind the gymnasium.[37]

George Pilcher

It was during the prosperous 1880s that my great-great-great grandfather immigrated to the United States, in pursuit of economic opportunity afforded by the Elgin National Watch Factory. George Pilcher born on September 28, 1863 heralded from Liverpool, England. His wife Mary Fallon, my great-great-great grandmother, was born on April 14, 1865 in Manchester, England. They married on January 26, 1884, and together had nine children.[38] The story of the family's passage to the United States began with George's long-time friend, Thomas Donahue, a former shipmate from Liverpool. Tom later moved to the United States and wrote a series of letters back to George in England concerning the employment opportunities in America and specifically those found at the Elgin National Watch Company. After some correspondence with Tom, George came to the difficult decision to travel to the United States in pursuit of employment at the watch factory and a future for his family. In February 1888, George arrived in Newport News, Virginia, alone, as Mary and the first two children, John and Mae, stayed behind in England.

George began working at the Elgin Watch Factory in September of 1888, initially working in the yard force before a transfer to watchmen's force after a productive and well-lauded, two months of work. It was nearly a year after George's arrival in America, in 1889 that Mary and the children were financially capable to make their way to the United States. After arriving in their new home Mary began to miss her homeland and doubt the notions of raising her children in the New World. This homesickness inspired Mary in secret to ask of her employer, at the private house she was employed, to garnish her earnings, and put aside a portion of her income, so that she could save enough money to travel back to England with the children. The employer at Mary's requested did this until she had enough to move back to England with both John and Mae. Once in England; however, she began to miss him and opted to return with the children to the United States to be with George, this time for good. All of the moves between England and the United States occurred between February 1888 and June 1890, a period in which the travel time of a transatlantic voyage was nearly three weeks. [39] After her return, Mary was once again with child. During the pregnancy Mary became ill, rendering her paralyzed for the remaining 45 years of her life; however, the baby named Annie was delivered safely without complication.

George, on November 5, 1894, after establishing himself and his family went to Geneva,

Illinois and successfully became an American citizen.[40] During his time at the Elgin National Watch Factory, George also served in the NFEC, which by this time had its own steam fire engine equipped with five hose carts, 3,000 feet of hose, large extension ladders, 1,200 fire grenades, and a Holly water works system which could produce an eight-fold formation of one inch streams.[41]

George worked in the watchmen's force until January of 1901, at which point he was then transferred to the gilding department. He worked in the Gilding Department for a little over two years and then switched again to the Screw Department in July 1903, where he worked until he fell ill in 1921 and passed away. The Elgin Watch Factory employee publication, *Watch Word*, devoted an entire column to George's obituary, notably saying "George Pilcher, well known Screw department employee, died in St. Joseph's hospital early Friday evening, December 2, following an illness of six weeks. ... Mr. Pilcher was on the automatics. He made a great many friends during his years in the shop, all of whom learned with regret of his death."[42] Later in the same issue under the "Timely Ticks: Newsy Notes from the Departments" section George is mentioned again, "George Pilcher will be greatly missed, but not forgotten. He made many friends during his year in the Screw department and was well liked."[43] George was not the only person in the family employed by the Elgin National Watch Factory; fourteen others went on to also work there over the years.[44]

The Annual Pilcher Family Picnic

When George and his family lived on the 600 block of Raymond Street, near the watch factory, he would rent a horse and wagon, so the family could picnic at Camp Commons, now known as Tyler Creek Forest Preserve. This was the beginning of the annual Pilcher Family Picnic tradition, which is held every June. For many years the picnics were held at this same location. In order to reserve the same spot for the picnics the reservations would have to be made on January 2 of that year. A relative, Bob Biesterfeld, knew the Forest Preserve's caretaker, so he was the one who made the reservations for many years. The picnics have grown to be quite large over the years, and in order to best plan and organize the picnics committees directed by a chairman were selected to oversee each picnic. The committee would oversee choosing the picnic date, deciding on a menu, a picnic theme, sending out invitations, picking out games for the children and adults, calculating the picnic expenses, and figuring out how much each family needed to pay to cover costs. After the picnic the committee was in charge of cleaning up. The committee was also in charge of choosing the committee for the next year's picnic. The committee chairman would record everything in a logbook, and these records have been kept since the 1954 picnic. Starting in 1973 picnic, with the 75th anniversary, the number of picnic attendees has been recorded. The picnic location changed after 1978 when the Kane County Forest Preserve directors banned alcohol in the Forest Preserve, with the rule taking effect in 1979. The Pilcher Family Picnic was held at the Randall Oaks Park in West Dundee in 1979. From 1980 to 1983 the picnic was held at the Eagle's Home in Elgin and was moved in 1984 to Ken and Sharon Henryson's home, descendants of Mae Pilcher, George Pilcher's daughter, just west of Elgin. The picnics were held at this location for the next decade. The 1994 Picnic was held at Bill Schmitz, Jr.'s property along the riverfront, in South Elgin. The centennial anniversary Pilcher Picnic and was held at the YWCA Camp Tu-Ende-Wei, which is located on Route 25 south of Elgin. The turnout for this picnic included over 150 relatives. T-shirts were sold and the *Daily Herald*, a local newspaper covered the event.

The themes, food, locations, etc., have changed over time, but the meaning and significance of the picnics, the coming together of generations from across the country to spend time together and share food, stories, love, and laughter, has continued. The connection of family members to one another is important for this intangible heritage. The Pilcher Family Picnics have even been featured in local magazines. On June 25 in 1958, the *Elgin Daily Courier-News* wrote, "The annual picnic of the Pilcher family took place at the Forest Preserve, with 70 in attendance. A ham dinner was served by John Stolt, assisted by Mrs. Darrell Monteith, Walter Stolt and Ray Pilcher. Later, games were played, with races for the children."[45] In acknowledgement of the centennial family picnic, the *Daily Herald* wrote, "in an age where families splinter, and children move thousands of miles away from their parents, the Pilcher clan has found a way to stay close. ...It would be just like any other picnic, with games for the children and beer for the grown-ups, if the Elgin-area family had not been getting together every year since 1897...While the original members of the family have long since died, the tradition is alive and well."[46] The Pilcher Picnic traditions ties our family to George Pilcher, his life in Elgin, and the Elgin National Watch Company, dating to the 1890s.

Factory Life and Departments

Bells woke the watch factory employees at 6:00am in the morning; reminder bells ran at six-thirty, and at seven signaled the starting of the machine engines and the beginning of the workday. Employees received a one-hour lunch break at noon, and then worked until the completion of the workday at five. Until the Panic of 1893 this ten-hour, six-day a week schedule was standard for all employees. Mechanical watches were very complex devices containing hundreds of tiny individual parts, which were powered by the winding of the owner and the energy stored within the mainspring. Elgin streamlined their watch production through the creation of machines that were specific to each component of the watch, which were divided into different departments, also known as "rooms."[47]

The production of a watch movement would begin with the Plate Department, which produced the plates in which all other components would be placed and set in-between. These plates were cut into strips from sheets of brass or nickel, and the strips were then flattered and cut followed by a drilling process that cut threaded holes for the tiny screws, which attached the other components to the plates. The department with the most employees that produced the most diverse components in the greatest volume was the Screw Department, which used an array of machinery for various tasks. This department was responsible for producing not only the tiny screws, but also the winding stems, shafts, cams, and levers used in the watch movements. Rubies, sapphires, and garnets were transformed into extremely tiny donuts, cups and blocks in the Jeweling Department. These jewels were used in the watch movements as bearing surfaces for the moving gears and shafts. The stones were hard, but also allowed for movement that metal on metal wouldn't permit. When a watch was referred to as "fully jeweled" it meant that it had 15 or 17 jewels. These jewels, allowed better movement in the watch gears and aided in the preservation of components allowing the watches to last indefinitely, provided they received maintenance periodically.[48]

Sheets of brass and gold were used to cut the watches gears, called wheels, from the Train Department. The wheels attach to shafts, held in place by the plates. At the shaft's end was where the watches' hands were attached. These connected pieces were referred to as the gear train, hence the department's name. The Escape and Balance Departments created components that controlled the mainsprings, known as the escape and balance wheels.[49] Originally the watch dials were hand-painted by employees in the Dial Room, located in a separate building from the main factory building complete with its own enameling furnaces then later this process was done by machine on polished metal.

Figure 5.1: Employees at work at the Elgin National Watch Company factory in the 1910s. Source: Library of Congress Prints and Photographs Division.

The Elgin National Watch Company offered a variety of dial designs, with more than 142 by 1889 for their many customers to select from.[50] The Engraving Department was responsible for the lettering and numbering of the watch movement plates. All of the components were put together into a finished watch movement in the Assembling and Timing Department, which was responsible for putting together everything except the dial, hands, and balance. This was the responsibility of the Timing Department, where employees known as "finishers" specifically renowned for their skill in watch making did this task.[51]

The mainspring and hairsprings were produced in the Spring Department. New machinery and watch models were created by the Modeling and Design Departments, who worked with engineers. The workbenches and building maintenance were fulfilled by the Carpentry Department. One of the most important departments was the Machine Department responsible for producing, "the dies, gauges, files, bits, polishers, cutting tools, chucks, jogs and hundreds of other devices needed for the highly precision work of the watchmaking."[52] This department created machine part replacements and entire machines, making it extremely vital in the efficiency and success of the watch factory production. This assembly line-like division of labor into specific departments with different jobs allowed for a reduction in training time and an increase in productivity for each department and the whole factory.

The creation of watch movements was extremely complex even with the streamlining of the process through machinery and labor division. A typical watch movement was comprised of over a hundred separate parts, which required almost 4,000 individual steps performed by different employees in different departments in order to reach completion. Watch movement production runs were usually about 1,000 movements in size and could take up to a year to complete an entire order. [53]   Elgin's watch factory was extremely productive through its constant updates, machinery creation, and improvements, allowing the company to reduce expenses, and to employ less skilled workers, who required shorter training periods. While the work was tedious, it was clean and safe, rarely experiencing injuries or accidents.[54]

The Elgin National Watch Company employees were considered to be part of "Father Time's Family," and they were accordingly treated very well, and they were very loyal because of this. Up until 1886, the factory employees were paid once a month, which changed in that year to be three times per month.   The only time the employees received payroll late was after the Great Chicago Fire of 1871, which caused a shortage of currency.[55] The Elgin Watch Company was one of the first to create welfare services sponsored by a private enterprise; which are called fringe benefits today. [56] In 1913, the company introduced a Mortuary Fund, a system similar to life insurance, where an employee before death could select a beneficiary that would receive $500 when the participating employee passed.[57]

The Watch Company's Impact on Elgin, Illinois

The watch factory drew people from far and wide with opportunities and appealing work conditions and benefits, allowing both the town of Elgin and the company itself to expand and prosper. The dramatic rise in population from 5,341 to 17,723 between 1870 and 1890 can be attributed to the major expansion of the watch factory. [58] The Elgin National Watch Company was doing so well in this period that it was accountable for 60 percent of the domestic market for fine-jewel watches in 1891.[59] In response to this successful growth, more people came to Elgin seeking opportunities, and where between 1890 and 1893, the town's population increased to 21,528.[60] Along with the new residents Elgin gained new factories that produced a variety of goods, such as shoes, watchcases, and casket hardware. The Elgin National Watch Company's newest employees constituted totaled more than the summation of all employees for all new watch factories combined, employing over 3,000 individuals.

The population growth caused in increase in demand for housing by employees, resulting in new houses being built all around the watch factory, filling in vacant tracks of land. In addition to the standard employee single-family homes, impressive housing for the Superintendent, the two assistant superintendents, two foremen, and a company cashier were constructed near the factory.[61]

Figure 5.2: The Elgin National Watch Company factory as it appeared during the mid 1910s. Source: Library of Congress Prints and Photographs Division.

Railroad Watches

Due to the increasing number of railroad workers and dramatically faster trains in use across the country, which in everyday use demanded precise adherence to more complicated and rigorous scheduling, railroad watches became a key source of the Elgin Watch Company's prosperity. As the railways advanced in locomotive speed and track network complexity, with an increase in the number of individual trains now running at the same times, both sharing and sometimes even intersecting tracks, the desire to remain on schedule changed from a luxury to an imperative safety concern and highlighted the need for increased protocol and coordination.[62] In addition, radio communication was yet to be developed and the railway employees utilized precision timetables and dramatic hand signaling in order to maintain safe distances between trains, which required the use of precision pocket watches produced by Elgin.[63]

The merit of Elgin watches was found not only in their accuracy and precision, but also in their synchronization as they were placed in the use of thousands of railway workers spanning across the country. In 1868, one of Elgin's most popular advertisements promoted the company's six models of watches for sale with text describing the flagship B. W. Raymond movement as:

> One of our leading Railroad Companies have been so well convinced of the superiority, that they have furnished it to their Engineers, and it is pronounced by them to be the closest running American Railway Watch yet manufactured, and full

equal to some of the finest imported watches as a correct time-keeper.[64]

The ever-increasing market for railroad watches became a key revenue stream for Elgin even in the company's earliest days as they attempted to conquer the market and their competition.[65]

To gain the patronage of the railway companies; however, was no easy feat. The railway companies, in order to protect their assets and adhere to the increasingly more complicated and strict schedules as rail traffic increased, demanded their railway watches to meet rigid performance standards and requirements, which contributed to the popular symbolism of the watch as a beacon of technological advancement and societal progress.[66] The Elgin railroad grade watches were considered not only superior time telling devices but among the finest scientific instruments during the period. This is underscored in the nineteenth century media, with an example being an excerpt from an 1869 edition of *Harper's New Monthly Magazine*, which stated:

The railroad is a great critic. Nowhere else is a watch so severely tested, nowhere else is accuracy so absolutely essential. After a careful trial, solely upon its own merits the Elgin watches have been adopted as the standard upon several of our leading trunk lines. On the Pennsylvania railroad alone, more than a hundred locomotives are run by them, and they are in use among conductors and engineers, upon every railway in the Northwest, and upon the great transcontinental line from Omaha to San Francisco.[67]

The renowned success and publicity brought to the Elgin Watch Company from the railroad cannot be overstated. By conquering this market, the Elgin watch became not only known for its products individual merit, but it also for the standards the pieces individually held, due to their use by the railway enterprises. The precise and affordable timepieces accompanied by the railways' endorsements found subsequently not only fare reception, but also sales in the civilian watch markets, which held less rigorous standards.

The standards for railroad watches increased when in April 1891, two trains collided head-on, in an accident that was the result of a malfunctioning watch. A list of specifications for railroad watches was created by a commission in an effort to prevent a tragedy like the 1891 accident from ever happening again. Railroad employees were required to carry the list of specifications on their person, and any watches that did not meet the specifications were not permitted for use on the railroad. This list was made official, and was used starting in 1893, featuring specifications such as: "the watch had to be open faced, that is, without a covered case; be size 16 or 18; have at least 17 jewels; keep accurate time to within 30 seconds in a 7 day period; be lever set and have the winding stem at the 12 o'clock position; use Arabic numerals instead of Roman numerals; use a plain white dial with black colored hands and numbers; have "heavy" hands that were easy to read under adverse conditions."[68] Once a watch was approved for railroad use it was inspected every fortnight and records of its performance were kept daily.[69]

Figure 5.3: An antique Elgin pocket watch from the early twentieth century, which originally belonged to the editor's great-grandfather. Source: Photograph by Barry L. Stiefel.

The Panic of 1893

Starting in 1892 the United States began to experience an economic decline, which for the Elgin Watch Company ultimately resulted in a significant drop in sales. The company's inventory became uncomfortably stagnant causing the management to come to the decision of closing the factory on Saturdays starting in June 1893. This attempt to mitigate the juncture between manufacturing costs and incoming revenue was simply insufficient. Soon the fact that the Elgin watch simply was not selling in the numbers it once had become all too apparent. As the economy continued to decline, the Watch Company announced on July 26 to its factory employees that beginning August 1, that the work force of the company would be reduced by fifty percent. This blow was gargantuan; the company over the course of a year let nearly 1,400 employees go, which slashed the payroll nearly in half, as the company had employed approximately 2,873 individuals prior to the cuts. The Elgin Watch Company, despite its attempts to reduce payout and preserve a steady level of manufacturing, sales, and revenue, felt the repercussions of their decision in a documented span of dropping production numbers with total time pieces manufactured as low as half those recorded in the previous year, and eventually even a decrease in operating hours to only four work days per week. The situation worsened in September, as factory wages were cut again, ranging from 10 to 30 percent.[70]

In addition to the issues at the factory itself, a new complication began to emerge in the local economy, as the newly unemployed citizenry were no longer allowed to board at the National House.[71] As a result, the City of Elgin found itself reeling after a dramatic decrease in population from what can only be described as a mass exodus, when nearly 1,600 residents left over the course of a year, beginning in 1893.[72]

What was ultimately dubbed the "The Panic of '93" remained a significant issue for the Elgin Watch Company for nearly three years with little sign of recovery until the late spring of 1897. As years passed, the financial setbacks began to fade and in 1899 the Elgin Watch Company's factory employees were allowed to work half Saturdays during the summer and by January 1st, pay returned to its original pre-panic levels with an increase of approximately ten percent along with the elimination of road blocks preventing promotions and raises for certain employees. This upward trend in increasing employee wage and scheduling benefits continued into 1901, when the company established shorter hour workdays without a pay decrease. [73] The company's president, Charles Hulburd, declared, "1901 has been the most successful for the company of any. We have made and sold over 600,000 movements and have on hand at present but a running stock of 10,000".[74] The Elgin National Watch Company was once again the top American watch manufacturer, and its employees were earning wages that were the highest in the company's history.[75]

Factory Expansion

With time and increase in demand it became apparent to management at the Elgin Watch Company that additions to the factory were required. Construction began in 1902 on a western wing for the factory that added an additional 88,000 square feet. Construction of a new front factory building was begun in 1904, and completed within a year, adding 116,000 square feet of factory workspace.[76] The new additions to the factory not only gave the company room to produce more, but it also provided Elgin with a boost in publicity that was described saying,

> The visual impact of the exterior of the building was impressive. The front façade was dominated by a 144-foot clock tower, which was anchored by an archway over the main entry doors leading to the administrative offices. The four-story front wings, with an additional floor on the corner towers, conveyed the massive size of the company it represented. Hundreds of windows, recessed into well-proportioned and detailed bays gave the building an inviting air of light and openness, despite its immense size. The finished brick surface resembled a school or office building more than a factory.[77]

The clock tower of the new addition would come to be a renowned landmark and symbol not only of the Watch Company, but of the City of Elgin as well. The clock tower featured four Seth Thomas clock faces, each with a diameter of 14 feet 6 inches. The clock faces were even visible at night, illuminated by lamps. This clock tower also featured a large two-and-a-half-ton bell.[78] The new working areas were made of narrow, well-lighted, well-ventilated rooms. In addition to the new factory building, the company also had a new powerhouse constructed.[79] A new refrigeration plant took 600 gallons water per hour from the artesian well and cooled it.[80]

The Elgin National Watch Company Observatory

The invention of the quadrant in the eighteenth century allowed the passage of time to be measured by the distance between the sun or a star and the horizon. By 1890, telegraphs and electro-mechanical devices could be used to transmit electrical impulses, which communicated the correct time determined by observatory clocks. The Elgin Watch Factory decided to use this technology to increase its precision in timekeeping by building its own observatory using the stars to determine the correct time for its watches. The company chose a professor from Carleton College, William W. Payne, to select the location for the new observatory as well as decide on the necessary equipment. The location that Payne chose was a knoll located at the corner of Watch and Raymond streets. This site was chosen because the gravel of the knoll absorbed most of the earth's vibrations, allowing for accurate readings in the Observatory building. The company then selected George Hunter as the architect for the construction of the new facility.[81] William Payne was later hired as director of the department in February 1910 when the observatory opened.[82]

The equipment Payne chose were four Riefler clocks, a well-respected German brand, and a 3-inch transit telescope. The celestial observations were used with these clocks to allow for precise time keeping. The time was sent to the main factory through underground cables. The Timing Department received the correct time from the observatory and set the new watch movements by it. The observatory was equipped with meteorological equipment, as it was commonly postulated the weather had the ability to affect the accuracy of the clocks. This building also featured a bedroom, which the astronomer used for naps when he took breaks from his celestial observations.[83]

The Elgin National Watch Company's movements' popularity grew with their star-timed accuracy. The use of the observatory led to the use of one of the slogans for the Elgin National Watch Company, "Timed by the Stars". The construction of and use of the observatory truly set the Elgin Watch Company apart from the country's other companies, as Elgin was the sole enterprise to operate its own observatory and use it to time its movements.[84] From 1910 through 1926, the U.S. Weather Bureau utilized the Watch Factory Observatory's instruments to record temperature and rainfall. The observatory was added to the National Register of Historic Places in 1994, under Criterion A, for its influence in broad American history between 1910 and 1944.[85]

Wristwatches

After 1900, European watch manufacturers began designing and producing watches that were created for wear on the wrist, rather than storage in a pocket. This new type of watch was initially dubbed the bracelet watch and was primarily marketed to women. Despite the growing trend in Europe it was not until 1910 that the Elgin Watch Factory produced a 5/0 movement bracelet watch designed for women. At the same time a pocket watch was designed for men that featured loops on either side to allow after-market straps to be attached and then worn on the wrist. During the outset of this new fashion men were initially unreceptive to the notion of a wristwatch. Elgin, after a markedly unsuccessful push, then began an advertising campaign associating the design with masculine themes. The watches remained unpopular in the United States until World War I when the United States' Military ordered wristwatches for troops due to the tactical advantage of the watches accessibility during combat.[86] After the war, Elgin took advantage of the military's promotion of the wristwatch through a continued advertising push associating the design with masculine themes and patriotism, gradually winning over fickle public perception of the device.

The rise in popularity of wristwatches in the 1910s and 1920s reflected the national trend towards a preference of smaller watches. Wristwatches were more visible than pocket watches; therefor, their design was meant to draw attention and this style-appeal increased popularity. The Waltham Watch company chose to focus on mechanical fuses during this period, rather than wristwatches, which Elgin also took advantage of. Despite the Elgin Watch Company's active orders for, "aviation clocks and watches, stopwatches, navigation compasses, barograph clocks, and the development of a chronometric tachometer" placed by the Army Air Corps, they continued to push the wristwatch through aggressive production and advertising campaigns, which in the end paid off.[87]

The Elgin Watchmakers College

The Elgin Watch Company's president, Hulburd, understood the need for skilled watch repairmen who could both repair and maintain the watches the company produced, inspiring him to establish a horological school. The Elgin Watchmakers College was founded in 1920 with the construction of a three-story brick building located near the factory. At first, the first floor was occupied by the Elgin National Watch Company, the second floor was used by the Watchmakers College for instruction, and the third floor was used as a dormitory for the students.[88] The college taught students for 11 months of the year, with weeks comprised of 35.5 hours of bench work, four hours of lecture, and four and half hours of technical drawing. The college provided each student with three years of education, the first year ended with a Horological Institute of America examination that if passed certified the student as a junior watchmaker, the second year resulted in the student becoming a certified watchmaker, and the third year led to students being certified horologists. In the first year, students learned how to repair American watches and make alterations. In the second year, students learned how to adjust the more complicated Swiss watches and American railroad watches. In the third year, students were taught to design watches and chronometers on their own.[89]

Aircraft Instruments

As demand for Elgin watches continued to grow, the company was required to produce 4,000 movements in a day, rendering the current factory space inadequate. Additions were promptly undertaken as, "a new wing directly in the rear of and parallel to the front building was completed in 1923. Five stories in height, 365 feet long by 32 feet wide. The office and stairway potion was six stories in height and 88 feet in depth."[90] This addition proved to not add enough square footage to the work area, and in 1927 the final additions of two mirrored wings were constructed, completing the ever-expanding main factory to a total area of twenty-one acres.[91] At the same time the company was working on expanding the factory in 1923 it created a tachometer, "an instrument that measures the revolutions per minute of a revolving shaft under different conditions".[92] The U.S. Navy and the U.S. Army began using the Elgin tachometers in their aircrafts. The plane that Charles A. Lindbergh used in his nonstop flight from New York to Paris in 1927, the *Spirit of St. Louis* was even equipped with an Elgin tachometer.

The success of the tachometer led to the company designating an entire Aircraft Instrument Division in 1928. This division even had its own trademark, *Avigo*, complete with an official associated winged symbol. This division utilized the entirety of the factory's second floor of the east wing. Mechanisms produced by this division included a barometric-type altimeter, a speed indicator, magnetic compass, oil and pressure gauges, aircraft clocks, and ball bank indicators. Glow in the dark dials and watch hands were also painted with radium.[93]

Decline in the 1920s and the Great Depression

The extremely successful years the Elgin National Watch Company experienced were followed by a decline, as the American watch industry began to struggle during the late 1920s. As times worsened in the country economically, the employees of the watch factory suffered as they were dismissed, from 4,379 in 1927 to 3,400 in December 1929.[94] When the stock market crashed, the market for watches in the United States was so small that the factory dismissed another 1,100 employees in 1930, and by the end of that year all departments were only working three days a week. In 1931, times were so bad that factory completely shut down production from May 27 until July 6.[95] The company was forced to make changes in 1932 in an effort to cut costs including reducing wages and paydays within a month, ending the production of numerous watch styles, and even discontinuing the beloved publication of *Watch Word*.[96] During this period the residency at the National house reached historic lows forcing the company to demolish the structure due to an inability to keep up with maintenance costs. The attached National Gymnasium was also demolished in 1937, in an additional effort to reduce expenses.[97] The land that once housed he employees of the watch company during its peak now only housed automobiles, as it was converted into a parking lot during the company's decline. [98] Workers continued to be dismissed reducing the number of employees on payroll to a record low of 480 in 1933. These dwindling numbers represented less than fifteen percent of workers employed by the watch factory only four years earlier in 1929.[99] In 1934, the company began to recover hiring additional employees, raising the number of workers to over 1900. Not until 1936 were employee wages again reestablished at the amount before 1929. During this period the Elgin Watch National Company was the highest paying watch company in America.[100]

Innovations and Changes in the 1930s

Despite the hardships presented by the Great Depression, the Elgin Watch National Company survived the low points in its history through a focus not only on production but also on innovations. In the midst of the turmoil, the company was able to produce in 1932 the smallest American made watch movement. The company created new equipment, the binocular microscope and contour projector during this period as well.[101] In working with the Western Electric Company, the Elgin Watch Company also created a timing machine, which benefited the watchmaking process by reducing the observation time required.[102]

Changes were made within the company in the 1930s. Father Time, who had represented the Company for decades, was replaced in 1935 by a heraldic crest that resembled a Scottish coast of arms. In 1937, the company introduced new wristwatches to the market, named The Lord Elgin and Lady Elgin series.[103] The former was an 8/0 size, 21 jewel movement complete with a filled or solid gold case; this watch cost between $50 and $125. The Lady Elgin movement was a 19-jewel movement, featuring a gold case, with the cost beginning at $47.50.[104]

In response to that a majority of watch repairs were due to defective mainsprings, the Elgin Watch Company enlisted the Battelle Memorial Institute of Columbus, Ohio in 1935, to create a new material for manufacturing more durable mainsprings. [105] One of the Institute's research metallurgists, Oscar E. Harder, assigned to develop the new material, which the company named Elgiloy. This alloy was made of eight elements, was rustproof, non-magnetic, and almost unbreakable. It was exactly what the Elgin Watch Company had been hoping for. The new mainspring made from Elgiloy was named the DuraPower mainspring.[106]

World War II Efforts
The Elgin National Watch Company employed 3,400 workers by the end of 1937. The recession of 1938-39 caused this level to drop down to 2,250. The beginning of World War II resulted in the watch factory employment rising to 4,000 as the company worked to fill military orders. At the time of the Pearl Harbor attack, 20 percent of production by the Elgin National Watch Company was devoted to military orders. The company produced civilian watches through June 1942, when it shifted its production to solely focus on military orders. During this period the watch factory employees were photographed and fingerprinted for security reasons. The War Department contracted with the Elgin National Watch Company in April 1940 to develop equipment and a production plan for the creation of mechanical time fuses to be used in war efforts. To fulfill this obligation another

building was constructed, which was named Plant No. 2, making the main factory Plant No. 1. The factory employees worked tirelessly to fill the $6,029,188 order for fuses that the War Department issued in January 1941.

As new machinery was necessary for production of fuses, beginning production was no easy feat. Despite the difficulty in startup, experts at the Elgin Watch Factory had production well under way before the United States entered World War II. [107] The watch company excelled at the production of these fuses and three of the company's scientists, Dr. Carl N. Challacombe, Walter Kohlhagen, and George G. Ensign, received a War Production Board citation for their success. The company's Plant No. 2 received the prestigious Army-Navy 'E' Award for Excellence for high production achievement in 1942. In addition, Plant No. 1 also received the award in 1944, for its production of "times, chronomantic tachometers, aircraft compasses, navigation watches, special clocks and watches, ground speed indicators, and torque control mechanisms."[108]

The military then requested watches, which the troops could read in the dark; however, the device could not reveal their location to enemies. Elgin responded with the production of watches featuring dials with glowing figures and hands painted with radium. Precautions were taken by the watch company to protect the health of the employees by employing extra ventilation in the workspaces and health examinations with argon lamps to check for radium on the skin.[109] During World War II the government assigned soldiers to learn how to repair watches at the Elgin Watchmakers College between April 1943 and July 1944, who received this education in an express eight-week course.[110]

Recovering from World War II

After World War II the government cancelled all its production contracts, causing the Elgin National Watch Company to reorganize itself for a primary civilian consumer base. [111] The company did not fully recover until 1948 when production of civilian watch movements finally reached their pre-war levels. Elgin was able to recover from the war with greater success than any other American watch company due to its "impressive lead in consumer preference". [112] During World War II as it was exclusively producing for the war efforts, the Elgin Watch Company continued to market its watches to the general public on both the radio and print media. The advertisements featured the various products the company created for the military advocating readers to "Hold fast to your desire… there will be more Elgins." [113] After the war, the company advertised with even greater intensity; the Elgin Watch Company spent more than all other American watch companies combined on their marketing campaign during World War II.

The company made the decision in November 1945 to purchase a 218,000 square foot factory building in 900 North 16th Street in Lincoln, Nebraska. The building belonged to the Elastic Stop Nut Corporation, from which Elgin was able to purchase the property for $290,000 and the equipment inside useable for watch production for $60,000.[114] This purchase was made because it had lost a fourth of its male employees to the war and veterans were leaving for education or other job opportunities. The company saw the Lincoln Plant as a resource of extra production area, in a town of new skilled labor. This decision and purchase marked the first time that Elgin Watches would be produced outside of Elgin, Illinois.[115]

Elgin supplied the Lincoln plant with machines, tools, and designs and by spring of 1949, where the plant soon produced its millionth Elgin watch movement. The Lincoln plant was expanded in 1952, with the addition of two entire floors of workspace, bringing the building to a total of 312,000 feet of workspace. Back in Elgin, plants No. 1 and No. 2 had a combined square footage of 519,700. Eventually, the Lincoln plant was producing 80 percent of the watch movements and casing them at the Elgin locations.[116]

Expansion and Diversification of the Watch Company and the Korean War

In 1950 the Elgin National Watch Company decided to diversify into other industries in order to, "ensure a steady supply of materials and allow long term stability."[117] By borrowing $10 million, the Elgin National Watch Company purchased the Wadsworth Watch Case Company, of Dayton, Kentucky as its first effort of expansion and diversification.[118] Next, in 1951, the Elgin Watch Company purchased the Hadley Company, Inc. of Providence, Rhode Island, which produced watchbands and jewelry accessories. After the acquisition of these two companies the Elgin Watch Company employed 6,715 people.[119]

During this period the company began producing and selling an abrasive, called "Dymo", which was made of diamond dust and improved oils. The company also began producing rotary cutting and grinding tools to go along with its new abrasive in 1954. A move in the same year that was outside of watch production was the acquisition of Neomatic, Inc., of Los Angeles, a company that developed small electronic components and sub-miniature relays, which are powered switches used in electronics. The Elgin Watch Company continued with this trend by acquiring both the American Microphone Company of Pasadena and the Advanced Electric and Relay Co. of Burbank in 1955. The purchase of the array of companies resulted in doubled sales volume, but unfortunately only $2 million in profit, which was low compared to the pre-diversification profits of $1.6 millions.[120] The Elgin National Watch Company began once again producing devices for the military during the Korean War, when the Defense Department issued a $60 million contract for the production of "precision ammunition components and other military equipment".[121] Plant. No. 2 in Elgin had not been in use since 1949 but was reopened to fill these orders in 1951. The Lincoln factory also worked to fulfill the military request by making proximity fuses to be used by the armed forces. In 1953, 20 percent of the production at the Lincoln factory was for military orders.[122]

Decline of the Elgin Watch Company

The great decline of the Elgin National Watch Company began after the Korean War, "consumers lost interest in expensive watches as status symbols." [123] By 1955, the company had dramatically dropped in rank to 428th out of the United States' largest 500 industrial companies, based on sales. The company's efforts to enter the electronics market were unsuccessful, the military contracts were declining, and the competition of Swiss and Timex watches continued to mount. [124] All of these factors led the company to reduce expenses, by way of reducing the quality of their products. [125] Between 1956 and 1968 costs continued to be cut every year, and the Wadsworth and Lincoln plants were dissolved when the company could no longer afford to operate multiple facilities at the same time as the demand for watches continued to decline. Despite these setbacks the company continued in its attempts to stay competitive. In 1957, it unveiled two new lines of watches, the Starlite line for women, and the Sportsman for men. These watches were actually Swiss movements that Elgin was importing.

In 1960, the company was forced to close down the Elgin Watchmakers College, which at the time was only educating a mere 44 students. People were repairing their watches less frequently, and the individual fee of $48 per month was no longer sufficient with so few students. The observatory had not been utilized to time the watches for years, and so the company chose to deed it to the local public school district in 1960.[126] The company suffered greatly in 1958, with a net loss of $2.4 million, the largest to date in the company's history.[127] The desperate diversification efforts continued, and the company acquired the Welby Corporation of Chicago and the Bradley Time Corporation of New York, which were both clock producers. The Elgin Watch Company also purchased Lohengrin Diamond Ring Company and the Syndicate Diamonds, Inc., both ring manufacturers in the same year. The Helbros Watch Company and the Columbia Diamond Ring Company of Axtel Brothers, Inc., of New York were also acquired.[128]

Another expansion effort was made in 1962 when the company began construction of a new factory in Blaney, South Carolina, a town that was so grateful to be the location of new enterprise that it changed its official name to Elgin. This new factory was 73,000 square feet when completed in 1963. Rather than only hiring employees from the local town, this plant had 600 employees from the Elgin factory transferred to it. By 1964, only 900 employees remained working at the factory in Elgin, Illinois. As operations at the new site came underway, the original Elgin Factory was eventually abandoned. In 1965, just a year after the company's centennial, the original main factory complex was put up for sale. The company's net loss in 1965 was $6.8 million. The operations at the factory in South Carolina only lasted a few years, where it produced the very last domestically made Elgin watch in January 1968.[129] In the same year, The Elgin National Watch Company merged with Thompson-Starrett, Inc., a company that produced construction equipment and scientific instruments. This new firm was named Elgin National Industries.[130]

Demolition and Preservation Issues

The Elgin National Watch Company's main manufacturing complex began demolition in 1965, the same year it was sold. This landmark of not only the company, but also the City of Elgin was torn down in sections by wrecking ball, until only the iconic clock tower remained as a testament to the innovation and success of what was once the world's leading manufacturer of watches.[131] The destruction of the site was devastating to the identity of the surround area as "few things in the City of Elgin were better known of and have been seen more often than the big clock in the tower of the Elgin National Watch Company."[132] The only remaining part of this huge complex is the main entrance posts, which now serve as the entrance to a shopping strip mall. The decline of the Elgin National Watch Company was a gradual one over many years, which allowed the City of Elgin's economy to survive when the company was officially dissolved. Other industries came to Elgin, and workers found new jobs with these companies.[133] The only significant structure directly associated with the company is the observatory, which is still utilized by the school district as a planetarium. The legacy of the company is still evident in this city; Elgin watches and tools are displayed at the Elgin Area Historical Museum, the first watch produced by the company, the B. W. Raymond serial number 101, is enshrined and on display at the Hemmens Cultural Center in Elgin.

The City of Elgin has made many efforts towards preserving its rich history, especially as the consequences of the demolition of the watch factory became understood in retrospect. The city created the Elgin National Watch Historic District that encompasses the residences associated with the factory workers, representing the growth of the community as a direct cause of the growth of the watch factory. Notable structures identified within this district are the Watch Company Observatory and the Fire Barn No. 5.[134] In 1984, the city created the Elgin Heritage Commission, who is responsible for all preservation efforts in the city.[135]

The Elgin's city government decided to review its Historic Preservation Ordinance in 1988, and it ended up rewriting the entire ordinance, introducing a design review process overseen in partnership with Elgin Heritage Commission. This process guarantees that all building permits within the historic district are reviewed by the aforementioned organizations, and that the Secretary of the Interior's' Standards for Rehabilitation are followed.[136] The City of Elgin again made progress in its preservation efforts when it introduced its Historic Architectural Rehabilitation Grant Program in 1995, which financially helps owners in rehabbing their property.

Within the Elgin National Watch Historic District is the Elgin National Company Neighborhood, which is important for its vernacular buildings constructed between 1880 and 1925, coinciding with the growth of the watch factory complex. A Historic Buildings Plaque is managed by the City of Elgin as well.[137] A Survey of the

Elgin National Watch Historic District neighborhoods which involved evaluating all the properties in the neighborhood and creating a database which includes photographs of the properties as well as information on "use, condition, integrity, architectural style, construction date, architect or builder when known, architectural features, alterations, and a significance rating" on each structure.[138] This database is archived by the Department of Code Administration and Neighborhood Affairs in the City of Elgin.

The Elgin National Watch Company no longer exists, and its manufacturing complex is long gone, however, through the vernacular homes of the workers in the surrounding area, the company, its workers, and their influence can be appreciated, understood, and preserved. [139] How could this monument to American industry and watch manufacturing be demolished? E.C. Alft explains that "preservation was not feasible for a number of reasons. Since the heating plant had been torn down, it would have been a deteriorating shell. The clock works had been sold and shipped out of state. The tower's size would have interfered with use of the property for other purposes. Community resentment of the 'take over' by outsiders would not have favored purchase of the land by the city, even if funds had been available."[140]

Architecture Associated with the Factory

The National Watch Factory neighborhood's architecture was developed in phases, mirroring the progression and expansion of the factory in times of prosperity. The first period of real residential development associated with the factory works was between 1873 and 1880, and this period produced simple vernacular house types that were typical of the period.[141] In the 1880s, many residences were constructed in the neighborhoods, mainly of the same vernacular style of the previous era of development, but in this period the high-style structures were primarily Queen Anne.[142] Through the 1890s, development continued, but at a lesser level, and this period introduced the Colonial Revival and Dutch Colonial Revival styles to the area.[143] In the 1910s, the American Foursquare style residence was constructed and introduced, and this style was the main one of the time.[144]

The 1920s reflected the last period of growth of the factory and therefor was the last period of considerable development of residences in the neighborhood. These homes were mainly American Foursquare, but Craftsmen Bungalows and Tudor Revivals were also constructed.[145] This progression of vernacular architecture in the neighborhood mirrors the influence of the watch factory and the workers who resided in the area. This use of architecture styles is not only important in respect to the watch factory and the City of Elgin, but also in the scope of American architectural history as the main styles of each decade are represented through the development spurred by the success of the factory over such a long period.

Not located in the Elgin National Watch Factory Neighborhood, the First Universalist Church, is still a significant structure associated with this history. The church was designed by George Hunter, the same architect who worked on the first sections of the main factory and was completed in 1892. This Richardsonian Romanesque church was designed to resemble a pocket watch from above and was listed on the National Register of Historic Places in 1980.[146]

Conclusion

Whenever my family drove through Elgin, my grandfather would express how awesome he thought it was that his great-grandfather had come to this country specifically to work for the Elgin National Watch Company. I grew up understanding the importance of this past to my family, but now after researching the company and its influence I realize how significant this watch company was at a national level. This research and understanding have made me feel closer to an ancestor I have never known, but whom I deeply respect and admire. I also feel closer to my grandfather who helped me choose the topic of this paper, and who passed away several weeks into the semester. I am grateful for the long talks we had discussing ancestry, Elgin, and the watch factory. I appreciate all the tours and stories he gave me of Elgin, a town he grew up in and loved, and a town whose watch factory is the entire reason my family exists in the United States. The significance of this factory and the historic built environment of Elgin is not solely important to my family; but also, for thousands of the other workers and their descendants.

After my dad passed away earlier this year, as I was beginning my research for this project, I traveled home to northern Illinois to organize and clean out his house, which led me to the discovery of hundreds of family pictures. Pictures that stood out to me were of my mom and I at the Centennial Annual Pilcher Family Picnic. I recalled going to the Pilcher picnics, but until the discovery of these pictures I did not know I was able to attend such a monumental year in the history of this family tradition, with my mom when I was two years old. I also found pictures of my mom, dad, and I attending the 103rd Pilcher family picnic in 2000 when I was five years old. These pictures of me with my parents, grandparents, and great-grandma, whom are all since deceased, are important to me as reminders of being together. The connection of the family tradition of the picnics, which ties me to generations of past relatives all the way back to 1897 is amazing, and I am grateful to have such a wonderful family tradition that has endured. Not until this project did I realize how remarkable this annual picnic event is. My family may not boast anyone famous, but the people, their lives, their impacts, their connections are all worthy of remembering, understanding, and preserving. Through my research I found what may be considered the little things and facts to be the most interesting and important to me. Learning the history of Elgin, Illinois, and its development, understanding my ancestor's place in all of it, and the thought of them enjoying a horse and carriage ride on their way to picnic in the warm sun, in a growing small town in the middle of rural Illinois, at the end of the nineteenth century, is what I loved to reflect about most on this past.

A watch represents more than just the current time. The Elgin Watch represents the past century-long history of struggles and successes for a company that was once the biggest manufacturer of watches. As this company and city's histories are examined the future most be considered. Aside from the observatory, the Elgin Watch Factory complex has all been demolished. The influence from this once great company is still evident in the neighborhood and its progression of architecture through the various vernacular styles. The company and its history remain important not only in the broad scope of American industrial history, but in a much smaller, more personal sense to all those who are descended from those who worked at this factory and lived and helped create this past. The factory George worked at and its company are gone, but the tradition he created is still strong in our family today. It is my hope that I can do what I can to help preserve this incredible tradition that links me and my descendants to our predecessors.

Chapter 6: The Trinkets We Carry

By Alec Meier

Foreword
Careful where I place my feet. Boots with heavy soles have little control and one misstep is a violation of the silence that has been protected by the lonely thicket. Life felt still and sharp in this place: like even breathing was disturbing the trees as the cold air pierced my lungs to be exhaled as smoke rising to the lowliest branches before disappearing. I continued with my calculated steps drawn further in, though the briars and brambles tore at my skin and clothes. Forward the trees whispered as the wind shook their needles into my hair and onto my shoulders. Forward said the soft crunch that were dried leaves below my boots: and forward is where I went.

The incline was steep, and the aches build as the forest thickens and the way seems less clear. Yet the higher I climb the more I can smell the air at the top, clean air blowing from the south: where the heavy smell of manure and peat bogs travels with the wind and reminds me that this mountain protects the south. It is rugged because it saves the gentle lands and rolling hills from the life of heaths. Strong winds and heavy rains are the life of the moor land but not home. Home is safe and green because this forest and mountain stand. It is a sacred place. The crunch of leaves begins to turn to the beating of stone. The loose stones catch my feet and roll my joints: a final test, but through the mist the purpose of this endeavor can be seen.

Figure 6.1: Stone carving near Carrigeenshinnagh: a short distance from my great-grandmother, Lile Pascal Kavenagh's childhood home. Source: From the personal collection of the author.

I approach and feel the rough stone with my padded hands. Its worn but grabs at the skin calling me in. I crawl onto it and head for the apex. The uneven peaks and troughs of the stone bruise my knees and leave indentations into my skin. It wants to mark me as its own. I have left with a part of me changed by it. I hear the falling of dust below me the higher I climb, hands and knees, until the summit is before me. I reach out my hand, cracking my knuckles in the cold; I feel the curves made long before me. How they flow together in a dance of water and life; memorialized in stone to never be lost. I stare at the markings, the same markings which cover the tile of my family's home. The same markings engraved onto people suggesting the old ways do not die but change. I feel these carvings and realize: this is family, and this is home.

Introduction

The question "What is your heritage and the state of its preservation?" was a topic which roused many philosophies of how to address my family's history. My patrilineage is a well-documented and extensive list of names and artistic renderings of the grandfathers and grandmothers whom have lived in the last millennium. Thus, in my research to understand my Irish ancestry, which I most strongly relate, it became apparent that the abundance of information on the subject could threaten this exploration of understanding by becoming a timeline with no greater depth. Rather than telling the story of a singular person or specific time I could explore how, through all of these generations before my father and I, heritage both tangible and intangible have been passed down to the modern day by the total effort of all of these people. Not least of all the people who have no names, who's work, and life continue to change the present and strike into our memory unforgettable recollections.

The significance behind this process is one which attempts to aid in allowing future generations to appreciate not only objects from the past, or my past, but attach to them the meaning in which they were first acquired or used. The tangible heritage discussed further are objects, that while they hold little monetary value and similar examples from the same time periods can be found with relative ease, are important because of the specific people who used them. They relate to myself and my family regardless of economic value, but rather a sentimentality that makes these objects important to the progression of previous generations, leading into our modern times. The past echoes throughout our lives and within my own experience through these heirlooms, even though I presently reside in South Carolina, far away from Ireland.

Geography of the Past

Much of my heritage relies on the geography of the land that nurtured my ancestors and shaped who they were. Leinster Province has always been the stomping ground of my father's family. With Carlow and Wicklow being dearest to my sentimentalities. Carlow is southwest of Wicklow and remains an agricultural region due to its nutrient rich soil and rivers fed by the nearby mountain runoff. In the northeast Wicklow remains a testament to the last ice age which shaped the mountains, moors, heaths, and rugged terrain which has always protected the gentler southern landscape of Carlow. It is these mountains that have been used to deflect the blows of foreign armies and later hide refugees from unfair punishment. Wicklow is the protector of Carlow.

Though the fathers of my father have lived in Carlow for much longer than many care to remember, or admit, my family's heritage has been made flowery or more diverse by many of the wives having been from other counties or even abroad: as often the village and all the people who lived there were closely related. Thus, many times significant others were looked for away from home in the more modern era. Wicklow and Dublin have without a doubt been the closest ties to areas outside of Carlow; but there was an incident with a Turkish woman that still is both a mystery and staple of family jokes. Thus, to understand my Irish heritage a fair bit of traveling was required. This makes the geography of the past far more interesting as these seemingly distant places were interlaced with history and heritage which can only be appreciated with the culture passed from parent to child. For the most part however, this history is centered in the small villages in the eastern border of Carlow, the land of my forbearers.

The Way Ahead

For the entirety of my life, family and heritage has been a concept well-rehearsed and understood as a history but not attached to the present. When I was a lad of nine I could recite my grandfather's going back four hundred years, repeating their names to the delight of my grandfather and great uncles. Yet the names meant nothing to me. I had known that each had done something worthy of remembrance, but I never met them nor did I particularly care. This black-and-white explanation of family history lead to boredom, thus losing my interest. However, when I was a teenager I began noticing little objects around my parents' home, which without explanation had always been there for as long as my memory served. This was the turning point for how I viewed my heritage. It was not a simple list of names but a cultural patrimony that was always in my periphery waiting to be noticed.

The short creative memoir that is used as a forward to this paper is my summarization of how I feel about the culture my family, passed down to me through the efforts of previous generations. The story of my hike in the Wicklow mountains most closely relates to my great grandmother's tiles, yet even in the stories about my grandfather, as well as the descriptions of the few other objects left to me by my family: relationships between the feelings of that hike and the feelings of my heritage will have similarities; and can be related to that memoir. Thus, when I describe my heritage it is several small things that have links to specific people in my family's past but also it is broader in the sense that the ideas that have stayed with me were instilled by ancestors' past. Rather, this will not be about my grandmother or grandfather, but about a family whom used all their resources to keep their traditions and beliefs alive. To explain my heritage in a method that is meaningful there will be a series of shorter stories from my family's or my own past, and how my life experiences were deeply affected by my ancestor's actions.

The purpose of this endeavor is not to learn everything I can learn about a few people, but about a family whom created me and nurtured my passion for all things old. Through stories and memories, as well as tangible cultural objects I hope to comprehend the magnitude of my family's effect on me. This is, in a manner of speaking, a story about heritage identity making. I will approach intangible and tangible aspects of my heritage in a method that brings more knowledge and ensure their future. All of these stories have a similar theme, and they seek to further the idea of pride in Irish heritage.

As a side note I must mention that for the past several centuries my family has been, as they say, very "green." My ancestors fit within the context of Southern Catholic Republicans as they have been described by historians throughout the centuries. In these attempts to understand whom they were, as well as myself more thoroughly, often political strife and conflict is involved. Irish history is known for its dark and often violent nature, yet these are issues that have influenced my heritage. With that said I do not wish to make these conflicts the center of attention, and as such will be noted and used to forward the stories of my ancestors rather than my ancestors being used to forward the stories of these conflicts. In the most respectful way I do not want my heritage to incite anger or negative feelings about any historical or modern parties who may have been involved. Thus, we must view history with a humbleness and insight into our ancestor's lives to allow an understanding of why they made the choices that they did.

Lile's Tiles

As a child I remember being told by my mother about the tiles in our house. How my great-grandmother Lilly bought them in the younger years of the last century: and now they adorn the kitchen, bathroom, and various other places in my parents' home. It is for the most part white tiles that predate my great grandmother but set in place between every few planer tiles there are dark green ones with hand-formed motifs. These motifs swirl in various directions with their peaks and troughs lining up to create beautiful spirals, which are nearly symmetrical throughout the design. I used to gaze at these tiles and wonder, "who came up with these shapes and swirls?" Where did this artist retrieve this idea?

The ancient peoples who lived in southeastern Ireland were pivotal to the material culture passed down within my family. While their names are forgotten, and little is known of their society, or their daily lives, they formed a culture that shaped the country for the entirety of its existence. In this way, not to mention the biological relationship between modern people and those early Gaels, they have become heritage or rather "family" to every person with Irish blood in their veins. Those gentle carvings with their watery designs carved into un-forgetting and unforgiving stone have shaped people with pride for their Irish heritage unto the present. Examples can often be seen tattooed onto people, and imprinted upon objects sold at tourist destinations, or passed down as heirlooms through families.

Figure 6.2: Lile's tile as they stand in my parents' kitchen in Carlow. Note the similarities of the tile pattern with the stone carving shown in Figure 6.1. Source: Photograph by the author.

Stone carving started before the advent of Christianity with these early Gaelic peoples finding large boulders or stones to carve and continued up into the fourteenth century.[1] Many of the original carvings were pagan in nature as they depicted gods and goddesses: as well as fairies and monsters. Their hypothesized purpose was to please the gods; allowing the carver's people to benefit from that appeasement.[2] Often, simple symbols are used to depict those deities and other times swirls and waves are used as a background to the more humanistic motifs. These carvings and evidence of Gaelic life can be seen easily when in the country as they left them to stand, and in some way keep watch of their descendants.

To understand the affect that these carving have had and why they are so awe-inspiring to modern people a brief synopsis of the process is needed. The stones with petroglyphs often weighed over several metric tons.[3] The Gaels would use very rudimentary tools, often carving stone with stone, and later used iron.[4] How they were able to make such intricate designs with such primitive technology is astounding in the same way as any ancient monument or megalith. The petroglyphs attract the eye and grab the attention. Never to wholly gone because of this incredible and nearly vernacularized medium. Relating to my traceable family however, many of these stone carvings can be found in Leinster province with a large proportion being in the Wicklow Mountains, scattered through both wild landscapes and close to homesteads and village centers. These carvings remained a part of our lives for millennia, shaping our perception of who we are.

My great-grandmother was born Lile Pascal Kavenagh in 1896. She was one of six children in her family to grow up in the small mountain town of Carrigeenshinnagh in County Wicklow.[5] She lived in a cottage which has since been torn down but was likely only two rooms during her childhood there: living a humble life as the daughter of a peat moss harvester. Her daughter, Mary Lou (my grandmother), told me in an interview about her younger years that Lile would often walk with her father down from their cottage to the village: and be mesmerized by the goods being brought from

Dublin. [6] My grandmother described her as, "a woman whom loved beauty." It's a picturesque thought to imagine Lile going to the village to admire the clothing, furniture, and foods, among an assortment of things. From a young age she loved style and fashion, and this is exhibited within the house's furnishings.

However, she did grow up in a village set in a rugged landscape where her front yard had heaths and moors, mountains and thickets, peaks and troughs; and as such lived a life with less technological advancement as well as a need to interact with the land to be sustainable. This rugged landscape of her home required people to use the land to live most comfortably: having to often walk everywhere because the trails were too rough or small for horses, thus exploration of the local area was commonplace. She probably hiked very often with her father and siblings, as my grandmother claims, meaning she had stumbled upon the several carved stones in her local vicinity. The stone motifs that surrounded her home would be a part of her for the entirety of her life.

When Lile eventually moved to Dublin, she met her husband working for the same lawyers' office. [7] She was nineteen when they married and soon after moved to her husband's family home. [8] Having been in Dublin just before and during the Easter Uprising, and coming from a southern Catholic family, there were feelings of nationalism sweeping the island. During this period there was heightened tension between various groups in Ireland as well as between Ireland and Great Britain. [9] These tensions fueled the need for a

237

distinctly "Irish" identity separate from everyone else, known as the Celtic Revival. Revivalists sought to bring art, literature, poetry, and culture back from the abyss to justify Irish nationalism: thus, goods were made with motifs which related to Stone and Bronze Age art of Ireland.[10]

It was during these years that Lile began to collect furniture and decorative objects for her future home. Several pieces of furniture which were fashionable at the time she had shipped from Dublin to Carlow, her husband's native county, as well as she began collecting distinctly Celtic Revival goods. At one point in the early years of her marriage, circa 1915, Lile purchased several crates of tiles for the house she now lived in, away from Dublin or Carrigeenshinnagh. [11] These tiles though, brought Celtic Revivalism to the small village and on them were likened designs to stone carvings found in County Wicklow. She had seen the carved stones in her mountainous home and brought them with her to her husband's home in the rolling hills of Carlow.

The designs she seemed to favor, as evidence of leftover tiles that she did not have installed, prove that she was picking the forms from the local vicinity. What I find truly interesting about her preferences was firstly she was using material culture to tell the story of her own life. I realized this after pondering the tiles in the early morning before I went hiking in the Wicklow Mountains. Very near her childhood home, perhaps a kilometer away, there are ancient carved standing stones in several directions. Some are large and simple, and others small and ornate, but the carvings are prevalent on all of them. When I chose to hike through the wilderness around Lile's childhood home I expected to see beautiful scenery and the foundations of a life that has been all but forgotten. This was the case, yet it went deeper. When a passing motorist told me that the roads are often so small you have no choice but to finagle and decide how to best pass each other, that the state had fenced off a section of land, which surrounded a large megalith due to vandalism, my interest was piqued. I began the short hike from the old road that was at one point a passage of great importance but now was no more than a sheep trail flanked by crumbling stonewalls. While the bramble and briars clung to my clothes, the pine trees began to close in about me shaking needles onto my head and shoulders. The higher I went the vegetation turned into a rocky and moss filled mountaintop with little but sky ahead. I reached the chain link fence that was untethered at the bottom, allowing for a single person to crawl under at a time. While I do not condone trespassing, a chance to see a megalith so close to my family's home was worth the risk of embarrassment of being caught inside the fence.

I approached the stone and felt the face; it had texture so planned that it could never be mistaken as a natural boulder. That's when from the edge of the stone very close to the top, I noticed the shape. Lying in the top right of this megalith was a swirl of water. Rather it was interlaced curls with a triangular end, where they met near a cup or trough in the center. Memories of everyday activities were instantly released, as this was the design of several tiles throughout my home. In the bathroom and kitchen this shape pervaded my life there. I saw this and thought of the tile. I sat on a nearby earthen mound and realized my great-grandmother would have come here. She likely stood exactly where I was, in awe of the incredible carvings she saw before her. A little girl who would expand the family and be a pivotal part of my heritage would be here in her everyday life. I never met my great-grandmother Lile, but my father remembered her and spoke of her. My grandmother would claim her to be the most caring and beautiful woman to walk the country though my relation to her was never more than a name on a list.[12] Yet now I can relate to her in a way that is almost like saying hello for the first time, nervous and excited. I sat and remembered all of the memories from the house that had tiles, which were exactly the same as this carving. When my grandmother purchased these green tiles with Celtic designs she too had seen the petroglyphs and experienced these same feelings. I see the carvings and think of tiles; she saw the tiles and thought of carvings. She chose to bring her heritage with her into the present and future. The people who carved the stone at the apex of a mountain left designs into the standing stone, which reverberated through the generations, eventually affecting my great-grandmother and (later) me. A family history in which the first early stone carvers will remain nameless but goes back through this tile. The history of modern Ireland is spoken through it, as these designs have been a part of my family's culture long before St. Patrick.

My great-grandmother's tiles struck me as an important part of my heritage simply because they are an allusion to my grandmother's beliefs, as well as to a culturally important past that reminds people of the history of ourselves. She brought her personal memory from her youth with her into the new places she lived. This love of memory was passed down, as can be seen in the remarkable state of preservation of the tiles. Those tiles, which are installed throughout my parents' home, have withstood time and are a part of everyday life. Those that my grandmother did not favor remain safely padded and protected from the elements. They remain as a testament that the art of Ireland and the culture of its people from millennia past still have a grasp on our modern sensibilities. At the risk of seeming like a stereotype of a superstitious culture, these tiles allow me to remember that where my father's family is from is a place with a long history, only waiting to be recognized.

Past generations have not disappeared, but only become softer in their methods of communication. If ghosts exist, as the superstitious culture of Ireland would have us believe, it is through the legacies of what past generations have left to us in the present to further to those who will come after. Lile chose these tiles herself, picked their placement, and cared about her culture enough to include it in her everyday life. This heritage, similarly to Lile's experience, is part of my family's daily life too. What she did has allowed me to think to myself when I see these tiles, "Hello Lile."

The Songs of My Grandfathers

History and heritage can often seem like abstract ideas with little effect on our daily lives. We know some of the stories and can use them like impressive trivia when asked about our knowledge of our ancestors. But we often cannot relate or even think of them as living beings whom have a tremendous baring on who we have become. This was for the majority of my life the way I had felt; yet, I would see heirloom artifacts scattered throughout my life. It was not until I understood the meaning from the stories of these objects did I realize that material culture keeps heritage with us, reminding us of where we have come from. From these objects are stories of the peoples' lives who used them and, as with my grandmother's tiles, provides a sense of who they were. As I write, just behind my computer rests a harmonica, with spots of rust on its top cover, and dings and dents dotted over its body. Yet, while this harmonica may be worn, the reeds continue to sing with a sweet tone of life: using breath to create a melodious sound that mirrors the smooth movement of water when played. It was my grandfather's instrument that dances with the tunes of water and life.

Whenever my parents host a family party, whether it is Christmas or Samhain (the Gaelic version of Halloween), various aunts, uncles, cousins, grandparents, and parents tell stories about the past while the younger generations gather around for the bonfire to grow and emit enough heat in the frigid outdoor air. We also revel in the freedom from adults as we play football or hurling; cursing at each other before returning to the polite conversation expected by our elders. Nestled by the fire in my parent's garden, the moorland can be seen to the north as a reminder of the danger and protection it offers. To the south, a river that waters the fertile farmlands rushes and swirls, giving the garden an ever-present white noise as proof of its dependency. My grandfather would say, "this is the land we fought for." The fertile green land that provides ease of life. Rolling green hills is the landscape of Carlow, hardwood forests, clear streams, and bountiful crops make it the jewel of Leinster province. Whenever my grandfather would say "we fought for this land," I had always assumed that he was claiming how he devoted his life to acquiring property here. Understanding this family history better now than I did before he passed in 2005 has since given me a deeper perspective.

My grandfather, Val O'Byrne, had always loved music; it was said he played in Dublin during his years at university and performed at venues like the Hairy Lemon, a pub that has hosted many talented and well-known musicians.[13] He went to Trinity College in Dublin and claimed to take law classes to make money and music classes to stay sane. My grandmother claimed he could play any instrument since his father taught Val and all of his siblings many instruments.[14] Thus, my grandfather came to love music and played the entirety of his life. His favorite instrument was the harmonica.

At the parties there was a traditional membership of the band: my grandfather, Val, would play harmonica and sing, while his younger brother took the banjo, and my aunt would play the fiddle. After a brief warm up period of testing the strings or clearing the chambers, the first song would be played. It would start with various traditional songs often "Star of the County Down" or "The Waxie's Dargle": more upbeat and happy tunes that would liven the party. My grandmother would grab the closest male relative with intense fervor to begin dancing, and the children whom were learning river dance in school would line up to compare their skills. As the night grew older the food would be eaten and the attempts to keep the fire ablaze weakened as us lads began to become weary from the hoisting of logs onto our shoulders from the edge of the forest. This was when the song choice would drift to more somber songs while everyone conversed around the music with heavy eyelids and weary tones. Yet, the most memorable song my grandfather, great uncle, and aunt would play would always be the last tune of the night.

Looking back on why they would play it last, I believe was their way of striking up energy with the tiring crowd as the evening came to an end. My grandfather Val would whisper into me and my cousin Joseph's ears to rally the troops, as such my cousins and I would grab our footballs, sit around the band, and act as impromptu drummers. All of us knew the appropriate times to beat on our footballs in the song, as we were far from the first generation to be the percussionists, which was visible in seeing our grandmothers and grandfathers stomp their wellies into stone patio or gently pat the tops of their thighs with crooked and cracked hands. With the coals from the bonfire lighting our faces and the smoke rising to disappear into the black star lit sky the song went "Fiach McHugh has given the word,": our cue to hit our footballs twice and as loud as possible, reminiscent of the battle marches for which the song was made, followed by, "Follow me up to Carlow."

The song "Follow Me Up to Carlow" is the song of my father's family, the O'Byrnes. It is the tale of my many great-grandfathers and his battle against the Royal troops of Queen Elizabeth I of England. [15] The lyrics tell of Fiach McHugh O'Byrne's brilliant battle plans, using the terrain of the Wicklow Mountains to protect Carlow at the Battle of Glenmalure; as well as his men performing valiant acts of bravery against the foreign foes. [16] My grandfather believed it was our duty to remember what lives were lost to protect our home, even if it was against an enemy from five centuries ago whom no longer were a threat. He had grown up during the Irish Civil War and raised seven children through the period known as the "Troubles" in Ireland. These experiences would make him value the safety of his family and home and connect him with the great Fiach McHugh O'Byrne. Carlow was my grandfather's life and thus this song meant much to him. "Follow Me Up to Carlow" was his heritage and the state of its future preservation lies with my cousins and I, singing along and beating our footballs to the song.

Val played this song on his harmonica the entirety of his adult life. It was meaningful to him as a way to appreciate his own past. Combined with his favorite song, Val would play the harmonica almost as a metaphor for the modern attempts to understand who we are and where we come from. It was his method, by playing this song, of preserving his personal heritage. The harmonica as such is almost a metaphor for the entirety of the need to preserve and appreciate our own heritage. He was preserving it in a way that was non-tangible while also creating a tangible piece of history by doing so. The meaning behind it as such is one with a message of remembrance.

Since the passing of our grandfather Val, my cousins and I have learned how to play instruments because it is our way of connecting to a period gone by and furthering it into the future. While we may not always play the same songs, or use the same rills, our culture created this passion. This intangibility behind my grandfather's instruments or the broader history of our family's past continues to echo through our strings, reeds, and voices. My cousin, Abbey, plays violin just as beautifully as her mother; and Bryan McDonald plucks at his grandfather's banjo improving every day: deciding which songs he most likes to play, whilst I whistle a tune through Val's old chromatic harmonica. Often to the notes and lyrics that combine to form "Follow Me Up to Carlow."

Figure 6.3: One of Val's harmonicas, this one dating from the 1980s and his favorite from the last decades of his life. Photograph by the author.

Bata/Shillelagh

Tangible cultural heritage is the focus of much of my interest when researching my family's past. Each unique piece connects you with a different part of or person from the past. The object speaks to the social climate and interests of the time, opening up an understanding of the period's culture and beliefs when investigated or attached to the life of the person whom owned it.[17] One such object in my possession is my twice great-grandfather's *batá,* or more commonly known as a *shillelagh*, which is a type of cane or stick. Connected to this stick are stories that sway between fact and fable. While there is little evidence to prove that the claims made on this legendary cane are real the cultural telling of stories and pride in such an artifact of Irish tradition is one which can be understood and valued likened to mythology. As a disclaimer to that statement these kinds of weapons were often seen within Irish mythology, dating back to the High Kings of Ireland (seventh through twelfth centuries). One such mythology in which fighting sticks were described, being very similar to modern variations of today, was the tale of "The Destruction of Da Derga's Hostel" which discusses the death of one of Ireland's High Kings: considered one of the finest Irish Sagas next to stories of Cu Chulain.[18]

While the shillelagh is one of those symbols of Ireland that has pervaded the culture and history of Ireland, as seen by popular belief in the modern era, the true history of the cane (or sometimes weapon) is one filled with both intrigue and drama. The story of the batá/shillelagh begins rather obscurely since the word "shillelagh" is one with unclear origins of its etymology. The word is dissimilar to the lexicons of Gaelic and English spelling and grammar systems yet continues to be used to describe both the "batá," Irish fighting stick, as well as the name of a large forested area of County Wicklow, Ireland.[19] The first use of the word "shillelagh" to describe the stick fighting tradition was in nineteenth century England, yet it is unclear if there is any earlier evidence for this name. However, stick fighting with similarly shaped sticks has been a part of Irish martial art forms since long before the written record. The sport most likely came from the Stone Age when it was a formidable weapon in the tumultuous period of human settlement over nine thousand years ago, and it continued to evolve and change as time passed.[20]

Throughout the Middle Ages the batá/shillelagh was considered an effective weapon, increasing in popularity throughout the following centuries. When Ireland fought England from the fifteenth through the twentieth centuries there would be an ebb and flow of penal laws placed upon the country.[21] After the Desmonde (1569-1573) and Osmonde (1579-1583) rebellions in Ireland against Elizabethan England, a series of laws were instated banning Irish people from carrying weapons unless under the service of the English crown.[22] This would occur again under the Stewart monarchs and after. These penal laws were placed on Ireland into the twentieth century in order to maintain control over the citizenry and dissuade rebellion, or at least rebellion with better armament. These laws are what lead to the use of fighting sticks becoming so important to the Irish. As armaments were illegal, walking sticks and canes began to be relied on for defense.[23]

A batá/shillelagh should be understood when taken within the context of my grandfather's story. Traditionally it was a stick close to a meter (or yard) in length and made from oak, ash, or blackthorn. They would take tree saplings with a portion of the root ball as it was heavier than the rest of the wood; leaving the bark. A craftsman would then apply a metal cap, most often copper, ferule at the end of the trimmed stick to discourage splitting up the length of the piece. After the metal cap was fitted to the stick it was then greased with butter to allow for a slower drying time, making it stronger in its molecular makeup. Once this was done the craftsman would hang the sticks in a chimney to cure for a year or longer. The soot from the fireplace would attach to the butter and eventually penetrate into the wood, turning the entire piece black as tar. After the drying period in the fireplace, the head (root or burl section) was polished while the rest was sealed creating a black haft with a polished brown head strong enough to withstand substantial abuse. This was the method of creating batás/shillelaghs for the longest time and can still be seen done this way in many parts of County Wicklow.

The artform of stick fighting in Ireland is known as *Bataireacht* and traditionally was a skill passed down from father to son. Throughout the eighteenth and nineteenth centuries it was not uncommon for villages to not only have the tradition of fathers teaching their sons to use the stick as a weapon, but an actual instructor to assist too.[24] By the time a male was of age his skills in stick fighting would often be of incredible depth and magnitude. This widespread knowledge of stick fighting, often used against foreign oppressors on the island, began to be seen in a more negative light.

The xenophobia of the English towards the Irish would use the batá/shillelagh as a testament that the Irish were prone to (or even enjoyed) violence for the sake of fighting. This was of course, absurd as the sport came from necessity of unstable conditions due to the political strife within the country. Yet, Irish people seized this idea in a different way creating a cultural phenomenon. The historian John Hurley outlined this cultural phenomenon in his scholarship about Irish stick fighting, which he called Shillelagh Law. It began as a series of rules for combat to create an even position for both sides, disallowing unfair advantage. This code of conduct for combat soon transgressed to a deeper political meaning towards the end of the nineteenth century. [25] It was a political ideology that spoke against unfair treatment and misrepresentation of Ireland by its English overlords, fueling the animosity during this period and furthering the Celtic Revival in Ireland. If Irish fighters can agree to equality and fairness in rules than the argument was that it was not the Irish who were in love with violence, but the English whom sought to oppress through unfair means. If the English used unfair means in their subjugation of Ireland, then according to Shillelagh Law, so could the Irish when they fought back.

My great-great-grandfather, Aonghus O'Byrne, was born into this world of stick fighting. He grew up near the location of my family's home in County Carlow. Where he lived was close to the famed Shillelagh forest known for its old growth blackthorn trees. These trees were prized not only for their use in building construction, but the smaller saplings made the best and hardest batás/shillelaghs. Where he grew up was also a very "green" part of the country in political ideology (not the landscape), and thus he grew up both having a dislike for royalist ideas and knowing how to fight with a stick.

Aonghus was a known citizen of dissent: often having various issues with lawmakers of the region. He was also known to distill his own alcohol, known as *poitin*, to sell to the local villages whilst avoiding taxes imposed on such goods, dating to the Elizabethan law that prohibited distillation save for a licensed handful. Aonghus's recipes are still in the possession his descendants. This was the beginning of his life outside of British law. Short terms of incarceration eventually lead to Aonghus fleeing to the safety of the Wicklow Mountains, where he joined separatist groups colloquialized as factions. Factions in Ireland were more or less gangs with political or familiar leanings, a predecessor to the Irish Republican Army, and were known to create large brawls involving hundreds, sometimes thousands of people. [26] Aonghus was a part of one of these nineteenth century factions. He was involved in brawls against soldiers under royalist leaders and throughout this time he carried his batá/shillelagh.

This weapon was both aid in walking on rough terrain as well as protection and considered to be a staple for those people whom lived this kind of life. It was said Aonghus used it in various fights, ranging from Cork in the south of the island to Antrim in the north.[27] Many tales tell of how he defeated his adversaries with less than favorable odds. He was, as they say, a "ruffian" in life. This would end however, when he would be apprehended and killed in Swords: a village outside of Dublin, for resisting arrest under charges of violent acts against the crown. His batá/shillelagh was not with him at the time. The story goes that before he went to do some illegal activity in Swords he left this prized possession with his mother to ensure he would be coming home, which of course did not happen. As such his mother, Mary O'Byrne, gave the batá/shillelagh to her grandson – Aonghus's newborn child – my great-grandfather. The batá/shillelagh was passed down through the male line as a symbol of fathers teaching their sons to defend themselves, as well as the freedom from corrupt English rule. Hence Aonghus's cane was passed to me, where it now sits proudly in the corner of my room retired from its life of fighting.

Though this batá/shillelagh remains in excellent condition throughout its century-long lifespan, the meaning of its intended purpose is one that was always considered with a passing glance after it ceased to be used for fighting. That this object *was* passed down to me, a pseudo-legacy, is one with such historical significance to have affected not only the life of my ancestor, Aonghus, but those who it has passed to since – besides those that were on the receiving end of the batá/shillelagh's actions. The historic context of the batá/shillelagh has literally affected the formation of contemporary Ireland.

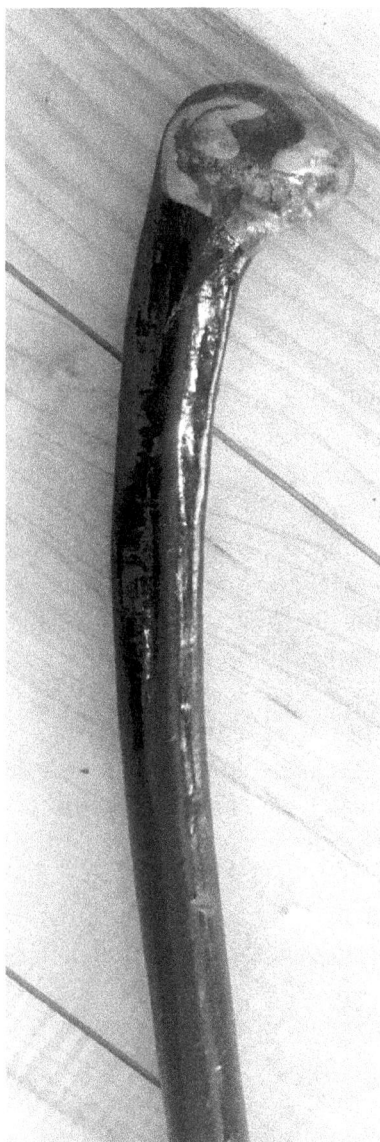

Figure 6.4: Head and upper portions of Aonghus' batá/shillelagh showing the root ball at the top of the shaft. Source: Photograph by the author.

This batá/shillelagh is considered one of the foremost family heirlooms from this time period. While political motives are attached to the object it should be addressed that it was during this tumultuous time that laid the foundation for later events in the early twentieth century that would lead to a sovereign nation of Ireland. Meaning while this stick was used to commit crimes now long forgotten, it is cherished as an artifact, such as any weapon from the past. The batá/shillelagh symbolizes the struggles that lead to the formation of freeing the Irish people. As such, the batá/shillelagh should be considered a relic of times now past to evoke memory and meaning from the violent periods that allowed for the growth of the nation. I do not condone the actions of Aonghus O'Byrne but understanding the history of this period can allow for a better appreciation of this artifact.

State of Tangible Heritage

The focus of looking into my heritage has predominantly been involved with artifacts that have been ever present in my life. This is sometimes difficult when discussing the state of its preservation in comparison to intangible traditions or stories because there are protocols for stewarding objects for future generations.[28] It is also difficult for myself, having been a student of Historic Preservation and Community Planning because my education focused on large structures and landscapes, and little on hand-held artifacts. Small objects do not lend themselves to the conventional manners of preservation practice as taught at university. Thus, what can be said about small objects more than they will be preserved in my lifetime? My feelings on the matter; however, is somewhat disappointing. Artifacts are important for telling the stories of the people who made myself (and imminent generations), and should be ensured to remain for their enjoyment, studies, and everyday appreciation. My goal as such was to come up with some level of insurance that these objects will remain for my descendants to enjoy and understand far into the future.

Thus, while the application of preserving these artifacts seems too small for my formal preservation education of buildings, there is another, broader philosophy to consider for community planning: "If you fail to plan, you plan to fail." And while this adage can be given credit to many people it is a statement that has shaped my perception on many issues in life, and thus I hope for this philosophy to be my own addition to the family's heritage. The way forward as such will be my ambition to guarantee this tangible cultural heritage be maintained well into the future of my family, but also my attempt to add my own effects on its future, which one day will be seen as worthy of being remembered alongside Aonghus's batá/shillelagh, Val's harmonica, and Lile's tiles. This is my effort to justify breathing in a place of history that remains sharp and relevant in hopes that it will not disturb the heritage but betters it.

With artifacts in hand it is easy to forget that while today they are here in seemingly good condition, or rather lasting condition, that eventually these objects will approach a period of destruction or loss. As the poet Robert Herrick wrote, "all things decay with time" and perhaps unfortunately for these items time knows no end.[29] The difficulty is however, not in preserving objects per se, but rather maintaining the stories and meanings which the objects are cherished for. Without their stories the tiles, harmonica, and batá/shillelagh are not as important as standalone artifacts. Rather, they are important because each one is a glimpse into the life of a person, or my heritage, which without the knowledge leaves that person all but forgotten. My love for these artifacts comes from a place of understanding the lives of those who came before and is the same value assigned to such objects by preservationists and historians. So, the question is how does one preserve the objects and the stories behind them? To address the easiest solution is to discuss how to preserve material culture. However, each type of material has to be treated differently but can be preserved with relative ease.

Beginning with the batá/shillelagh, which is both the oldest and easiest to preserve in respect to the physicality of the object. Firstly, because of the construction method discussed previously, it is incredibly durable and hard, which naturally protects the untreated inner portions of the wood fiber from water, thus decreasing the chances of rot. However, as the finish has gained scratches from the century or so of use and abuse, treating the batá/shillelagh with a special wax compound, called Renaissance Wax (made for the priceless items of the British Museum), further protects the organic material from decaying. It is acid neutral and resistant to water and alcohol.[30] This compound ensures that the batá/shillelagh will be preserved for a remarkable period if the layer of wax is maintained periodically. Meaning in the future when it is handed down to the next generation, my impact on this piece will be for prolonging its longevity using these contemporary means.

Secondly, Val's harmonica is slightly more difficult to preserve due to the inner workings of the instrument. Similar to Aonghus's batá/shillelagh the same wax compound is used to protect it from any further rust build up on the outside casement, as there is some light rust from the many years of its life. But the reeds and comb are far more delicate and thus need more careful treatment. The best method of preservation however, as stated by the Society for the Preservation and Advancement of the Harmonica (SPAH), is to ensure that the inner workings remain dry and to use moderate breath strength when playing the instrument.[31] While it may not be the best to play such an object very often, as it may quicken its useable life, using the harmonica ensures the working of its parts if played gently. Meaning in a more succinct fashion: use it with care and keep it dry.

Lastly, Lile's tiles were made durable and to last. The U.S. National Parks Service provides recommendations on how to preserve tiles on their website and discusses the cleaners to use and protective coatings.[32] The methods vary depending on the type of tile and though they caution using certain types of sealants or protective coats due to the porous nature of tile, even with a glaze, as this can harm the finish or make them more apt to discolor. For the most part the Nation Park Services recommends vacuuming or dusting grit and grime off of the tiles and continue to use a non-acidic cleaner to wipe them down.[33] This method seems to be the most simple and effective as it has preserved Lile's tiles for around a century without damage. In the future it will be, as a preservationist, my prerogative to ensure their existence and maintenance well into the future.

With the physical state of these objects in a rather good condition, and methods to further protect them already under hand, the more difficult question is addressed of how to preserve with them the memories that make them so important. This is an area that is more difficult due to the small nature of the object as well as the inability to ensure the furthering of oral history through future generations. This is the struggle of history and preservation, because of ignorance or indifference, and the challenge of memory.

While a simple solution to preserve these stories would be to write them down (as I have done with this paper), the method of making the information accessible can be more difficult. If written down and printed the information could become separated and lost, thus making the information and the object irrelevant to one another. If the oral history is stored digitally, technological advancements may make the information inaccessible when software and hardware platforms become outdated. If the object is simply handed down accompanied by oral history, meaning may be forgotten and lost. To preserve this oral history may be an exercise in futility but perhaps all preservation is a constant battle of prolonging the inevitable. The way to success may seem unclear but through the mist of oral tradition the purpose of this endeavor can be seen. To do as was done in part for myself when learning these stories, so that my ancestors may have a voice that can be echoed far into the future.

The first method of preserving this heritage has already been underway. With my attempt at bringing family history to light, as the colloquialism would have it, the past is for the first time written down. My ambition to further my family's history is in the act of preserving these stories. This narrative has made it possible for these three lives to be further connected to and the objects that symbolize their stories given meaning with evidence. This written historical account of the objects is not only preserving these stories but also making them accessible to others who would be interested. While I cannot ensure the lifespan of this account, I can ensure that the objects will be accounted for in relation to it. The pictures are an act of preservation as they cover small details of the objects that allow for further study and understanding of cultural heritage.

The intangibility of memory and tangible objects preservation do clash, as one can be held and the other must be contemplated.[34] This is made more difficult with small objects like the harmonica, batá/shillelagh, and tiles; whereas a societal cultural heritage can be addressed more readily, as was done by UNESCO.[35] The small-scale of moveable artifacts effectiveness can heighten passing down culture to future generations. UNESCO adopted the following method for recognizing cultural heritage, which relates to my family's artifacts and how to go forth with their preservation:

> The intangible cultural heritage means the practices, representations, expressions, knowledge, skills—as well as the instruments, objects, artifacts and cultural spaces associated therewith—that communities, groups and, in some cases, individuals recognize as part of their cultural heritage. This intangible cultural heritage, transmitted from generation to generation, is constantly recreated by communities and groups in response to their environment, their interaction with nature and their history, and provides them with a sense of identity and continuity, thus promoting respect for cultural diversity and human creativity.[36]

The answer lies within all three techniques of preserving intangible culture. Oral history passed down through the generations and recorded as well into a document that can be accessed either in hand or through technology. While it may not be perfect, and room for error and loss still remains, the beginnings of preserving history are through these means. To simply make this information common knowledge within the family as well as community will preserve the history of these artifacts until or if possible, an infallible answer can be reached. The information is now there and throughout my life it will be my endeavor to spread it to those whom care to know or receive the objects within their lifetime. Thus, the state of preservation of the tangible cultural objects and intangible cultural heritage is, for my lifetime, in remarkably well condition; but with most things it is up to the future members of the family to decide how to further these ideas. Hopefully, instilled with the love of history and passion for heritage, these objects will continue to inspire future generations. For my part it is to allow descendants to access the information and keep it close to the harmonica, tiles, and batá/shillelagh so that it may not be lost. The plan is in place to preserve, and much like culture it may change depending on the social environment but adapting to modern life. This is the ambition to better the heritage so that it won't be forgotten or distorted. To steward the history so that it will remain honest and true for the entirety of its lifetime passed down.

For the future it is important to promote an interest in history as well to maintain the history itself. How to foster a relationship between heritage and future generations is something that has been debated within society for the entirety of human existence. The Southern Historical Association attempts to do this by investigating history rather than repeating it.[37] Reaching to the humanistic need to uncover and question rather than simply to memorialize: as I had done with the list of ancestors' names when I was younger. To protect the stories best, as in relation to my heritage and cultural objects, is to incite interest by challenging to find more. To challenge the future to understand better, relate the information to their modern times, and appreciate the efforts of the past that give them the privilege to do so. Hopefully, the artifacts will be treated with respect and remembered for their significance.

Conclusion

Throughout the process of researching heirloom artifacts a new love has been aroused within myself and my family for stewarding our past. This has created a renewed fervor for remembering and recording the information passed down to us so that it does not become lost, because much of the family history has been forgotten due to the passage of time. It should be noted that the entirety of my efforts has been to promote this interest among those who share my heritage too.

For example, I spoke with my cousin Bryan McDonald, who plays the banjo, about his view of heritage as it relates to our common grandfather and the music he played.[38] It struck a note with him that the instruments he plays or owns are part of a history longer than he had thought. It has been his purpose as such to handle, care for, and preserve instruments passed to him by our shared grandfather, so that he may pass them to his children and grandchildren one day. Bryan now displays this part of his heritage, though unrelated to Val's harmonica in my possession, in a method that keeps them safe and inspires devotion or interest among those who see them. This research has created a competition among family members for various trinkets, so we may all share a piece of the past. Val's harmonica, which is in my possession, is an object of interest among several family members.

The batá/shillelagh that I have always considered my birthright, is now documented in a way I can share with those around me. While many of my cousins wish to have it themselves, their want for such a funny piece of wood is proof of growing interest, which has been generated by including them in this study. Showing them that this is the beginning of the plan to preserve our heirlooms, as well as also our shared heritage, has brought about a successful response. This endeavor is coming to fruition more quickly than previously thought by repeating the stories of our ancestors in a way that relates to us in the younger generation. Appreciation creates the desire to preserve.

Lastly, Lile's tiles, which I have to admit that above all else, had the greatest connection with me. These tiles gave me an insight into Lile's life and allowed me to appreciate something which was always present but seldom recognized. How she brought heritage with her is something that we may not be able to appreciate in our ancestors, as we do today. She made the decision to continue this effort and spread it to the future, so we may understand her life in such a subtle way. Allowing us to see the little girl, now over a hundred years ago, running around these ancient sites in the Wicklow Mountains. Not only did this idea strike me in such a way as to allow my connection with her to grow, but my mother too. My mother, related to Lile through marriage to my father, has taken it upon herself to better care for the tiles than simply using non-acidic solutions to clean them. My mother is reaching out to the future by treating them with respect by informing those closest to this heritage about their importance. The tiles now have been ensured to retain their color and finish for many years. Not only does this mean that the efforts made have begun to work in making a difference in how we perceive this part of our heritage, but how to make it last. The interest simply needed to be awakened within us, and now more heritage can be saved from the abyss of ignorance.

The parts of our collective past whisper to us every day. Whether it is a story remembered or the smallest of objects that sit unadorned in a drawer, to be held on the rare occasion that they enter our minds. If we listen as I have attempted to do and inspire others to do so with their own heritage, we can ensure that the state of preservation can be remarkably good. While these objects are small the devotion to the associated memories behind them can better the understanding of ourselves, as well as the experience of generations past. This is the effort of preservation for my heritage. While we may not be able to meet these ancestors, often nameless or with little information known of them, we can relate to understand that they felt as we do today.

Reverberate the initial passage regarding my experience wandering through the Wicklow Mountains, where I learned about the life of Lile O'Byrne, this heritage marks us as its own, which is how the past influences the present. I see – or rather we see – that these events are a dance of life; fluid like water and ever changing with each decision, echoing throughout the ages. Memorialized in ourselves to never be lost if we maintain this appreciation, we can see these effects on ourselves. That our history and the people within it have done something that stays with us. I see these markings impressed upon me by ancestors, like carvings on stone, and I realize the old ways do not die, but change. The feeling that permeates my mind is that this is family, and this is home.

Appendix A

Transcription of interview with Mary Lou O'Byrne (M refers to Mary Lou, whilst I refer to the Interviewer)

I: "So what can you tell me about Lile's tiles?"

M: "Well I remember she used to talk about where she got them which was erm, somewhere in Wicklow. Perhaps (unintelligible), but sometime in the first couple years of their marriage. She got them in crates".

I: "The crates which hold the unused pieces?"

M: "Yes, but she didn't like all of them, so she had to pick and choose. She was picky about her decorations and wouldn't just use any. She cared so much that her home was pretty. She always dressed beautifully and drew attention everywhere she went. Your father would remember that about her she was always to the nines."

I: "So was there rhyme or reason behind which tiles she liked and didn't like?"

M: "Besides her being picky... erm Well she told me they reminded her of where she grew up in Wicklow."

I: "Where did she grow up?"

M: "Carrigeenshinnagh in Wicklow. It's a little heath village, but you know you've been to her house. Remember the one that's falling down by the little hedge road."

I: "I remember Grammy. Did she talk about her childhood there much with you?"

M: "Yes, she adored her Da. She would walk him to work every day and hold his packed lunch."

I: "so where did Lile meet your dad?"

M: "They met in Dublin, erm she worked for him I think. He was a lawyer in Dublin you know. She would've been, let's see, nineteen or twenty when they got married. It seems young now, but people go married earlier back then you know."

I: "After they were married they moved to Carlow?"

M: "Yes, maybe some time passed, I don't know for sure love. But I know the villagers used to talk about her being too posh. They were all jealous (inaudible, laughter) because she would ship all her clothes from Dublin, so she wouldn't have to only buy stuff from the erm village. She even shipped furniture."

Appendix B

Transcription of interview with Bryan McDonald

(B refers to Bryan, whilst I refer to the Interviewer)

I: "Hey Bryan how's the banjo?"

B: "Alright, I think I'm going to break out Val's things and make sure it's not rotting."

I: "Good to hear mate."

B: "What you think I should, like, do with them?"

I: "Hang them up? I just keep the harmonica on the table."

B: "Yeah, I D K but I'll probably hang them make the house look artistic or whatever."

I: "(Laughter) you do that"

B: "Yeah alright talk to you later."

I: "Adios."

Appendix: *Human Centered Built Environment Heritage Preservation: Theory and Evidence-Based Practice*

Co-edited by Jeremy C. Wells and Barry Stiefel (New York: Routledge, 2018).

Description

"What is Your Heritage and the State of its Preservation" is a pedagogical approach discussed within *Human-Centered Built Environment Heritage Preservation.* This book addresses the question of how a human-centered conservation approach can and should change practice. For the most part, there are few answers to this question because professionals in the heritage conservation field do not use social science research methodologies to manage cultural landscapes, assess historical significance, and inform the treatment of building and landscape fabric. With few exceptions, only academic theorists have explored these topics while failing to offer specific, usable guidance on how the social sciences can actually be used by heritage professionals.

In exploring the nature of a human-centered heritage conservation practice, we explicitly seek a middle ground between the academy and practice, theory and application, fabric and meanings, conventional and civil experts, and orthodox and heterodox ideas behind practice and research. We do this by positioning our approach in a transdisciplinary space between these dichotomies as a way to give voice (and respect) to multiple perspectives without losing sight of our goal that heritage conservation practice should, fundamentally, benefit all people. We believe that this approach is essential for creating an emancipated built heritage conservation practice that must successfully engage very different ontological and epistemological perspectives.

Endnotes

Introduction, by Barry L. Stiefel

[1] Susan Kammeraad-Campbell, "About", *Storyboard America*, (2015), <http://www.storyboardamerica.com/about.html>, (20 June 2018).

[2] Barry L. Stiefel, "Beyond Names and Dates on a Tree: How Librarians Can Help Explore Family Heritage and Preservation," *Genealogy and the Librarian*: *Perspectives on Research, Instruction, Outreach and Management,* Carol Smallwood and Vera Gubnitskaia, eds. (Jefferson, NC: McFarland, 2018), 156-63.

[3] Barry L. Stiefel, "'The Places My Granddad Built': Using Popular Interest in Genealogy as a Pedagogical Segue for Historic Preservation," in *Human Centered Built Environment Heritage Preservation: Theory and Evidence-Based Practice*, Jeremy C. Wells and Barry L. Stiefel, eds. (New York: Routledge, 2018).

Chapter 1: Cultivating Heritage in North Carolina Soil, by Rebecca Lawing

[1] "North Carolina State Research Guide: Family History Sources in the Tar Heel State." Ancestry's Red Book: American State, County, and Town Sources.

[2] United States. Census Bureau. *Report Number: Statistical Abstract of the United States: 1900.* By Bureau of Statistics. Vol. 23. Washington, DC: Government Printing Office, 1901.

[3] Laura A. Phillips, *National Register of Historic Places Registration Form (10-900): West Main Street Historic District*. National Park Service, Department of the Interior.

[4] John L. Hancock, "Planners in The Changing American City, 1900-1940." *Journal of the American Institute of Planners*, vol. 33, no. 5, 1967, pp. 290–304., doi:10.1080/01944366708977936

[5] "Urban and Rural Dwellers." *NCLS Research*, www.ncls.org.au/default.aspx?sitemapid=2294.

[6] *The History of Lincolnton | Lincolnton, NC - Official Website*, City of Lincolnton, www.ci.lincolnton.nc.us/226/History-of-Lincolnton; and Phillips, *National Register of Historic Places*

Registration Form (10-900): West Main Street Historic District.

[7] Marjorie M. Applewhite, "Sharecropper and Tenant in the Courts of North Carolina." *The North Carolina Historical Review*, 31: 2, April 1954, 134–149.

[8] David W. Galenson, "The Rise and Fall of Indentured Servitude in the Americas: An Economic Analysis." *The Journal of Economic History*, vol. 44, no. 01, 1984, pp. 1–26., doi:10.1017/s002205070003134x

[9] Although Irene's brothers passed long ago, due to the illegal nature of their business their names will not be specified out of respect for living relatives.

[10] Aaron Ennis Lancaster, "Chasing the Good Ol' Boys and Girls of Wilkes County, North Carolina." *Appalachian State University*, 2013. iv

[11] *Moonshine--Historical Overview*, www.ibiblio.org/moonshine/drink/historical.html

[12] "North State Hotel - Lincolnton - NC - US." Historical Marker Project. https://www.historicalmarkerproject.com/markers/view.php?marker_id=HMTT9.

[13] "Appalachian Music." *The Library of Congress*, www.loc.gov/item/ihas.200152683/ Dobney, Jayson Kerr.

[14] "Nineteenth-Century Classical Music | Essay | Heilbrunn Timeline of Art History | The Metropolitan Museum of Art."

[15] "Home Sweet Home Life in Nineteenth-Century Ohio." Special Presentation: Parlor Music (Performing Arts Encyclopedia, The Library of Congress). Accessed April 19, 2018. http://memory.loc.gov/diglib/ihas/html/ohio/ohio-piano.html.

[16] David Lowenthal, "Stewarding the Past in a Perplexing Present." In *Values and Heritage Conservation*, 18-25. Los Angeles, CA: Getty Conservation Institute, 2000.

[17] "Guidelines for Evaluating and Documenting Rural Historic Landscapes, National Register of Historic Places Bulletin (Nrb 30)." National Parks Service. 19 April 2018. https://www.nps.gov/nr/publications/bulletins/nrb30/.

[18] "Intangible Cultural Heritage," Link to the Intangible Cultural Heritage Website. 19 April 2018. https://ich.unesco.org/en/what-is-intangible-heritage-00003.

Chapter 2: What's in a Name: Establishing My Heritage through the Perpetuation of a Neglected Surname, by Flannery Wood

[1] Minich Family History Document, private collection.

[2] Kathryn Minich Mossburg. Telephone interview, 16 January 2018.

[3] Louise Wood Royal. Telephone interview, 19 January 2018.

[4] Ingrid Winther Scobie, "Family and Community History through Oral History," *The Public Historian* 1:4 (1979): 29-39. doi:10.2307/3377279. Pg. 32.

[5] Scobie, "Family and Community History through Oral History," 33.

[6] Scobie, "Family and Community History through Oral History," 35.

[7] Scobie, "Family and Community History through Oral History."

[8] Scobie, "Family and Community History through Oral History," 33.

[9] Jacquelyn D. Hall, et. al., *Like a Family: The Making of a Southern Cotton Mill World* (Chapel Hill: University of North Carolina Press, 1987), 31.

[10] Hall, et. al., *Like a Family*, 31.

[11] Hall, et. al., *Like a Family*, 32.

[12] Hall, et. al., *Like a Family*, 31.

[13] Elsdon C. Smith, *New Dictionary of American Family Names* (New York: Gramercy Publishing Co., 1988), xiv.

[14] Patrick Hanks and Flavia Hodges, *A Dictionary of Surnames* (New York: OUP, 1988), v.

[15] Smith, *New Dictionary of American Family Names*, pg xiv.

[16] David Hey, "FAMILY NAMES AND FAMILY HISTORY," *History Today* 51, no. 7 (July 2001): 38. History Reference Center, EBSCOhost (7 February 2018), 38.

[17] Hey, "FAMILY NAMES AND FAMILY HISTORY," 38.

[18] Smith, *New Dictionary of American Family Names*, xiv.

[19] Hey, "FAMILY NAMES AND FAMILY HISTORY," 39.

[20] Smith, *New Dictionary of American Family Names*, xiii.

[21] Patrick Hanks, ed., *Dictionary of American Family Names* (New York: Oxford University Press, 2003), 3:630.

[22] Hanks, ed., *Dictionary of American Family Names*, 2:569.

[23] Minich Family History, private collection of author.

[24] Smith, *New Dictionary of American Family Names*, xxii.

[25] Patrick Hanks and Flavia Hodges, *A Dictionary of Surnames* (New York: Oxford University Press, 1988), viii.

[26] Hanks, ed., *Dictionary of American Family Names*,2:569.

[27] Hanks, ed., *Dictionary of American Family Names*,384.

[28] Hanks, ed., *Dictionary of American Family Names*.

[29] Minich Family History, private collection of the author.

[30] George Redmonds, David Hey, and Turi King, *Surnames, DNA, and Family History* (New York: Oxford University Press, 2011), xvi.

[31] Minich Family History, private collection of the author.

[32] Minich Family History, private collection of the author.

[33] Minich Family History, private collection of the author.

[34] Minich Family History, private collection of the author.

[35] 1910 US Census, Philadelphia, Pennsylvania, population schedule, district 1062, pg. 8A, Household 164, Daniel Minnick Family; digital image, Ancestry.com, March 3, 2018.

[36] Minich Family History, private collection of the author.

[37] Minich Family History, private collection of the author.

[38] Minich Family History, private collection of the author.

[39] Minich Family History, private collection of the author.

[40] Minich Family History, private collection of the author.

[41] 1920 US Census, Philadelphia, Pennsylvania, population schedule, Burholme Township, pg. 13A, Household 278, Daniel C. Minich Family; digital image, Ancestry.com, February 21, 2018.

[42] Minich Family History, private collection of the author.

[43] Minich Family History, private collection of the author.

[44] Minich Family History, private collection of the author.

[45] Kathryn Minich Mossburg. Telephone interview, 16 January 2018.

[46] Mary Anna Wood, in discussion with the author, 2 February 2018.

[47] Wood, in discussion with the author, 2 February 2018.

[48] Lyons Family History, private collection of the author.

[49] 1910 US Census, Anderson, South Carolina, population schedule, Varennes Township, pg. 2A, Household 17, J.A Lyons Family; digital image, Ancestry.com, 23 January 2018.

[50] Lyons Reunion Family History Skit, private collection of the author.

[51] Lyons Reunion Family History Skit, private collection of the author.

[52] Lyons Reunion Family History Skit, private collection of the author.

[53] Eddie Lyons. Telephone interview, 19 February 2018.

[54] Thomas Henry Wood Life and Employment History, private collection of the author.

[55] Thomas Henry Wood Life and Employment History, private collection of the author.

[56] Thomas Henry Wood Life and Employment History, private collection of the author.

[57] Louise Wood Royal. Telephone interview, 19 January 2018.

[58] Thomas Henry Wood Life and Employment History, private collection of the author.

[59] Thomas Henry Wood Life and Employment History, private collection of the author.

[60] Thomas Henry Wood Life and Employment History, private collection of the author.

[61] Eddie Lyons. Telephone interview, 19 February 2018.

[62] Thomas Henry Wood Life and Employment History, private collection of the author.

[63] Thomas Henry Wood Life and Employment History, private collection of the author.

[64] Eddie Lyons. Telephone interview, 19 February 2018.

[65] Eddie Lyons. Telephone interview, 19 February 2018.

[66] Richard Tyler, "The John B. Stetson Company." Written Historical and Descriptive Data, Historic American Building Survey, National Park Service, U.S Department of the Interior, pg. 3. From Prints and Photographs Division, Library of Congress (HABS No. PA- 1227; http://lcweb2.loc.gov/master/pnp/habshaer/pa/pa0900/pa0912/data/pa0912data.pdf. 17 February 2018.

[67] Tyler, "The John B. Stetson Company," 2.

[68] Tyler, "The John B. Stetson Company," 3.

[69] Tyler, "The John B. Stetson Company."

[70] Tyler, "The John B. Stetson Company," 1.

[71] Tyler, "The John B. Stetson Company," 4.

[72] Tyler, "The John B. Stetson Company."

[73] Tyler, "The John B. Stetson Company."

[74] Tyler, "The John B. Stetson Company," 5.

[75] Tyler, "The John B. Stetson Company," 5.

[76] Jennifer S. Revels and Mary Sherrer, Historical and Architectural Survey of Anderson County, South Carolina: Final Report. Columbia, SC: TRC, 2002.pg 48.

[77] Revels and Sherrer, Historical and Architectural Survey of Anderson County, South Carolina.

[78] Revels and Sherrer, Historical and Architectural Survey of Anderson County, South Carolina.

[79] Elizabeth Belser Fuller, ed., *Anderson County Sketches* (Anderson, SC: Anderson County Tricentennial Committee, 1969), 60.

[80] Elizabeth Belser Fuller, ed., *Anderson County Sketches,* 60

[81] Revels and Sherrer, Historical and Architectural Survey of Anderson County, South Carolina, 48.

[82] Revels and Sherrer, Historical and Architectural Survey of Anderson County, South Carolina, 54.

[83] Hey, "FAMILY NAMES AND FAMILY HISTORY," 38.

[84] Revels and Sherrer, Historical and Architectural Survey of Anderson County, South Carolina, 54.

[85] Revels and Sherrer, Historical and Architectural Survey of Anderson County, South Carolina, 54.

[86] Revels and Sherrer, Historical and Architectural Survey of Anderson County, South Carolina, 54.

[87] Revels and Sherrer, Historical and Architectural Survey of Anderson County, South Carolina, 54.

[88] Revels and Sherrer, Historical and Architectural Survey of Anderson County, South Carolina, 54.

[89] Minich Family Documents Collection, private of author.

[90] Minich Family Documents Collection, private of author.

[91] Minich Family Documents Collection, private of author.

[92] Letter to Francis Minich, Minich Family Documents, private collection of the author.

[93] Letter to Francis Minich, Minich Family Documents, private collection of the author.

[94] Katarina Wegar, *Adoption, Identity, and Kinship: The Debate over Sealed Birth Records* (New Haven: Yale University Press, 1997), 22.

[95] Wegar, *Adoption, Identity, and Kinship: The Debate over Sealed Birth Records,* 22.

[96] Kathryn Minich Mossburg. Telephone interview, 16 January 2018.

[97] Katarina Wegar, *Adoption, Identity, and Kinship: The Debate over Sealed Birth Records* (New Haven: Yale University Press, 1997), 64.

[98] Wegar, *Adoption, Identity, and Kinship*, 64.

[1] Bibliography for Chapter 3: "New Orleans Mardi Gras: More Than Just a Wild Party" By Ellen Feringa

"Arrival of the Grand Duke." *New Orleans Republican* 13 February 1872: 1.

Barber, Kristen. "Mardi Gras and Post-Katrina Politics." *Everyday Sociology Blog*, W.W. Norton & Company, Inc., 24 Feb. 2009, www.everydaysociologyblog.com/2009/02/mardi-gras-and-post-katrina-politics.html. 31 March 2018.

Bookhardt, Eric D. "Designing Pandemonium: An Art History of Mardi Gras in New Orleans," *New Orleans Art Institute.* http://www.insidenola.org/p/designing-pandemonium-art-history-of.html. 23 January 2018.

John Brasted, "The Achaeans Ball 2018." *Nola.com.* http://photos.nola.com/4500/gallery/the_achaeans_ball_2018/index.html. 31 January 2018.

Christian Brown, Email Interview. 14 January 2018.

Burnett, John. "Mardi Gras Adjusts to Post-Katrina New Orleans." *NPR*, NPR, 27 Februart 2006, www.npr.org/templates/story/story.php?storyId=5234970. 31 March 2018.

Cabildo, 2018. Louisiana State Museum. http://louisianastatemuseum.org/museums/the-cabildo/. 17 January 2018.

Lissa Capo, "Throw Me Something, Mister": The History of Carnival Throws in New Orleans," Dissertations and Theses. University of New Orleans, 20 May 2011.

"Care-Free New Orleans Celebrates Mardi Gras." *The Shreveport Times* 9 March 1935: 7.

"Carnivals around the World." *UNESCO*, 7 Mar. 2017.
en.unesco.org/news/carnivals-around-world. 5 March 2018.

"City Intelligence." *The New Orleans Bee,* 14February1872: 1.

Paige Cooperstein, "These Vintage Photos of Mardi Gras in
New Orleans Show It's Always Been A Wild Party." *Business
Insider*, 4 March 2014. http://www.businessinsider.com/
vintage-photos-of-mardi-gras-2014-3. 23 March 2018.

Audie Cornish, "Zulu Coconuts: A Prized Catch." *NPR*, NPR,
1 Mar. 2006, www.npr.org/2006/03/01/5239877/zulu-
coconuts-a-prized-catch. 31 March 2018.

Kris Cusanza, "A Carnival Tradition: Rex Members Give Out
Pins to the Ladies." *WGNO.* 9 February 2015a.
http://wgno.com/2015/02/09/a-carnival-tradition-rex-
members-give-out-pins-to-the-ladies/. 18 February 2018.

---. "Crown Jewels of Carnival: A History of the Jewelry
Worn by Rex and His Queen." *WGNO*, 11 February 2015b,
wgno.com/2015/02/10/crown-jewels-of-carnival-a-history-of-
the-jewelry-worn-by-rex-and-his-queen/. 18 February 2018.

Janissa Delzo, "Mardi Gras 2018: 90,000 Pounds of Beads
found in New Orleans Storm Drains." *Newsweek.* 27 January
2018. http://www.newsweek.com/mardi-gras-beads-new-
orleans-storm-drains-793032. 4 March 2018.

Charles L. Dufour and Leonard V. Huber, *If Ever I Cease to
Love: One Hundred Years of Rex 1872- 1971.* New Orleans:
The School of Design, 1970.

"Endymion." *Krewe of Endymion.* Krewe of Endymion: 2012.
https://endymion.org./ 4 March 2018.

Brian Ettinger, "Rex Appeal." *New Orleans Magazine,* 33: 5,
February 1999, 72. EBSCO*host*,
nuncio.cofc.edu/login?url=http://search.ebscohost.com/login.
aspx?direct=true&db=f5h&AN=1558217&site=eds-
live&scope=site. Accessed 14 January 2018.

Lee Farrow, *Alexis in America: A Russian Grand Duke's Tour,
1871-1872.* Baton Rouge: Louisiana State University, 2014.

Richard Fausset, "Mardi Gras Beads Cause Environmental
Hangover." *Los Angeles Times*, 15 February 2012,
articles.latimes.com/2012/feb/15/nation/la-na-mardi-gras-
beads-20120216. 14 January 2018.

Fav4eva. "Intangible Cultural Heritage: The Pride and Celebration of Festival of Saint Francis of Assisi, Columbia." *Global Heritage.* 29 Nov. 2016. https://thinkglobalheritage. wordpress.com/2016/11/29/intangible-cultural-heritage-the-pride-and-celebration-of-festival-of-saint-francis-of-assisi-columbia/. Accessed22 March 2018.

Linda Bouden Feringa, Telephone Interview. 10, 14, 19-20, and 28 January; 9 and 13 February; 1 and 3 April 2018.

Megan Feringa, Email Interview. 1 Jan.; 4 April 2018.

Peter Anthony Feringa, Interview by author. 9, 14, and 28 January; 10, 12, and 16 February; 15 and 17 April 2018.

"Festival of Saint Francis of Assisi, Quibdó." *Intangible Cultural Heritage UNESCO.* 2012. https://ich.unesco.org/en/RL/festival-of-saint-francis-of-assisi-quibdo-00640. Accessed 5 March 2018.

"The Gion Festival." *Enjoy Kyoto.* 2014. http://enjoy-kyoto.net/issue/issue05/the-gion-festival. 5 March 2018.

Grand Marshal of the Empire. "Proclamation." *New Orleans Republican* 13 February 1872: 4.

"The Great New Orleans Fire" *Frenchcreoles.com.* http://www.frenchcreoles.com/CreoleCulture/creoleexperience /new%20orleans%20fire.html. Accessed 23 January 2018.

Kevin Gotham, *Authentic New Orleans: Tourism, Culture, and Race in the Big Easy.* New York and London: New York University Press, 2007.

Stephen W. Hales, Rex*: An Illustrated History of the School of Design,*_China: Arthur Hardy Enterprises, Inc., 2010.

Arthur Hardy, "The History of Mardi Gras." *Arthur Hardy's Mardi Gras Guide*, Arthur Hardy Enterprises, www.mardigrasguide.com/history/. 16 April 2018a.

---. "History of Mardi Gras." *New Orleans Online.com*, http://www.neworleansonline.com/neworleans/mardigras/mar digrashistory/mghistory.html. 22 January 2018b.

---. "Lundi Gras Riverfront Celebration an Old Tradition Reignited in 1987." *The Advocate*, 8 February 2016, www.theadvocate.com/new_orleans/news/article_b23222a4-3817-56c8-86ed-0805c435d86f.html. 5 March 2018c.

Ned Hemard, "Mardi Gras Memories." *New Orleans Bar Association*, NEW ORLEANS NOSTALGIA, 2016, www.neworleansbar.org/uploads/files/Mardi Gras Memories 2_10_16.pdf. Accessed 5 March 2018.

History.com Staff. "Mardi Gras 2018." *History.com.* 2010a. https://www.history.com/topics/holidays/mardi-gras. Accessed 18 April 2018.

---. "Prohibition ends." *History.com.* 2010b. http://www.history.com/this-day-in-history/prohibition-ends. 24 February 2018.

Leonard Huber, *Mardi Gras: A Pictorial History of Carnival in New Orleans.* Gretna: Pelican Publishing Company, 2003.

"Japan's Commitment to the Protection of Oral and Intangible Heritage." *Permanent Delegation of Japan to UNESCO.* 2013. http://www.unesco.embjapan.go.jp/htm/intangibleheritage. htm. 5 March 2018.

The King of Carnival, "Edict No. 11. " *New Orleans Republican* 13 February 1872: 4.

"The King of the Carnival." *New Orleans Republican* 13 February 1872: 1.

Klusby, "Krewe of Rex special pins date back to the late 1800s." *WGNO.* 31 January 2018. http://wgno.com/2018/01/29/krewe-of-rex-special-pins-date-back-to-the-late-1800s/. 18 February 2018.

Errol Laborde, *Marched the Day God: A History of the Rex Organization.* New Orleans: The School of Design, 1999.

---. "The Greatest Mardi Gras Ever." *New Orleans Magazine,* *New Orleans Magazine,* February 2016, www.myneworleans.com/New-Orleans-Magazine/February-2016/ The-Greatest-Mardi-Gras-Ever/. 5 March 2018.

Charles Lipson, *How to Write a BA Thesis: A Practical Guide from Your First Ideas to Your Finished Paper.* Chicago & London: The University of Chicago Press, 2005.

"Local Intelligence." *New Orleans Republican* 1 February 1872: 5.

"Local Intelligence." *New Orleans Republican* 3 February 1872: 5.

"Louisiana's Biggest Annual Celebration: Mardi Gras" *Lou!s!ana.* https://www.crt.state.la.us/tourism/pressroom/festivals-events/mardi-gras/index. 23 January 2018.

"Mardi Gras Floats." *All About Mardi Gras | Mardi Gras Floats*, Rebecca McCormick, 2018, www.allaboutmardigras.com/Features/Tradition Features/floats.html. 23 January 2018.

"Mardi Gras is Observed with Gaiety." *The Monroe News-Star* 5 March 1935: 3.

Mary Foster – Associated Press, Writer. *New Orleans Celebrates Mardi Gras.* AP Online, The Associated Press, 02/24/1998. EBSCO*host*, nuncio.cofc.edu/login?url=http:// search.ebscohost.com/login.aspx?direct=true&db=n5h&AN=9 98e01209d43463fd78a4015fad33b84&site=eds-live&scope=site. 11 January 2018.

Lisa Feringa McLean, Interview. In print. 11 January 2018.

Trimiko Melancon, "The Complicated History of Race and Mardi Gras." *African American Intellectual History Society.* 9 February 2018. https://www.aaihs.org/the-complicated-history-of-race-and-mardi-gras/. 25 March 2018.

"Muses2016Throw_EG1_1140B." *Krewe of Muses,* Krewe of Muses, New Orleans, kreweofmuses.org/shoes/

"New Orleans Brings Mardi Gras to Brilliant Close." *The Shreveport Times* 14 February 1934: 3.

Nell Nolan, "Nell Nolan: Meeting of Rex and Comus courts ends Carnival." *The Advocate.* 17 February 2016. http://www.theadvocate.com/new_orleans/entertainment_life/ nell_nolan/article_c844bac5-74a2-556d-9536-c60bad815bba.html. Accessed 25 March 2018.

Bruce Nolan, "Bitter Mardi Gras Debate of Race, Class Evolves 20 Years Later into a Diverse Celebration." *MardiGras.com*, 12 February 2012, http://www.mardigras.com/news/2012/02/mardi_gras_debate_ of_race_clas.html. Accessed 16 April 2017.

"Notice." *The Times-Picayune.* 2 February 1872: 4.

Rosar O'Neill, *New Orleans Carnival Krewes: The History, Spirit and Secrets of Mardi Gras.* Charleston: The History Press, 2014.

Wayne Philips, Interview by author. 6 January 2018.

John Pope, "Butterfly King Float to Join This Year's Rex Parade on Mardi Gras." *MardiGras.com*, 24 January 2012, http://www.mardigras.com/news/2012/01/butterfly_king_float _to_join_t.html. 30 March 2018.

Pro Bono Publico Foundation
http://www.probonopublicofoundation.org. 9 January 2018.
"Queen of Mardi Gras." *The Monroe News-Star.* 5 March
1935: 5.
Katy Reckdahl, "Rex Foundation Donates $1M to Aid Local
Schools*." The Advocate.* 14 January 2018.
David Redmon, "The Destructive Life of a Mardi Gras Bead."
The Conversation. 24 February 2017.
https://theconversation.com/the-destructive-life-of-a-mardi-
gras-bead-71657. 21 March 2018.
"Rex: King of Carnival." *Rex: King of Carnival*, School of
Design, www.rexorganization.com/. 11 January 2018.
Rex Organization. "L'Ancienne Nouvelle-Orléans." 2018.
---. *1934 Rex Court.* 1934. The Rex Den, New Orleans,
Louisiana.
---. *1935 Rex Court.* 1935. The Rex Den, New Orleans,
Louisiana.
---. *1960 Rex Court.* 1960. The Rex Den, New Orleans,
Louisiana.
---. *2006 Rex Court.* 2006. The Rex Den, New Orleans,
Louisiana.
"Rice Export Co. is Formed; Has N.O. Home Office." *The
Monroe New-Star* 22 January 1927: 5.
"Rice Export Unit Formed." *The Shreveport Times* 23 January
1927: 18.
"The Rich Heritage of Mardi Gras in New Orleans." *Arcadia
Publishing.* 1 February 2017.
https://www.arcadiapublishing.com/Navigation/Community/A
rcadia-and-THP-Blog/February-2017/The-Rich-Heritage-of-
Mardi-Gras-in-New-Orleans. 22 March 2018.
Mark Romig, "Rex Fact Sheet." *Rex Organization.*
http://www.rexorganization.com/static/Downloads/2018/RexF
actSheet2018.pdf. 22 March 2018.
Lily Rothman, "How Mardi Gras Became a Party for
Everyone." *TIME.* 17 February 2015.
http://time.com/3703165/mardi-gras-crew-history/. 4 March
2018.
Royal Design House. Interview by author. 15 January 2018.
Alison Satake, "Biodegradable Mardi Gras Beads." *LSU
Media Center.* 6 February 2018.

http://www.lsu.edu/mediacenter/news/2018/02/06bio_kato_be
ads.php. 21 March 2018.

Saving Antiques. "Why Cultural Heritage
Matters." *SAFE/Saving Antiques For Everyone*, SAFE,
savingantiquities.org/wp-content/uploads/2016/05/why-
cultural-heritage.pdf. 15 April 2018.

Henri Schindler, *Mardi Gras Treasures: Invitations of the
Golden Age.* Hong Kong: Pelican Publishing Company, 2000.

---. *Mardi Gras Treasures: Float Designs of the Golden Age.*
Gretna: Pelican Publishing Company, 2001.

"Shoes." *Krewe of Muses*, Krewe of Muses,
kreweofmuses.org/shoes/. 31 March 2018.

Stephen Stenning, "Destroying Cultural Heritage: More than
just Material Damage." *British Council.* 21 Aug. 2015.
https://www.britishcouncil.org/voices-magazine/destroying-
cultural-heritage-more-just-material-damage. 24February 2018.

Sue Strachan, "Meet the Debs: 67 Members of the 2017-18
New Orleans Debutante Coterie." *NOLA.com*, NOLA.com, 19
July 2017,
www.nola.com/society/index.ssf/2017/06/meet_the_debs_64_
members_of_th.html. Accessed 24 February 2018.

---. "Rex, Comus Continue 100-plus Year Tradition at Their
Carnival Balls." *Nola.com*, 14 February 2018.
www.nola.com/society/index.ssf/2018/02/rex_and_comus_con
tinue_100_plu.html. 24 March 2018.

---. "Stars Align for The Achaeans bal masque." *Nola.com,* 1
February 2018.
http://www.nola.com/society/index.ssf/2018/02/stars_align_fo
r_the_achaeans_b.html. 15 April 2018.

"Tuesday Evening, Mardi Gras Night." *New Orleans
Republican.* 13 February 1872: 1.

World Heritage Convention: United Nations Educational,
Scientific and Cultural Organization (UNESCO). 1992.
UNESCO World Heritage Centre. https://whc.unesco.org. 5
March 2018.

"Yamahoko, the Float Ceremony of the Kyoto Gion Festival."
UNESCO. https://en.unesco.org/silkroad/silk-road-
themes/intangible-cultural-heritage/yamahoko-float-
ceremony-kyoto-gion-festival. 5 March 2018.

Chapter 4: Landscapes of Memory: Exploring Family Heritage Through Place and Travel, by Madison Alspector

[1] Jennifer Alspector, "What is our family's heritage." Interview by Madi Alspector. 27 February 2018.

[2] John Koenig, "'Anemoia.'" Class Lecture/Discussion of YouTube Video, 17 April 2018.

[3] Jane Cohen, "What is our family's heritage." Interview by Madi Alspector. 28 January 2018.

[4] Wayne Phoenix, "What is our family's heritage." Interview by Madi Alspector. 24 March 2018.

Chapter 5: A Pilcher Tradition: The Legacy of the Elgin National Watch Company, by Madison Moga

[1] Alexis McCrossen, "The 'Very Delicate Construction' of Pocket Watches and Time Consciousness in the Nineteenth-Century", *Winterthur Portfolio*, 44:1, (Spring 2010). 2.

[2] E. C. Alft and William Briska, *Elgin Time: A History of the Elgin National Watch Company 1864-1968*. (Elgin, IL: Elgin Historic Society), 5.

[3] Alft and Briska, *Elgin Time*, 7.

[4] Alft and Briska, *Elgin Time*, 8.

[5] Alft and Briska, *Elgin Time*, 8.

[6] Alft and Briska, *Elgin Time*, 9.

[7] Alft and Briska, *Elgin Time*, 10.

[8] Alft and Briska, *Elgin Time*, 11.

[9] Alft and Briska, *Elgin Time*, 13.

[10] E. C. Alft, *Elgin: An American History*, (Elgin, IL: Crossroads Communications, 1985), 56.

[11] Alft and Briska, *Elgin Time*, 11.

[12] Alft and Briska, *Elgin Time*, 14

[13] Alft and Briska, *Elgin Time*, 14.

[14] Alft and Briska, *Elgin Time*, 15.

[15] Alft and Briska, *Elgin Time*, 13.

[16] Alft and Briska, *Elgin Time*, 16.

[17] Alft and Briska, *Elgin Time*, 17.

[18] Alft and Briska, *Elgin Time*, 17.

[19] Alft and Briska, *Elgin Time*, 17.
[20] Alft and Briska, *Elgin Time*, 18.
[21] The Elgin Chapter of the National Secretaries Association, *Bicentennial Booklet on the Elgin National Watch Company*, 6
[22] Alft and Briska, *Elgin Time*, 26.
[23] Alft and Briska, *Elgin Time*,15.
[24] Alft and Briska, *Elgin Time*, 16.
[25] Alft and Briska, *Elgin Time*, 16.
[26] Alft and Briska, *Elgin Time*, 16.
[27] Alft and Briska, *Elgin Time*, 21.
[28] Alft and Briska, *Elgin Time*, 22.
[29] Alft and Briska, *Elgin Time*, 22.
[30] Alft and Briska, *Elgin Time*, 23.
[31] Alft and Briska, *Elgin Time*, 23.
[32] Alft and Briska, *Elgin Time*, 23.
[33] Alft, *Elgin: An American History*, 60.
[34] Alft and Briska, *Elgin Time,* 24.
[35] Alft and Briska, *Elgin Time*, 24-25.
[36] Alft and Briska, *Elgin Time*, 40.
[37] Alft and Briska, *Elgin Time*, 41.
[38] Gary P. Biesterfeld, *Pilcher Cousins* (Elgin, IL: Gary P. Biesterfeld, 2001), 3.
[39] Biesterfeld, *Pilcher Cousins*, 4.
[40] Biesterfeld, *Pilcher Cousins*, 5.
[41] Alft and Briska, *Elgin Time,* 26.
[42] Employee's Advisory Council, *Watch Word* (Elgin, IL: Elgin National Watch Co.), 8.
[43] Employee's Advisory Council, *Watch Word,* 33.
[44] Biesterfeld, *Pilcher Cousins*, 337.
[45] "Pilcher Family Has Annual Picnic", *Elgin Daily Courier-News*. 25 June 1958.
[46] Arthur Kane, "100th year family picnic draws all ages". *Daily Herald.* 30 June 1997.
[47] Alft and Briska, *Elgin Time*, 30.
[48] Alft and Briska, *Elgin Time*, 30.
[49] Alft and Briska, *Elgin Time*, 31.
[50] Alft and Briska, *Elgin Time*, 32.
[51] Alft and Briska, *Elgin Time*, 32.
[52] Alft and Briska, *Elgin Time*, 32.
[53] Alft and Briska, *Elgin Time*, 32.

[54] Alft and Briska, *Elgin Time*, 33.
[55] Alft and Briska, *Elgin Time*, 34.
[56] Alft and Briska, *Elgin Time*, 54.
[57] Alft and Briska, *Elgin Time*, 55.
[58] Alft and Briska, *Elgin Time*, 28.
[59] Alft and Briska, *Elgin Time*, 40.
[60] Alft and Briska, *Elgin Time*, 39.
[61] Alft and Briska, *Elgin Time*, 39.
[62] Alft and Briska, *Elgin Time*, 41.
[63] Alft and Briska, *Elgin Time*, 42.
[64] Alft and Briska, *Elgin Time*, 42.
[65] Alft and Briska, *Elgin Time*, 43.
[66] Alft and Briska, *Elgin Time*, 41.
[67] Alft and Briska, *Elgin Time*, 42.
[68] Alft and Briska, *Elgin Time*, 43.
[69] Alft and Briska, *Elgin Time*, 43.
[70] Alft and Briska, *Elgin Time*, 43.
[71] Alft and Briska, *Elgin Time*, 43.
[72] Alft and Briska, *Elgin Time*, 43.
[73] Alft and Briska, *Elgin Time*, 46.
[74] Alft and Briska, *Elgin Time*, 48.
[75] Alft and Briska, *Elgin Time*, 48.
[76] Alft and Briska, *Elgin Time*, 52.
[77] Alft and Briska, *Elgin Time*, 53.
[78] Alft and Briska, *Elgin Time*, 53.
[79] Alft and Briska, *Elgin Time*, 53.
[80] Alft and Briska, *Elgin Time*, 54.
[81] Kimberly Bauer, "Elgin Watch Factory Observatory", *Pedaling Preservation,* https://pedalingpreservation.wordpress.com/2015/08/14/elgin watch-factory-observatory/ (1 April 2018).
[82] Alft and Briska, *Elgin Time*, 58.
[83] Alft and Briska, *Elgin Time*, 58.
[84] David Briggs, *Circle of Time* (Elgin, IL: The Elgin Area Historical Society & Grindstone Productions, Inc., 2002).
[85] Bauer, "Elgin Watch Factory Observatory."
[86] Alft and Briska, *Elgin Time,* 61.
[87] Alft and Briska, *Elgin Time,* 62.
[88] Alft and Briska, *Elgin Time,* 64.
[89] Alft and Briska, *Elgin Time,* 65.

[90] Alft and Briska, *Elgin Time,* 71.
[91] Alft and Briska, *Elgin Time,* 77.
[92] Alft and Briska, *Elgin Time,* 73.
[93] Alft and Briska, *Elgin Time,* 73.
[94] Alft and Briska, *Elgin Time,* 74.
[95] Alft and Briska, *Elgin Time,* 74.
[96] Alft and Briska, *Elgin Time,* 74.
[97] Alft and Briska, *Elgin Time,* 74.
[98] Alft and Briska, *Elgin Time,* 75.
[99] Alft and Briska, *Elgin Time,* 75.
[100] Alft and Briska, *Elgin Time,* 75.
[101] Alft and Briska, *Elgin Time,* 76.
[102] Alft and Briska, *Elgin Time,* 77.
[103] Alft and Briska, *Elgin Time,* 77.
[104] Alft and Briska, *Elgin Time,* 77.
[105] Alft and Briska, *Elgin Time,* 83.
[106] Alft and Briska, *Elgin Time,* 84.
[107] Alft and Briska, *Elgin Time,* 78.
[108] Alft and Briska, *Elgin Time,* 78.
[109] Alft and Briska, *Elgin Time,* 79.
[110] Alft and Briska, *Elgin Time,* 80.
[111] Alft and Briska, *Elgin Time,* 82.
[112] Alft and Briska, *Elgin Time,* 82.
[113] Alft and Briska, *Elgin Time,* 82.
[114] Alft and Briska, *Elgin Time,* 83.
[115] Alft and Briska, *Elgin Time,* 83.
[116] Alft and Briska, *Elgin Time,* 83.
[117] Alft and Briska, *Elgin Time,* 87.
[118] Alft and Briska, *Elgin Time,* 87
[119] Alft and Briska, *Elgin Time,* 88.
[120] Alft and Briska, *Elgin Time,* 89.
[121] Alft and Briska, *Elgin Time,* 91.
[122] Alft and Briska, *Elgin Time,* 91.
[123] Alft and Briska, *Elgin Time,* 92.
[124] Alft and Briska, *Elgin Time,* 92.
[125] Alft and Briska, *Elgin Time,* 92.
[126] Alft and Briska, *Elgin Time,* 93.
[127] Alft and Briska, *Elgin Time,* 93.
[128] Alft and Briska, *Elgin Time,* 94.
[129] Alft and Briska, *Elgin Time,* 95.

[130] Alft and Briska, *Elgin Time,* 95.
[131] Alft and Briska, *Elgin Time,* 96.
[132] Elgin Chapter of NSA, *Bicentennial Booklet on the Elgin National Watch Company*, 8.
[133] Alft and Briska, *Elgin Time*, 97.
[134] "Elgin National Watch Historic District", *City of Elgin,* http://www.cityofelgin.org/index.aspx?NID=496, (1 April 2018).
[135] Historic Certification Consultants, *The Elgin National Watch District: A Summary and Inventory,* (City of Elgin, 1998), 1.
[136] Historic Certification Consultants, *The Elgin National Watch Historic District*, 2.
[137] Historic Certification Consultants, *The Elgin National Watch Historic District*, 3.
[138] Historic Certification Consultants, *The Elgin National Watch Historic District*, 5.
[139] Historic Certification Consultants, *The Elgin National Watch Historic District*, 10.
[140] Alft and Briska, *Elgin Time,* 98.
[141] Historic Certification Consultants, *The Elgin National Watch Historic District,* 14.
[142] Historic Certification Consultants, *The Elgin National Watch Historic District*, 15.
[143] Historic Certification Consultants, *The Elgin National Watch Historic District*, 16.
[144] Historic Certification Consultants, *The Elgin National Watch Historic District*, 18.
[145] Historic Certification Consultants, *The Elgin National Watch Historic District*, 19.
[146] Alft and Briska, *Elgin Time*, 37; and "Illinois Single Property Listings Finding Aid", catalog.archives.gov, 476.

Chapter 6: The Trinkets We Carry by Alec Meier

[1] "Heritage Park." *The Irish National Heritage Park, Failte Ireland*, www.irishheritage.ie/park-history/stone-age/.
[2] "Heritage Park."
[3] "Heritage Park."

[4] "Heritage Park."

[5] Alec C. Meier, "Interview with Mary Lou O'Byrne." 22 February 2018.

[6] Meier, "Interview with Mary Lou O'Byrne."

[7] Meier, "Interview with Mary Lou O'Byrne."

[8] Meier, "Interview with Mary Lou O'Byrne."

[9] C. Dewey, "Celtic agrarian legislation and the Celtic revival: Historicist implications of Gladstone's Irish and Scottish Land Acts 1870-1886," *Past & Present*, 64, (1974), 30-70.

[10] Thomas M. Curley, *Samuel Johnson, the Ossian Fraud, and the Celtic Revival in Great Britain and Ireland* (Cambridge, UK: Cambridge University Press, 2009).

[11] Meier, "Interview with Mary Lou O'Byrne."

[12] Meier, "Interview with Mary Lou O'Byrne."

[13] "The Hairy Lemon," www.visitdublin.com/see-do/details/the-hairy-lemon#53.341223|-6.263870|13.

[14] Meier, "Interview with Mary Lou O'Byrne."

[15] "Follow Me Up to Carlow – Story and Characters," *Irish Music Daily*, www.irishmusicdaily.com/follow-me-up-to-carlow-story-explained.

[16] "Follow Me Up to Carlow – Story and Characters."

[17] National Parks Service, "Tangible and Intangible Cultural Heritage," *U.S. Department of the Interior*, www.nps.gov/articles/tangible-cultural-heritage.htm.

[18] *The Destruction of Da Derga's Hostel*, celt.ucc.ie//published/T301017A/.

[19] John W. Hurley, *Shillelagh: The Irish Fighting Stick.* (Pipersville, PA: Caravat Press, 2007).

[20] L. Jenkins, "Real Irish Fighting: A History of Shillelagh Law and Hob-Nailed Boot Stomping." Fightland, 13 October 2016, fightland.vice.com/blog/real-irish-fighting-a-history-of-shillelagh-law-and-hob-nailed-boot-stomping.

[21] Pgraybil, "Laws in Ireland for the Suppression of Popery," *University of Minnesota Law School*, 15 March 2017, www.law.umn.edu/library/irishlaw.

[22] Chris Lawlor, "From a Spark to a Firebrand: Feagh Mac Hugh O'Byrne." *History Ireland*, 3 September 2013, www.historyireland.com/early-modern-history-1500-1700/spark-firebrand-feagh-mac-hugh-obyrne/.

[23] John W. Hurley, *Shillelagh: The Irish Fighting Stick* (Pipersville, PA: Caravat Press, 2007).

[24] Hurley, *Shillelagh: The Irish Fighting Stick.*

[25] Hurley, *Shillelagh: The Irish Fighting Stick.*

[26] Patrick D. O'Donnell, *The Irish Faction Fighters of the 19th Century* (Dublin: Anvil Books, 1975).

[27] "County Antrim, Ireland Genealogy." *FamilySearch,* www.familysearch.org/en/County_Antrim,_Ireland_Genealogy

[28] Eric W. Allison and Mary A. Allison, "Preserving Tangible Cultural Assets: A Framework for a New Dialog in Preservation." *Preserving Tangible Cultural Assets: A Framework for a New Dialog in Preservation*, 2008.

[29] Robert Herrick, "All Things Decay and Die," *Aninna Jokinen*, www.luminarium.org/sevenlit/herrick/decay.htm.

[30] *Renaissance Wax*, www.conservationresources.com/Main/section_39/section39_08.htm.

[31] SPAH, *Society for the Preservation and Advancement of the Harmonica*, Naylor Association Management Software, www.spah.org/.

[32] Anne E. Grimmer and Kimberly A. Konrad, *Preserving Historic Ceramic Tile Floors*. Washington, DC: National Park Service, 1998, www.ov/tps/how-to-preserve/briefs/40-ceramic-tile-floors.htm.

[33] Grimmer and Konrad, *Preserving Historic Ceramic Tile Floors.*

[34] Kelsey Mckinney, "How to Preserve Your Family Memories, Letters and Trinkets," *The New York Times*, 8 Feb. 2018, www.nytimes.com/2018/02/08/smarter-living/how-to-preserve-your-family-memories-letters-and-trinkets.html.

[35] UNESCO World Heritage Centre, "Managing Cultural World Heritage." *World Heritage Centre*, whc.unesco.org/en/managing-cultural-world-heritage/.

[36] UNESCO World Heritage Centre, "Managing Cultural World Heritage."

[37] Southern Historical Association, "Mission Statement," *Southern Historical Association*, thesha.org/.

[38] Alec C. Meier, "Interview with Bryan McDonald." 4 March 2018.